THE
ADMINISTRATIVE THEORIES
OF HAMILTON & JEFFERSON

THE
ADMINISTRATIVE THEORIES
OF HAMILTON & JEFFERSON

Their Contribution to Thought on Public Administration

SECOND EDITION

LYNTON K. CALDWELL

HM

HOLMES & MEIER
NEW YORK / LONDON

Holmes & Meier Publishers, Inc.
30 Irving Place
New York, NY 10003

Great Britain:
1–3 Winton Close
Letchworth, Hertfordshire SG61 1BA
England

First edition copyright © 1944 by The
University of Chicago. Composed and printed
by the University of Chicago Press, Chicago, Illinois.

This book has been printed on acid-free paper.

Library of Congress Cataloging-in-Publication Data

Caldwell, Lynton Keith, 1913–
  The administrative theories of Hamilton & Jefferson.

  Originally published: Chicago : University of Chicago, c1944.
  1. United States—Politics and government—1783–1809. 2. Hamilton,
Alexander, 1757–1804—Contributions in public administration. 3. Jefferson,
Thomas, 1743–1826—Contributions in public administration. 4. Public
administration—United States—History.
I. Title.
JK171.A1C3 1988   350'.00092'2   87-28535
ISBN 0-8419-1049-9 (alk. paper)
ISBN 0-8419-1050-2 (pbk. : alk. paper)

TO HELEN

Table of Contents

Introduction to the First Edition

TO FURNISH perspective in human affairs is the special province of the historian, notably the historian of ideas. In the great decisions of public issues which arise with ever more startling acceleration, a firm grasp of the basic stock of values and ideas with which any people begin the management of their common affairs and of their successive modification to meet emerging trends can never be without value.

The evolution of the constitutional precepts of the United States government has been fully analyzed by constitutional historians, lawyers, and judges; the implications of such underlying ideas as are conveyed by the terms "liberty," "equality," and "democracy" have been traced in their changing context by the political theorists; and the institutions of government—federal, state, and local—are well known in their twentieth-century forms, although less well known in earlier decades. The development of the administrative system of this country and of the ideas on which it has rested for over a century and a half of national experience remains, in large part, a closed book.

The author of this study, trained both as a historian and as a political scientist, deals with the crucial period when the theory and practice of administration in the new general government were in process of formation. The administrative system, as well as the political system, of the United States was founded on the divergent theories and objectives of two of America's greatest statesmen—Hamilton and Jefferson. Each developed a coherent, well-considered plan of administration supported by deep-seated but conflicting preferences concerning the type of society toward which they hoped America would grow and buttressed by equally deep-seated differences of personality and aptitude. Hamilton triumphed for a brief period of magnificent construction; but Jefferson's spirit ruled over the subsequent century. The American system of administration in the troubled years of this generation has moved back toward the ideals of Hamilton but against popular preferences set in motion by Jefferson which still carry extraordinary weight. Neither ideal has been able to secure certain dominance over the other; neither can be driven from the field; and their reconciliation remains in considerable measure an unsolved problem.

Dr. Caldwell's study is not a history of administrative events; it is a presentation of administrative ideas. The volume opens an important avenue of further research and study both of the evolution of thought about public administration and of the march of events in the management of the public business. That so substantial a contribution can be made with respect to such well-known and often described personalities as Hamilton and Jefferson suggests fascinating possibilities in store dealing with such subjects as the Lincoln family in Massachusetts, Josiah Quincy of Boston, or with more nearly contemporary figures such as Governor Frank O. Lowden or the elder La Follette.

The history of administrative institutions and theories in the United States has value not only to Americans but to any people who are concerned with the problem of gearing together democratic institutions of policy and execution sufficiently strong to meet the exigencies of the present and the future. This and subsequent studies are thus turned to great purposes; and of this book it may be justly said that its insight and clarity are worthy of the purpose which it serves.

LEONARD D. WHITE

CHICAGO
March 20, 1944

Preface to the First Edition

LARGELY deprived of the analytic methods of an exact science, administration must rely to an extent upon the methodology of John Stuart Mill and draw from the past as much evidence as can be obtained concerning the administrative art. Great administrators have never abounded in any nation or at any time, and such knowledge as can be acquired from the past concerning the qualities, methods, weakness, and training of men who were undeniably skilled in the process of administration should hasten the day when society may draw forth and more fully utilize the resources of organizing and managing ability which we are only beginning to exploit.

Fundamental in the establishment of the national administrative system of the United States were the contributions of Alexander Hamilton and Thomas Jefferson. In the formative years of the government created in 1789, these men exercised an influence over the organization and functions of the national administration not exceeded by Washington himself. Their thought on the problems of public administration is relevant to the problems of our day no less than theirs.

To Professor Leonard D. White the author owes a special debt of gratitude for guidance throughout this study, initially undertaken at his suggestion. His generous and constructive assistance helped immeasurably in every phase of the writing.

Particular acknowledgments are due Professors Charles E. Merriam, William T. Hutchinson, and C. Herman Pritchett, who read the original manuscript; to Frank P. Bourgin and Professor Donald F. Carmony for constructive suggestions; and to the library staff of the University of Notre Dame for their co-operation. Adequate appreciation cannot be expressed for the encouragement and unfailing assistance which my wife has given to this work.

Publication of this volume was made possible by a grant from the Public Administration Fund of the University of Chicago which the author gratefully acknowledges.

L. K. C.

Introduction to the Second Edition

> . . . that governments of the people, by the people and
> for the people shall not perish from the earth.
> Gettysburg, 19 November 1863

With these lines, Abraham Lincoln stated in elegant simplicity a moral proposition that, beyond its relevance to the war to preserve the union, affords a consensual foundation for the administration of government in America. These words express a standard in theory and practice to which Americans almost universally expect their governments to conform. And in this standard of republican democracy may be found the reason why the American people continue to find relevance in the contrasting views of Hamilton and Jefferson about how their government should be administered.

The national Constitution was adopted by representatives of "we the people of the United States," and it was by definition and in principle "government of the people." To this proposition, Hamilton and Jefferson were unequivocally committed. For Jefferson, however, government by the people was the governing principle of politics; for Hamilton, government for the people was the driving principle of policy.

In many ways Hamilton and Jefferson were in agreement—and many of their values, in the fullness of time, have proved in principle to be reconcilable. Yet, the practical expression of these values in our history has differed greatly from the expectations held by Hamilton and Jefferson and their contemporary followers regarding their implementation. The government of the United States has become very strong, but that strength has not been deployed wholly in ways that Hamilton preferred. "Government for the people" has not been guided by a capability for foresight, and "for the people" has too often been applied for the benefit of so-called "special interests." Jefferson's vision of a localized self-governing agrarian society has vanished in the reality of an urbanized America, dominated by nationwide centralized organizations in which most individuals have little or no voice. But Jefferson's insistence on the free participation of citizens in public affairs has been realized in a way that he could not have foreseen—through the growth of nongovernment civic organizations. Thus, basic values of both Hamilton and Jefferson have been realized in principle, but not wholly in ways that, from the perspective of their own times, they could have foreseen.

The administrative theories of Hamilton and Jefferson were not unique; both men drew extensively upon historical traditions of political thought to illustrate and reinforce their own ideas. But while their ideas were not unique, their theories were distinctive—they were strongly marked and firmly joined to the diverse and differing legacies of political thought as they were applied in America. Both men were truly statesmen, men of public affairs and architects of *novus ordo seclorum*—a new order of the ages— imprinted on the Great Seal of the United States. Although the societies that they envisioned differed greatly in certain respects, both Hamilton and Jefferson regarded republican government, res publica, as essential to the security and advancement of civilization. They would distribute the powers of government differently, but neither was opposed in principle to the appropriate and timely use of public power. Neither shared the antigovernmental views of present-day libertarians, but they differed on how and when the authority of government should be invoked, and by whom.

The establishment of a new nation comprising a union of states presented an opportunity for the creative design of political institutions that would provide the framework for the development of a self-governing free society. Such opportunities have been rare in human history, and it was the good fortune of the Americans to possess an extraordinary group of public leaders, whose knowledge and insight were equal to the challenge of the occasion. Among these, Hamilton and Jefferson were preeminent. They could view the state as politicians of present times cannot—as a work of art to be accomplished, a work of artifice or invention. Hamilton was preeminently the architect of an administrative state, and Jefferson, writing to John Adams (28 Februrary 1796) declared: "This I hope will be an age of experiments in government." Government in America in the 1780s and 1790s was a subject for invention, for design, and for the deliberate shaping of institutions to bring about the realization of *novus ordo seclorum*.

In their differing visions of this new order may be found the rational basis for their different views concerning the administration of republican government. The structure of the federal republic drafted in Philadelphia in 1787 had no true historical precedent. No democratic republic of such geographical extent had previously existed. At the time of its adoption, the Constitution constituted a limited democracy, dependent upon the states for the determination of the right of suffrage. Yet the Constitution was drafted in the name of "we the people" and, unlike the farflung Roman republic, it was not held together by military power. Also unlike the Roman republic, there was no system of administration in place to coordinate the relationship between the states and the national government. Through its legions, Rome created its empire; through their representatives, the United States created their general government, of limited powers.

Nevertheless, administration in the new government was not without historical experiences upon which to draw. One hundred and fify years of colonial government preceded the separation of the United States from Great Britain. The government of England with its legislative, judicial, and ministerial practices provided examples that the founders of the new republic wished either to emulate or to avoid. Yet the circumstances of the Americans differed in a fundamental way from any historical precedents. Government in America had not evolved over centuries and had not been imposed by force of arms. Many of the colonial charters and instruments of government were the considered inventions of free and thoughtful peoples. There were significant differences among these colonial states; some were administered by royal governors under charter from the Crown, while others were self-governing under democratically derived covenants. In framing new constitutions, contention was inevitable, given the differences among the American people in political experience, philosophical assumptions, and expectations regarding the future. In retrospect, it is remarkable that the elements of conflict did not overwhelm the impulse toward union.

Conflict over the administration of the new government under the Constitution was more philosophical than ideological. The principal division was between two differing beliefs concerning human nature. From different assessments of human capabilities grew different conclusions regarding the possibilities of relationship between people and government. It was possible to agree, as did Hamilton and Jefferson, that republican government (government based upon popular consent) was of all other forms the most rational and best suited to the new order of the ages, and yet to disagree over how the affairs of this government should be administered. The point of difference between Hamilton and Jefferson and those whose views they represented was over the extent of human capacity for self-government. No longer a salient issue in American society, it is nonetheless a latent one, and there is today apprehension in the minds of some people that findings in sociobiology and behavioral science may undercut or contradict some widely held democratic assumptions regarding the nature and distribution of human capabilities.

Jeffersonian political theory assumed the infinite perfectibility of human beings—a belief basic to the eighteenth-century philosophy of the Enlightenment. But neither Hamilton nor Jefferson believed everyone equally capable of administering the affairs of government. When circumstances warranted, Jefferson was not backward about the vigorous use of executive

powers, although he regarded such action as exceptional, that is, as respon-
sive to emergencies, and not the rule for the administration of public affairs.
Believing "that government to be strongest of which every man feels himself
a part," Jefferson's ideal was a highly decentralized, participatory democracy
in which every citizen, personally, would have some part in the administration of public affairs. Consequently, he was no friend to bureaucracy, to
professionalism in public administration, or to the abstract state as the shaper
and director of national development.

To fully understand Jefferson's contribution to political thought on the
subject of administration, one must distinguish between his actions as a
public executive and his writings as a political theorist. Jefferson's views
regarding democratic administration were strongly held, but nevertheless
pragmatic. For example, he did not believe at the time of the Louisiana
Purchase that the people of New Orleans were ready for self-government.
They wanted for experience, which only time and education could provide.
He did not believe that the American people were ready for the appointment
of women to public office. He doubted that his faith in the ability of people
to govern their own affairs in their localities could be realized in the anomie
of great cities. The protection of personal freedom was Jefferson's great
purpose, and it was the Bill of Rights rather than the Constitution itself that
expressed the principles that he regarded as basic and permanent. Constitutions, in his view, should adapt to changes in society and to the advancement
of knowledge, whereas the rights of man he regarded as established by
nature and therefore inalienable.

Ironically, for the most part, it has not been self-governing local communities that have nurtured the Jeffersonian principle of individual freedom
from the impositions of official government. The federal judiciary—that
branch of government most feared and distrusted by Jefferson—has been the
primary agent for the advancement of his theoretical principles through
expansive interpretations of the Bill of Rights. Moreover, participatory democracy has not grown primarily through direct citizen involvement in public
administration. The rise of nongovernmental citizen organizations could not
have been foreseen by Jefferson. Yet, Jefferson's political philosophy, in
principle, and his profound specific distrust of bureaucracy and administrative initiative continue to influence American attitudes toward public
affairs.

It may be true as N. E. Cunningham observes in *The Process of Government
under Jefferson*, 1978, that Jefferson's presidency was more harmonious, and
presumably more efficient, than those of his predecessors. But Jefferson
benefited from the work of those predecessors in that they established the

federal executive. He did not disturb that structure, which was largely designed by Hamilton, but neither did he intentionally extend its powers. He was the first president to combine the roles of constitutional chief executive and political party leader. And this, together with his personal talents for conciliation and persuasion, enabled his "republican" administration to proceed more smoothly than has characteristically been true of presidencies before or since. Paradoxically, the principal disturbance in his administration came from the source he trusted most—self-governing localities. He felt the foundations of government shaken under his feet by the New England townships opposing his embargo on trade abroad.

Jefferson undertook to hold the federal government to strict, narrowly construed limits, yet he inadvertently opened the way to an indefinite expansion of executive initiative through his assertion of emergency powers. There were occasions, he believed, when the president should not be bound by the letter of the Constitution. These occasions arose chiefly in relation to foreign affairs, as in the purchase of Louisiana, the trade embargo of 1807, and the naval war against the Tripoli pirates. His exercise of emergency powers under the presidential authority over foreign and military affairs confirmed a pattern that has persisted to the present. The historic tendency of the American executive with exceptions, has been pro-active in relation to external affairs and reactive in relation to domestic issues, where power must be shared with Congress. Thus America today has a powerful, costly, and energetic national executive that intervenes abroad whenever it perceives the necessity, but too often seems incapable of politically rational, informed forecasting or planning for the nation's future.

In contrast to Jefferson, Hamilton did not have an optimistic faith in the innate goodness and perfectibility of human nature. Like Jefferson, he favored republican government, but with guidance by those citizens who had demonstrated their ability in the management of their personal affairs. Both men thought that government should be led by an "aristocracy" of virtue and talent, but whereas Jefferson saw the role of government as protecting personal freedoms and advancing human capabilities through education, Hamilton saw a leadership role for government in the planning and directing of the nation's development. In reviewing *The Administrative Theories of Hamilton and Jefferson*, in the *Public Administrative Review* 5, (Winter 1945):87–89, J. Donald Kingsley declared that "both the political and administrative characteristics of the Hamiltonian state are identical with the organization and objectives of the modern business corporation," and concluded that "Hamilton's ideas are modern because for one hundred years or more history has been shaped by the class whose apologist he was." This opinion, in my view, misinterprets Hamilton, but it is consistent with the treatment accorded Hamilton's political views by American historians and political scientists generally. The anti-Hamiltonian bias of academics and journalists has been documented and analyzed with care by Clinton Rossiter in *Alexander Hamilton and the Constitution* (1964). Rossiter's explanation for this bias is that these scholars, often amongst the more prestigious, wrote within the context of their own civic religion, which was (and is) democracy of a broadly equalitarian character. Thomas Jefferson has been the symbol and prophet of this civic religion, and homage to Jefferson seemed to require hostility to his opponents—the most formidable of whom was Hamilton. Consequently, the "best" of Jefferson has been contrasted with the "worst" of Hamilton. The published and reported words of each have been taken selectively out of context to support the often passionate commitments of the writers.

But apart from the important area of civil rights, latter-day Jeffersonians live in a republic in which the structures and procedures of government correspond more closely to Hamiltonian than to Jeffersonian principles. Jefferson as president not only retained the administrative system largely designed by Hamilton, but in such cases as the embargo and the Louisiana Purchase, he appeared to some observers to have adopted Hamiltonian policies. From Jefferson's viewpoint, this was untrue because he regarded these acts as exceptions to his strict views of constitutional authority. Yet his rationalizations helped to legitimize a concept of executive and emergency powers, which remains to this day a point of contention in American politics.

The most objective and perceptive interpretation of Hamilton since Rossiter is by Gerald Stourzh in *Alexander Hamilton and the Idea of Republican Government* (1970). Stourzh cites the observation of Gouverneur Morris that "General Hamilton was of that kind of men, who may most safely be trusted, for he was more covetous of glory than of wealth or power." Stourzh then adds that "Present-day political thought, exclusively attuned to the dimensions of wealth and power, is ill-equipped to grasp the relevance of this judgment." Hamilton's concern for the advancement of commerce and manufactures was not as an apologist for an emerging capitalist class. His purpose was the development of a powerful republic, independent of Europe, prosperous at home, and influential in affairs among nations. His personal ambitions coincided with his urge toward the creation of a powerful state with imperial qualities, in the classical sense. Commerce, to him, was the great engine of the wealth of nations, and in his philosophy, business should benefit the nation in a relationship mutually advantageous to business and government. But he invariably put the public interest ahead of commercial advantage.

How then, after nearly two centuries of social and political change, are we to understand the contributions of Hamilton and Jefferson to political theory on the subject of public administration. What relevance do their ideas have today? These questions have no direct and simple answers; they belong to the larger debate on the relevance of human history to present concerns. Clearly, the principles that they represented—Hamilton's concern for the effective and responsible general government, and Jefferson's defense of individual liberties—remain issues of widespread public relevance.

That the lives and thoughts of these extraordinary men continue to have meaning is evidenced by the continuing flow of published work relating to their work and careers. Since the publication in 1944 of *The Administrative Theories of Hamilton and Jefferson*, more than sixty-five books and an uncounted number of articles have appeared, roughly divided equally between these two individuals. Nothing in this literature has caused me to revise significantly the conclusions that I reached in 1944 regarding their contributions to political thought and public administration. Yet, I now believe that there is more to be said regarding their continuing relevance to American government.

The question of how Hamilton or Jefferson might have viewed the present state of government in America is unanswerable. They were men of their times, and they would necessarily have viewed our circumstances today from their own eighteenth-century background. From this point of vantage, they would very probably have quite mixed feelings about what the republic has become. We may conjecture that they would often be disappointed were they able to apply their principles critically to the American government today. Jefferson sought an empire of liberty, Hamilton an empire of power and prosperity. Both goals have been achieved in part, but the costs have been heavy and they have not yet been fully paid. Jefferson hoped for a politically decentralized nation of independent yeoman farmers and small townsmen. Hamilton favored a centrally directed republic with the power of decision vested in a strong executive. Neither ideal has materialized as it was envisioned, although elements of both may be found in present-day assumptions regarding public policies and public administration. Yet these ideals and the administrative theories through which they have been expressed, have become standards against which the performers of contemporary government is judged.

And this may be the true significance of their ideas today. The United States in the twentieth century has become very unlike the federal republic of 1789. The venerated Constitution as drafted in 1787 is only in formality and in certain largely structural particulars the fundamental law of the

United States today. The Supreme Court has assumed the function of a continuing constitutional convention and has become the nation's supreme legislative body—a fundamental shift from that balance of power and responsibility that Thomas Jefferson hoped was firmly embodied in the Constitution. Because Jefferson was as greatly concerned with the means by which public policies were to be effected as he was with the substance of policy, it seems unlikely that he would have approved of a legislating Supreme Court today, even though he believed that constitutions should be adapted to changing times. To both Jefferson and his great adversary, Hamilton, the methods by which the republic was governed were important ends of policy. Virtue in the art of governance was fundamental to Hamiltonian and Jeffersonian theories of public administration; with few exceptions (chiefly involving misconduct in office) it seems no longer to be a subject for informed concern in American public life. An essential ingredient of the theory of republican government was the concept of "virtue." The quality of virtue was familiar to political theorists of the eighteenth century, but it is next to impossible to explain to a twentieth-century audience. Virtue represented a standard for citizenship, for the performance of official duties, and for responsibility in the conduct of public affairs. The essence of virtue was responsibility—to seek the public good and to accept responsibility for those actions required to attain it.

Jefferson's concept of virtue required a careful distinction between the observance of the letter of the law and action in the public interest, when the two imperatives were in conflict. In 1810 he wrote to J. B. Colvin that: "A strict observance of written law is doubtless *one* of the high duties of a good citizen, but it is not the highest. The laws of necessity, of self-preservation, of saving our country when in danger, are higher obligations. To lose our country by a scrupulous adherence to written law would be to lose the law itself, with life, liberty, property, and all those who are enjoying them with us; thus absurdly sacrificing the end to the means." Jefferson concluded that: "The line of discrimination between cases may be difficult; but the good officer is bound to draw it at his own peril, and throw himself on the justice of his country and the rectitude of his motives."

Virtue like health is not easily defined; it is recognized most vividly by its absence. Recurring scandal in the White House and the Congress in recent decades reveals an absence of virtue and a confusion of private with public interests. The art of governing with integrity of purpose and with foresight appears too often to have been neglected. A public, bemused briefly by investigations of misconduct, is told that the constitutional system is "working" to set matters right. One may doubt that either Hamilton or Jefferson would have agreed that after-the-fact retribution cured the ailment that it sought to correct. That Americans today, as a body politique, have made no serious efforts to remedy the causes of official misconduct and to revive in some form the concept of virtue in public life suggests that in the art of governance, the nation has fallen behind the level of public probity observed by the founders.

Possibly in time, informed public concern with the practice of governance may again gain salience. The circumstances and tasks confronting government today are infinitely more numerous and more complex than were those facing the statesmen of 1787 and 1789. Technical innovations have been made in the art of administration; organization theory has developed in scope and sophistication. Yet the fundamental issues of governance remain largely in the realm of philosophy. Perceived group interests and moral convictions are, as they were in 1787, the determining elements in political doctrine and practice. But their context has changed. The nation is no longer newly forming, and its leadership no longer has a sense of history. Political metaphysics (dogmas of the "right" and "left, unsupported by empirical evidence) have displaced a regard for the political experience of mankind. Yet, to the extent that rational political thought continues to influence the theory and practice of government, the writings of Hamilton and Jefferson will continue to have relevance.

Because their public lives and thought are part of the political legacy of America and because of the extraordinary force and lucidity with which their theories were expressed, they continue even in an ahistorical age to be regarded as standards against which other concepts of governance are and should be compared. In retrospect, those hopes and assumptions concerning responsible governance so forcefully expressed in the writings of both of these men are amongst the more important of their contributions to political thought on public administration, and these writings remain a valuable resource to which a self-governing people may have continuing recourse. The American administrative state is also a democratic republic; the design and shaping of its public institutions remain a continuing task of unfinished business.

Upon this optimistic note, most assessments of the contributions of Hamilton and Jefferson end. These conclusions are consistent with the self-congratulatory tenor of most commentaries upon the successes of constitutional government in America. But there is another way in which the political and administrative theories of Hamilton and Jefferson might be evaluated. Their ways of looking at human progress might be taken as points of departure for a critical examination of our orientation toward the nation's future. Both these men set forth future-oriented political ideals that can be tested, in part at least, against the evidence of experience. Reality may afford the most reliable laboratory for examining the validity of political theories and ideas, but governments and governors everywhere seem to be erratically out of touch with it. The readiness of governments today to confront reality seems doubtful because of the conspicuous failures of policies that presumably were perceived to be realistic. Political science has been of little help in the detection of error in policy, in part because this discipline is dependent, for the validity of its assumptions, upon a science of human behavior that is as yet in an embryonic stage and may as often be misleading as it is enlightening.

The success of the American republic may have been as much a matter of fortune as of foresight. The concept of guidance through government toward a sustainable future, implicit in the administrative theories of Hamilton, has remained unacceptable to the majority of Americans, who then as now preferred unguided individual choices to "public planning" in any sense. Yet, by the test of survival, the constitutional system that took effect in 1789 has worked well thus far. If its success is owed to an exceptionally favorable combination of circumstances, including political institutions, will the system work as well when circumstances have changed—as indeed they already have?

We continue to be a nation of speculators. Unlike the followers of Hamilton and Jefferson, we do not take the measure of our assets and liabilities and shape our policies for a preferred future. A new order to the ages was born in the formative years of the republic, but its survival has been assumed with little regard for its risks of failure. Reform movements, the growth of professionalism in public administration, and the transformation of the state into the distributor of welfare and the redistributor of wealth have changed the character of the republic. Its administration has become global in extent and its financial affairs affect the lives of people everywhere. None of this change has come about through deliberate design. The administrative capabilities of the republic have made possible the exploitation of many possibilites, but we rely on history to assess the wisdom of the choices that have been made. The American people have not attempted a rational assessment of alternative futures and perhaps cannot do so.

Judged by the idealist principles of either Hamilton or Jefferson, the American republic has drifted off course. There appears to be no one general direction upon which Americans in the late twentieth century would agree. Many courses are advocated, often with passion, and more often than not they go in incompatible directions. Even though their differences were great, Hamilton and Jefferson shared a common faith in the creation of a new order of the ages by purpose and design. For them the state, as the institutional structure within which society could develop, was a work of art. They proposed different but not wholly incompatible designs for America's future. In contrast to prevailing attitudes today, both believed in the ability of society to plan, although in different ways, for its future. This was not planning the future, nor was it the detailed, dogmatic, ideological planning of the centralized bureaucracies that prevail over large parts of the world today. Neither was it the *ad hoc*, incremental, reactive approach to social problems that characterize today's liberal democracies.

Within the limits of nature, human learning and volition seem capable of setting the goals and selecting the means leading toward that new order for humanity that motivated the public lives of Hamilton and Jefferson. Their administrative theories were purposive as well as prescriptive. They were designed to move America toward that new order of the ages that has not yet been truly attained. We understand these men best as prophets, showing us the way to look at the relationships between society and government, even though their particular value judgments differed in detail and are less to be relied upon than is the forward-looking direction of their thought.

We have learned little more than they knew regarding the potentialities of human society, but we know where improvement is needed, even if we don't know how it may best be attained. What we seem to lack is the will to create a better world, guided by the best knowledge we can obtain from science and experience. We cannot determine the future, but our actions guided by purpose and foresight may influence its circumstances. To achieve this purpose, a commitment larger than to the self or the present is necessary. To envision the best that the nation may be, and to lead the people toward its attainment, is the commitment to civic virtue exemplified by the public lives of Hamilton and Jefferson. This larger than personal concern for the future of the nation is our most enduring legacy from the political theories of Hamilton and Jefferson.

L.K.C.

THE
ADMINISTRATIVE THEORIES
OF HAMILTON & JEFFERSON

PART I

THE ADMINISTRATIVE THEORIES OF
ALEXANDER HAMILTON

ALEXANDER HAMILTON: A BIOGRAPHICAL NOTE

Alexander Hamilton, born January 11, 1757, on the British West Indian island of Nevis, was sent to America by relatives of his mother to complete his formal education and in 1773 entered King's College in the city of New York. He early became an enthusiastic advocate of American autonomy, writing tracts in defense of the Continental Congress and of the Colonial cause. After the outbreak of war in 1776 he took command of an artillery company and in 1777 joined Washington's staff as secretary to the Commander-in-Chief. Resigning from Washington's staff in 1781, he served as a regimental commander and took part in the siege of Yorktown in October of that year.

Hamilton's term of service as Washington's secretary covered the period when the maladministration of the Confederation was at its worst; and the impotence of the Congress and the factiousness of the states convinced him of the necessity of a strong, independent centralized administration to protect American freedom by insuring order and justice. The variety of comprehensive reports, plans, and political correspondence which Washington assigned to him added immensely to Hamilton's experience in administrative affairs. Equally important was the confidence which he won from Washington, for without that confidence his career as Secretary of the Treasury would hardly have been possible.

Hamilton's political theories appear to have taken shape about 1780, for in his letter to James Duane of New York on September 3, 1780, and in the series of six papers entitled *The Continentalist*, published in 1781 and 1782, he set forth nearly all the policies which he was later to champion. The significance of *The Continentalist* has unfortunately been obscured by Hamilton's better-known contributions to *The Federalist*, but it deserves recognition as the most succinct yet comprehensive statement of Hamilton's political views and is an indispensable background for an understanding of the doctrines which he expounded in *The Federalist* and in his great Treasury papers.

During the winter of 1782–83 Hamilton served as a delegate from New York to the Congress and was increasingly convinced of the "absolute necessity" of a change of government. In 1786 he was appointed as one of the New York delegates to the Annapolis Convention, and, after the failure of this assembly to achieve substantial results, Hamilton worked strenuously to bring about a national convention to revise the constitution of the Union. In 1786 he had been elected as a representative to the legislature of the state of New York, and there pursued an energetic campaign to support and to strengthen the federal government.

In 1782 Hamilton was admitted to the bar of New York State, and in June of that year he was appointed state receiver of Continental taxes. This was Hamilton's first civil administrative post, and he characteristically stipulated as a condition of his acceptance that he have the special right of conferring with the state legislature, thus approximating the close legislative-administrative relationship which he believed effective government required. But the reluctance of the state officials to co-operate in enforcing the policies of the Continental Superintendent of Finance, Robert Morris, convinced him that only through an independent and supreme national administration could national policies be effected.

Following the action of Congress calling for a national convention in Philadelphia, Hamilton endeavored to promote the adoption of a centralized constitution to provide for the needs of a united and energetic nation. As a member of the convention, Hamilton urged the strengthening of the central administrative machinery at the expense of state sovereignty. He asserted that the convention could do no better than to model the new government after the British constitution. Although the Constitution as finally adopted fell short of Hamilton's nationalist objectives, he urged its prompt acceptance and collaborated with John Jay and James Madison in the writing of *The Federalist*, a series of letters designed to secure acceptance of the new government by the people of New York. As delegate to the Poughkeepsie Convention of 1788 he succeeded in persuading the state to ratify the new Constitution without the attachment of crippling amendments.

In 1789 Hamilton, at Washington's request, became the first Secretary of the Treasury, and until January 31, 1795, he assumed a leadership in the formulation of policy which led enemies to charge that he presumed the role of "prime minister." During these years he attempted to shift the balance of power in the federal Union in the direction which he advocated in the Philadelphia Convention and, in so doing, aroused the bitter hostility of Jefferson, Madison, and the opponents of administrative centralization. His vital contribution to the literature of public administration is contained in the great public papers transmitted to the Congresses of this period. In chronological summary the major of these reports were: January 9, 1790, *First Report on the Public Credit;* December 13, 1790, *Report on a National Bank;* January 28, 1791, *Report on the Establishment of a Mint;* February 23, 1791, *Opinion as to the Constitutionality of the Bank of the United States;*[1] December 5, 1791, *Report on Manufactures;* January 16, 1795, *Second Report on the Public Credit.*

Following his retirement from the Treasury, Hamilton continued as ex officio adviser of the Washington administration and subsequently of the John Adams cabinet. In July, 1798, he was appointed Inspector-General of the new army which was being created in expectation of war with France. Conflict with John Adams over matters of policy and personality led to a bitter public attack by Hamilton which probably insured the defeat of Adams by Jefferson in the presidential election of 1800.

In July, 1800, Hamilton retired from the Army and took no further part in public office. He nevertheless remained an active critic of public policy until his death on July 12, 1804, from a wound sustained in a duel with Aaron Burr.

[1] Transmitted not to Congress but to President Washington at his request.

CHAPTER I

THE PERSONALITY FACTOR IN HAMILTON'S PHILOSOPHY OF ADMINISTRATION

BECAUSE administrative ideas are a product of human thought and involve social relationships which arouse the emotions, the mental nature of an administrator must be considered in any interpretation of his work. As the principles of administration are discovered and refined, the subjective element in administrative thinking may be reduced. But, wherever social relationships and purposes are concerned, factors of personal preference are as likely to influence administrative decisions as are objective considerations of managerial technique. Public administration is truly a branch of politics, and the administrative theories of great public administrators cannot be understood without reference to their political objectives, their emotional promptings, and the measure of their values. Although Alexander Hamilton anticipated an objective "science of administration," his administrative thinking projected deep personal political convictions; and so, before an appraisal of his administrative philosophy is undertaken, the bearing of his personality upon his public life deserves attention.

QUALITIES OF INTELLECT

.... my ambition is prevalent, so that I .... would willingly risk my life, though not my character, to exalt my station.—To EDWARD STEVENS.[1]

The career of Alexander Hamilton affords the life-study of a purpose. It affords a notable example of great natural talent directed by its possessor to a consciously determined objective. While the source of Hamilton's purposeful energy remains undiscovered, his accomplishments testify to the strength of his ambition. Tinctured with vanity and a romantic urge to fame, his purpose was to do some work of truly historic significance; the motive was conscious, was deliberately cultivated, and guided the fateful decisions of his career. He planned early for ends which he foresaw in terms of magnitude rather than in detail, but which always involved leadership in some great human struggle. The urge to leadership was evident in Hamilton's earliest correspondence and continued as a domi-

[1] November 11, 1769, *The Works of Alexander Hamilton*, ed. Henry Cabot Lodge (Federal ed.; New York: G. P. Putnam's Sons, 1904), IX, 37.

nating force in his personal development until the closing months of his life.

Hamilton possessed the abilities necessary to realize his ambition, and he developed some of them to an extraordinary degree as he rose to fame. Of these talents by no means the least was a sense of order and logic which found expression in the architectural quality of his great public papers;[2] he wrote as he thought—directly and emphatically—to a distinctly utilitarian purpose. Only in his more intimate correspondence does one find the light touch of humor, and never the discursiveness of a Jefferson. Indeed, his exposition, though orderly and explicit, is sometimes so weighted with unrelieved detail as to try the patience of the reader. But, although he may occasionally seem to labor the obvious, one must recall that Hamilton addressed a public which doubted the utility of banks, misunderstood the nature of credit, and resented even a minimum of governmental control.

This sense of order and logic complemented an extraordinary capacity for analytic thinking. Hamilton's ability to reduce a political problem to its component parts was a factor invaluable to his political and administrative undertakings, and only when violence of impulse distorted his perspective, or when his logic overbore an appreciation of the nonrational in human behavior, did his analytic approach to politics fail. His comprehension of relationships, proportions, and social processes was indispensable to the formulation and execution of his public policies. Hamilton's power of analysis would have been less valuable had he not the art to use it swiftly and pointedly. He could work with a concentration of effort that approached the limit of his physical endurance, and he repeatedly routed opposition by rejoinder so swift and incisive that his opponents were utterly confounded. Even the subtle Madison was reluctant to take the field against him. Probably no other American statesman has been able to persuade so effectively by reasoned argument; but his persuasiveness was fired by the inner conviction of rightness. Hamilton felt an urgency and an inevitability about his work that pervaded the most technical and utilitarian of his papers.

[2] The more accessible sources of Hamilton's writings are: *The Works of Alexander Hamilton Comprising His Correspondence and His Political and Official Writings, Exclusive of the Federalist, Civil and Military*, ed. J. C. Hamilton (7 vols.; New York: Charles S. Francis & Co., 1850–51), and *The Works of Alexander Hamilton*, ed. Henry Cabot Lodge (10 vols.; New York: G. P. Putnam's Sons, 1885). A second, or Federal, edition of the Lodge collection was published in 1904 with the addition of two volumes containing *The Federalist* and is the best general source for Hamilton's writings. Hamilton's major Treasury papers are printed in *American State Papers, Finance*, Vol. I, and in *Papers on Public Credit, Commerce and Finance by Alexander Hamilton*, ed. Samuel McKee, Jr. (New York: Columbia University Press, 1934).

Along with these more solid attributes of order, power of analysis, and concentration, Hamilton possessed a fertile and active imagination. Insight rather than fancy was the essence of the quality, and he was ever concerned with possibilities based firmly on actualities. Yet one cannot concur with charges that he was utterly devoid of idealism. Hamilton accepted the current notions of progress and perfectibility, but he did not believe that society could instinctively and without direction achieve its greatest good. One can therefore agree that he was out of step with eighteenth-century liberal thought in so far as adherence to the doctrine of individualism and the minimized state affords a test of orthodoxy.

The most apparent nonrational trait in the Hamiltonian mind was a capacity for swift and violent passion. Impulse, the key to Hamilton's personal charm, fitted also the lock to a veritable Pandora's box of trouble. Unerring in judgment when his head was cool, Hamilton was capable of colossal blunders when he substituted impulse for insight, and his impulsiveness was the more significant because of the sharpness and strength of his emotional reactions. He knew only friends and enemies; with him it was the peace pipe or the tomahawk. Hamilton evidently recognized the force of his emotions, but he overstated their effect upon his thought when he confessed to Henry Knox that "my heart has always been the master of my judgment."[3] Although he recognized the necessity of compromise, he was scarcely equal to conciliation; and his sense of personal rightness, seldom yielding to expediency, proved at times a political weakness of first magnitude.

Without doubt Hamilton was imperious. He was, nevertheless, capable of modesty and did not adjudge himself infallible; faith in his own conceptions did not blind him to the merit in the ideas of others. But he was possessed of an irrepressible zeal for command. He could not resist the appeal of military authority, yet he was no militarist; he accepted the subordination of military power to civil authority, and his dictatorial tendencies contained no element of tyranny. But his authoritarian urge accompanied a confidence of intellectual superiority rankling to men of lesser talents. Joined to an impetuous disposition, this imperiousness became a dangerous quality in so forceful a personality. These were emotional factors which defeated Hamilton's otherwise certain capacity for political management. He could not always bend himself to conciliate when conciliation was necessary in order to control, and his weapons of rational persuasion and analytic demolition of counterargument were so

[3] March 14, 1799, *Works*, ed. Lodge, X, 348.

strong that he slighted the arts of cultivation and manipulation in which Burr and Jefferson excelled.

Hamilton's political life was, in a sense, a tragedy of self-defeat, for, great as was his success as a political and administrative leader, he appears to have fallen short of his aspirations to statesmanship. To the psychologist his career affords a study in frustration. He alone prepared his descent from power by an unnecessary break with the Livingston family in New York, in the quarrels with Jefferson and Burr, and in his fantastic attack upon John Adams. The Reynolds affair reveals more clearly than his major political battles the inner weakness of the man. Here, as in politics, the strength of momentary impulse and vanity overbore insight and reason. Hamilton had redoubtable enemies, but the greatest of them he harbored within himself.

Without this intellectual-emotional frame of reference one can hardly attempt a true analysis of Hamilton's ideas. Seldom given to contradiction, he sometimes, in the impulse of occasion, overstated his opinions; conversely, because many of his writings were designed to win the cooperation of persons who were opposed to his theories, he sometimes modified his opinion to avoid arousing prejudice which would defeat his purpose. Particularly is this true of his speeches in the Poughkeepsie Convention of 1788, of *The Federalist*, and of some of his private letters actually intended to be made public. But Hamilton's exceptional frankness and repeated emphasis on his fundamental tenets largely obviate the difficulty of determining his true position on most matters.

QUALITIES OF LEADERSHIP

. . . . the public interest. This in my eyes is sacred.—To HENRY LEE.[4]

The nation's first dominating administrator, Hamilton possessed the qualities most needful to his role. His powers of intuition, imagination, and insight were the mental tools indispensable to forecasting policy and planning for execution. His sense of order and logic was the essence of his ability to organize. He could co-ordinate policy with procedure—he understood relationships. The dissection and the construction of ideas were so natural to him as to seem involuntary. His disposition to command, added to his extraordinary energy and intelligence, made him a natural leader among men, and he was said to have regarded himself as "prime minister" of the Washington administration. John Adams, speaking of his own administration, confessed that Hamilton was "commander-in-chief of the House of Representatives, of the Senate, of the heads of department,

[4] March 7, 1800, *ibid.*, p. 364.

of General Washington, and last and least if you will, of the President of the United States."[5] Never could such an administrator be confined within a single portfolio; his was ever the directing mind, the pervasive, commanding influence. With these intellectual powers was combined a detachment resulting perhaps from his alien place of birth but certainly reinforced by his executive disposition.

Hamilton possessed the patience, the perseverance, and the persuasiveness necessary to direct the actions of others, yet the art of managing men was the least of his executive talents. Overborn by his feeling for command, the manipulative-conciliatory qualities which he demonstrated on certain notable occasions failed to achieve full growth. The defect was injurious to his political efforts, for he never fully understood the necessity of popular leadership as the focus for that congealing of national feeling which he hoped to bring about. Although he seldom failed to appreciate the degree to which control is bottomed on consent, he never understood that popular consent does not automatically respond to wise and honest administration. He did not see that to convince the most enlightened strata of the population was insufficient. The consent of the uninformed and misinformed had also to be won. The necessity for securing consent in order to control irked his impulse to command, and that the statesman must find his sanctions in the predilections of the uneducated and illiberal mass of the people seemed contrary to nature and reason. It was this unwillingness to go to the people that afforded substance for the contention that Hamilton was antirepublican.

Hamilton's conception of leadership was based upon the premise that it is the business of politics to deal with things as they are and not as they ought to be. He believed that the "true politician" takes human nature and human society as he finds them, compounded of good and ill tendencies. In contrast to Jefferson's notion that political institutions should promote the perfecting of society, Hamilton sometimes argued that the wise politician would not seek to disturb the "natural direction" of social movements, that he would "favor all those institutions and plans which tend to make men happy according to their natural bent, which multiply the sources of individual enjoyment and increase national resources and strength."[6] Yet one cannot truly say that Hamilton disbelieved in the possibility of social progress, for his political program was aimed at creating what seemed to him a better society. Indeed, his enthusiasm for pub-

[5] *The Works of John Adams*, ed. Charles Francis Adams (10 vols.; Boston: Little, Brown & Co., 1856), X, 127–28.

[6] *Defence of the Funding System, Works*, ed. Lodge, VIII, 448–49.

lic planning and for governmental regulation of economic development belies faith in the wisdom of laissez faire. Convinced that the natural direction of society was toward his vision, he could contend that his effort merely facilitated the flow of social forces toward their natural direction, whereas his opponents disturbed the natural course of things. His interest in education, less compelling than Jefferson's, illustrates his belief in the capacity of man for moral and intellectual growth. But Hamilton premised his political program on the assumption that most men improve little from one generation to another, and he considered it folly to suppose that new political institutions could alter old ambitions and methods in politics.

It would be easy to overemphasize the contrast between Jefferson and Hamilton in terms of their reliance on the perfectibility of man in determining their programs and methods of leadership. But it is clear that, whereas Jefferson's political theories (although not necessarily his methods) made sense only if man's perfectibility were assumed, Hamilton's objectives and methods did not depend upon the doctrine of perfectibility for their logic. Rather Hamilton's political doctrines concerned what might be done by man as he was, not what might be done by man in the course of his moral and intellectual growth. Jeffersonian political and administrative institutions were thus conceived to change and permit change in man's ways of thinking. Jefferson's decentralized federal union was a vast school of citizenship, whereas the centralized national union of Hamilton was an instrument for canalizing the existing conflict of passions into generally acceptable policy.

Hamilton's political leadership was essentially administrative in character. It was leadership in getting certain things done; it was leadership concerned primarily with existing problems and secondarily with future possibilities. This leadership did not neglect planning for the future as an aspect of public administration but was based upon the assumption that men would behave in the future much as they had in the past. Jefferson's planning assumed, or at least professed the hope, that the man of tomorrow would be wiser and more generous than his forebears, and his leadership might be in this respect described as philosophic rather than administrative in character. It was less concerned with the doing of things than with what ought to be done.

The effect of Hamilton's political career upon the nature of his administrative ideas can be described only in generalities. His early enthusiasm for the American revolutionary cause and the natural rights of man, reflected in *A Full Vindication of the Measures of Congress* and in *The Farmer*

Refuted, was overshadowed during the era of confederation by a distrust
of popular theories of public administration and a recognition of the need
for stability and authority in political institutions. His experience between
the years 1776 and 1786 had changed the emphasis of his thinking; army
life and the incapacity of the Confederation appear to have strengthened
whatever latent tendency he may have had to admire strong and energetic
government. The intrigue and impotence of the Congress, the jealousy and
provincialism of many of the state leaders, and the suffering of the revolutionary army from want of effective co-ordinated support filled Hamilton
with fear of governments which failed through want of proper organization to create an effective, responsible directing power. His unsuccessful
efforts in Congress of 1782–83 to provide for the national debt, to pay the
soldiers, and to make public the debates of Congress served to deepen his
conviction that strong executive leadership was indispensable to the national safety and welfare. His responsibilities as receiver of Continental
taxes in New York in 1782, as a member of the Continental Congress in
1782–83, as a major organizer of the Bank of New York in 1784, and his
various military responsibilities during the Revolution aided in the development of Hamilton's techniques of administration and must have contributed to the growth of his theory of executive responsibility suggested
in *The Federalist* and applied during his service as Secretary of the Treasury.

The evidence suggests that Hamilton's personal qualities made for
greater success in administration than in party politics in the narrower
sense. Writing to James A. Bayard in 1802, he proposed a reorganization
of the Federalist party, with local, state, and national committees, party
funds, party propaganda, and benevolent aid to immigrants and to labor.[7]
The plan which Hamilton outlined indicates that his talents might have
served well in political organization and that he was prepared to turn them
in that direction.[8] However, his tendency toward inflexibility and ex-
clusiveness in formulating policy was hardly compatible with political
success and actually weakened his administrative leadership. Unwillingness to conciliate the opposition was not necessarily fatal to political
leadership, but failure to conciliate colleagues and followers constituted a
weakness which in part accounts for the disintegration of federalism within a decade after the death of its great leader. He became a "colossus" to

---

[7] *Ibid.*, X, 434–36.

[8] An interesting analysis of Hamilton's ideas regarding political parties was made by James
Bryce in *The Predictions of Hamilton and De Tocqueville* ("Johns Hopkins University Studies,"
Vol. V [Baltimore: Johns Hopkins University Press, 1887]).

those Federalists who, believing in him, followed his bidding; but he carried his independence of mind, his reliance upon his own extraordinary abilities, too far for successful party-building. Thus, in a sense, Hamilton's great abilities proved in fact a weakness to himself politically and to his party. Had he lived longer, he might have learned how to govern without appearing to dominate and how to formulate policy without appearing to dictate, for the letter to Bayard written two years before his duel with Burr showed that Hamilton's political methods were by no means crystallized at the end of his career.

Hamilton's analytic, logical, organizing intellect is apparent in every phase of his administrative program, and his independence of mind, love of command, and thorough patience in propagating ideas are unmistakably evident in his great state papers. His performance as an administrator reveals, to the extent that information is available, the same accentuated traits which have been noted in this chapter. The unique quality of Hamilton's personality lay not in its complexity (Jefferson was a more complex figure) but in its sharp accentuation. His was a leadership in ideas but even more in action. As he loved the creative use of power, so he hated its abuse. He attacked the perversion of public trust to personal self-seeking and labored in public office to the sacrifice of the fortune which private effort would have brought him. His ambition was indeed "prevalent," but, guided by his sense of personal integrity and respect for the public interest, it bore no element of danger to the republic which he served.

CHAPTER II

THE POLITICAL BASIS OF HAMILTON'S ADMINISTRATIVE IDEAS

HAMILTON believed that "society naturally divides itself into two political divisions—the *few* and the *many*, who have distinct interests."[1] If government were controlled by the *few*, they would tyrannize over the many; and, if in the hands of the *many*, they would tyrannize over the few. Political power, he held, ought to be in the hands of both, for he agreed with Hobbes that the object of government was to avert social conflict.[2] He perceived the role of government as the

[1] "Brief of Speech on Submitting His Plan of Constitution" (1787), *Works*, ed. Lodge, I, 375.

[2] However, Hamilton did not agree with Hobbes's theories concerning man in a state of nature, for he believed men always subject to restraints of moral (natural) law (see *The Farmer Refuted*, February 5, 1775, *ibid.*, pp. 61–62).

direction of divergent and conflicting social forces toward generally beneficial ends. Thus public policy was evolved out of the vortex of social controversy, and it was the duty of the statesman to guide the process to assure the general good.

If government were to act in the common interest of contending groups, society must achieve some common basis of agreement as to the powers and responsibilities of those intrusted with the formulation of public policy. About details of policy Hamilton conceded that differences of opinion might exist, but concerning the obligation to obey public authority, and the basis upon which that authority rested, essential unanimity ought to obtain. Creating this area of agreement Hamilton conceived to be a task of statesmanship. To this end he held that the political leader should utilize the psychological, economic, and constitutional materials at his disposal to construct an administrative system acceptable to the public at large and capable of undertaking all the responsibilities which might reasonably be intrusted to it. Government must be so constructed as to influence the views and actions of the governed. It should likewise reflect popular attitudes and interests. It should derive support from and exercise control over that most fertile area of social contention, the economic sphere. And, finally, government ought to represent a constitutional order in which the social processes could be carried on with a predictable continuity.

PSYCHOLOGICAL BASIS OF GOVERNMENT

No government, any more than an individual, will long be respected without being truly respectable; nor be truly respectable, without possessing a certain portion of order and stability.—"THE FEDERALIST," NO. 62.[3]

Foremost of all the powers which governments ought to possess, Hamilton placed the power to command respect, which at home or abroad was the indispensable attribute of authority. Public opinion and the attitude of foreign powers were the measures by which the prestige of a government was determined. During the Revolution and under the Confederation the status of the Union, so measured, sank far beneath Hamilton's conception of what the public safety required, and his constant objective, therefore, was to heighten the tone of public authority to the end that due deference be rendered the Union by the people at home and by the powers abroad.

Between the quality of public opinion and its significance as a basis for political authority Hamilton drew a sharp distinction. He placed a low

[3] Edward Mead Earle (ed.), *The Federalist* (Washington: National Home Library Foundation, 1937), p. 407.

value on popular views in the formulation of public policy, yet he granted that public opinion, whether well or ill founded, was the governing principle of human affairs. Recognizing that the views of the governed often differed materially from those of the governors, he held that "the science of policy is the knowledge of human nature."[4] For public opinion, the ultimate arbiter of every measure of government, must be brought to accept measures wise in the public interest. Popular confidence in political leaders was necessary to secure this consent, but he believed that confidence was gained not by the representation of diverse popular notions but rather by good administration.

While Hamilton did not believe that the role of the statesman was to reflect public opinion, neither did he believe that public sentiment could or should be ignored. "There are certain conjunctures," he declared, "when it may be necessary and proper to disregard the opinions which the majority of the people have formed; but, in the general course of things, the popular views, and even prejudices, will direct the actions of the rulers."[5] Of the relation of opinion to administration Hamilton observed that "if a general opinion prevails that the old way is bad, whether true or false, and this obstructs or relaxes the operations of the public service, a change is necessary, if it be but for the sake of change."[6] Yet, because Hamilton sometimes decried public opinion as valueless, one should not conclude that he underestimated its power. He had suffered bitter attack by opponents who professed to represent popular opinion, and his imperious nature sought compensation for a lack of popularity in contempt for the quality of popular thinking. He respected the power of public opinion but had little faith in its content, and he would never have agreed that the voice of the people was the voice of God.

Although skeptical of the quality of public opinion, Hamilton held that freedom to think, to express, to assemble for discussion, and to publish was essential to the preservation of free government. Civil liberty, he wrote, "is only natural liberty, modified and secured by the sanctions of civil society."[7] He considered it "the greatest of terrestrial blessings" and believed the whole human race entitled to it. Men as well as measures should bear the public scrutiny, for it was essential not only to criticize an unwise measure "but to hold up to the people who is the author, that, in this our free and elective government, he may be removed from the seat of power."[8]

[4] "Speech in the Federal Convention, June 22, 1787," *Works*, ed. Lodge, I, 407.

[5] "Speech in the New York Ratifying Convention, June 21, 1788," *ibid.*, II, 20.

[6] To James Duane, September 3, 1780, *ibid.*, p. 238.   [7] *The Farmer Refuted, ibid.*, I, 87.

[8] "Speech in the Case of Harry Croswell" (1804), *ibid.*, VIII, 390.

But respect for duly constituted authority was likewise a requisite for freedom, and civil liberty did not include license to bring the government into popular contempt by deliberate misrepresentation and irresponsible abuse of public persons and measures. Although Hamilton had initially opposed the Alien and Sedition Acts of 1798, exclaiming, "Let us not establish a tyranny,"[9] he supported the measures enacted as necessary to protect the government from subversion.

One may deduce that, from his observations, Hamilton conceived human conduct as the interaction of two major psychological forces: the internal drives of self-interest and the external coercion of social convention in part expressed through governmental constraint. In the Constitutional Convention of 1787 Hamilton described the forces which he believed to govern the behavior of men:

Take mankind as they are, and what are they governed by? Their passions. There may be in every government a few choice spirits, who may act from more worthy motives. One great error is that we suppose mankind more honest than they are. Our prevailing passions are ambition and interest; and it will ever be the duty of a wise government to avail itself of the passions, in order to make them subservient to the public good; for these ever induce us to action.[10]

The factors of self-interest and ambition did not of themselves conduce to public wisdom, particularly as they afforded a handle to the manipulative schemes of demagogues. Yet interests compounded to form public opinion constituted the mainspring of political action. Thus new meaning appears in Hamilton's assertion that "the science of policy is the knowledge of human nature." Likewise the directive role of the administrator becomes apparent, for without the judicious guidance of statesmanship the clash of interests would destroy society.

But were there not interests in society utterly opposed to the general good—forces which the most artful statesmen could never direct toward the public welfare? Hamilton conceded that there were, and he believed that coercive power was essential to the maintenance of public order. His logical mind rejected the lawlessness and confusion that threatened the orderly processes of government in the post-Revolutionary years. He viewed temporizing measures as necessary to governments unable or unwilling to maintain a force effectual to awe sedition and hostility, but he feared that widespread popular disobedience would in time destroy all respect for law and lead to the establishment of government by violence. The coercion of custom was preferable to coercion by arms, but the threat of force in support of the laws was essential to their firm establishment.

[9] To Oliver Wolcott, June 29, 1798, *ibid.*, X, 295.   [10] *Ibid.*, I, 408.

Hamilton was deeply concerned that the habits of the American people respecting the authority of the new Union be properly formed. " 'Tis with governments as with individuals," he explained; "first impressions and early habits give a lasting bias to the temper and character. Our governments, hitherto, have no habits. How important to the happiness, not of America alone, but of mankind, that they should acquire good ones!"[11] In *The Federalist*, No. 27, Hamilton elaborated this role of habit in society, declaring that

the authority of the Union, and the affections of the citizens towards it, will be strengthened, rather than weakened, by its extension to what are called matters of internal concern; and will have less occasion to recur to force, in proportion to the familiarity and comprehensiveness of its agency. The more it circulates through those channels and currents in which the passions of mankind naturally flow, the less will it require the aid of the violent and perilous expedients of compulsion.[12]

Motivated by his interests, man was nevertheless conditioned by his habits. Hence the canalizing role of government was not only to direct human passions toward socially desirable ends but also to induce the formation of popular habits which would facilitate the orderly operation of government.

Hamilton's picture of society seems to be drawn with reference to his own marked talents. The psychological factors relating to government called for a political leadership possessed of the qualities of objectivity, insight, and firmness which he in full measure possessed. Human nature required that leadership travel with the current of public opinion, but statecraft required of leaders that they attempt to guide opinion in the direction of the general interest, and it was to this directive role in society that Hamilton aspired. He saw society in terms of the need which he believed it had for his abilities, and perhaps it was because of the very personal quality of this vision that he was able to provide the administrative leadership which the American people needed in the establishment of a truly national government.

THE ECONOMIC BASIS OF GOVERNMENT

There is no stronger sign of combinations unfriendly to the general good, than when the partisans of those in power *raise an indiscriminate cry against men of property.*—"To THE INDEPENDENT AND PATRIOTIC ELECTORS OF THE STATE OF NEW YORK."[13]

[11] "Phocion," Letter II (1784), *ibid.*, IV, 288.

[12] Earle, *op. cit.*, p. 168. Curiously, Jacques Necker, commenting on the federal executive power in America, held conversely its removal from "the first movement of the individual passions," separated by the states from the common contentions of men, to be a source of strength (*An Essay on the True Principles of Executive Power in Great States* [London: G. G. J. & J. Robinson, 1792], II, 54).

[13] March 9(?), 1789, *Works*, ed. Lodge, II, 119.

However Hamilton may have viewed Madison's dictum that the most common and durable source of faction was the unequal distribution of property, he certainly concurred in the belief that this cause of faction could not be removed and that, therefore, the responsibility of government was to control its effects. Although on one occasion he contended that "providence has distributed its bounties in the manner best adapted to the general order and happiness,"[14] he was not adverse to assisting Providence in its work. Some public controls in the economic sphere he considered necessary to reduce the dangers of faction. Declaring that no man ought to be hated for being either rich or poor, he warned against the consequences of attacks by the government upon men of property. He held such abuse neither just nor wise, "because it tends to alienate those who are endeavored to be made odious, from the government under which they live, and to incline them to favor changes in the hope of bettering their condition; and because, in the second place, by destroying the confidence of the body of the people in men of property, it makes a cooperation between them for the defence of their common privileges and interests more difficult, and consequently renders it more easy for aspiring men, in possession of power, to prosecute schemes of personal aggrandizement and usurpation."[15]

Although he held the power of wealth in great respect, it does not necessarily follow that Hamilton accepted class domination as a political principle. Without doubt he wished the concentrated, fluid wealth of the country to be at the disposal of the government, and accordingly he valued the support of the moneyed classes above popularity with the numerically greater but financially weaker multitude. But his policies were shaped to the end that the power of the nation's purse would be vested ultimately in the government itself rather than in the hands of any particular class or group. For he believed that political power should lodge exclusively in the hands neither of the many nor of the few, and he declared that the "power which holds the purse-strings absolutely, must rule."[16] Because "property begets influence," he contended that representative government should be so constituted as to avoid the dangers of domination by a plutocracy.[17] He recognized that the advantages enjoyed by the rich and powerful might tempt them to enterprise against the common liberty, but he felt that the force of public opinion, appreciation of true interests, and a re-

[14] *Ibid.*   [15] *Ibid.*

[16] To James Duane, September 3, 1780, *ibid.*, I, 218–19.

[17] "Speech in the New York Assembly, January 27, 1787," *ibid.*, VIII, 27.

spect for the authority of the law afforded security against aristocratic usurpation of political power.

Hamilton agreed with Madison that regulation of the various and interfering economic interests forms the principal task of legislation. However, he parted company with the Jeffersonian advocates of localism and the minimized state in prescribing the way in which the regulatory task was to be undertaken. He did not believe that commerce could or should assume sole responsibility for its own regulation, and he would therefore have the general government insure the economic well-being of the Union through seasonably interposed aids to commerce, combined with such regulation and restriction as the public interest required. He would not restrict the government to police or philanthropic functions but would have it the nation's first entrepreneur. The state would enter the field of economic enterprise as a promoter of the economic interests of the whole people. It served private interests, but directed them in the name of the general welfare. Yet the role of government was co-operative rather than domineering, and at no time did Hamilton suggest the competence of government to undertake a thoroughgoing regimentation of the economic order.

Hamilton's economic doctrines corresponded to no contemporaneous theory in all respects but inclined most strongly toward mercantilism. Recognizing a right of individuals to property and profit, he nevertheless held that the government, on behalf of the public welfare, might act at variance with private interests. Illustrating this belief was his assertion that "wherever, indeed, a right of property is infringed for the general good, if the nature of the case admits of compensation, it ought to be made; but if compensation be impracticable, that impracticability ought not to be an obstacle to a clearly essential reform."[18] He declared that "if a government voluntarily bargains away the rights, or disposes of the property, of its citizens, in their enjoyment, possession, or power, it is bound to make compensation for the thing of which it hath deprived them; but if they are actually dispossessed of those rights, or that property, by the casualties of war, or a revolution, the State, if the public good requires it, may abandon them to the loss without being obliged to make reparation."[19] Equally revealing are his views concerning the relationship of private to public finance. "Public utility," he wrote, "is more truly the object of public banks than private profit,"[20] and of the first United States Bank he ex-

[18] *Vindication of the Funding System*, No. III (1791[?]), *ibid.*, III, 16.

[19] "Speech on Acceding to the Independence of Vermont, April, 1787," *ibid.*, VIII, 60.

[20] *Report on a National Bank* (December 13, 1790), *ibid.*, III, 419.

plained that it was not to be a "mere matter of private property, but a political machine of the greatest importance to the State."[21]

In discussing the necessity of vesting Congress with the power of regulating trade, Hamilton most specifically dissented from the laissez faire theory. He observed that "there are some who maintain that trade will regulate itself, and is not to be benefited by the encouragements or restraints of government. Such persons will imagine that there is no need of a common directing power. This is one of those wild speculative paradoxes, which have grown into credit among us, contrary to the uniform practice and sense of the most enlightened nations."[22]

Although Hamilton never developed his economic philosophy into a systematic thesis, the several general contentions which we have described are so emphatically and repeatedly stated in his writings that they afford a fairly accurate summary of his major doctrines. He saw government in the role of a dynamic intermediary, directing the classes contending for the control of wealth toward ends which seemed to him mutually beneficial. Leadership in the field of private economic enterprise he thought belonged to those groups or individuals who, by their acquisition of property, had given evidence of their ability to manage affairs. But no group or individual ought to aspire to domination of society. Economic leadership was distinguished from political control. And, although the preponderance of private economic power might pass into the hands of the wealthy and able, they were to be restrained by public opinion, by law, and by their own interests correctly understood from usurping political authority which belonged to all.

Hamilton viewed wealth as an essential condition for power and therefore as an element indispensable to the support of government. The public regulation of the great sources of wealth was a cardinal principle of his economic policy. His early and continued interest in public finance was but an aspect of this concern and can be placed in true perspective only when measured by the vaster scope of his economic and political ideas. For to Hamilton finance was ever the means to an end far greater than national banks and funded debts—the building of a unified and invigorated national state.

THE CONSTITUTIONAL BASIS OF GOVERNMENT

A government, the constitution of which renders it unfit to be trusted with all the powers which a free people ought to delegate to any government, would be an unsafe and improper depositary of the NATIONAL INTERESTS.—"THE FEDERALIST," No. 23.[23]

---

[21] *Ibid.*, p. 424.   [22] *The Continentalist*, No. V, *ibid.*, I, 267–68.   [23] Earle, *op. cit.*, p. 145.

In a society formed out of the fears and desires of the people, combining
its contradictory wills to form popular opinion and competing against itself for the goods and services of the world, how were the alternative extremes of anarchy or tyranny to be avoided? Hamilton believed that an
intermediary power must be provided to govern the conflict of social interests, but on the particular constitution of that authority he held no
certain dogma. One cannot be sure whether Hamilton, as charged by Jefferson, considered royal monarchy to be the best of all governments, but
it is clear that he did not deem monarchism feasible in America. In a letter
to Lafayette he declared the merit of a constitution to be a relative matter: "I hold with *Montesquieu*, that a government must be fitted to a nation, as much as a coat to the individual; and, consequently, that what
may be good at Philadelphia may be bad at Paris, and ridiculous at
Petersburgh."[24]

Regardless of the form of constitution, the purpose it served was always the same—to provide a legal system through which affairs of society
might be transacted in an orderly manner. Predictability was the essential
quality of law; uncertainty induced by erratic social change, the symptom
of threatening anarchy. Hamilton's legal conservatism represented a reasoned conclusion that a stable social order required uniform and continuing methods of resolving differences. He could not agree with Jefferson that occasional revolutions might be desirable and that each generation ought to be free to determine the rules governing its affairs without
reference to tradition. Law to Hamilton was what history was to Burke—
the pole star by which political helmsmen guided free society between the
shoals and reefs which threatened destruction. Thus Hamilton expounded
a philosophy of law as the cohesive and enduring force in society. He
declared:

> Government . . . . is that POWER by which individuals in society are kept from doing
> injury to each other, and are brought to cooperate to a common end. The instruments
> by which it must act are either the AUTHORITY of the laws or FORCE. If the first be
> destroyed, the last must be substituted; and where this becomes the ordinary instru-
> ment of government, there is an end to liberty![25]

"Nothing is more common," he asserted, "than for a free people, in
times of heat and violence, to gratify momentary passions, by letting into
government, principles and precedents which afterwards prove fatal to
themselves."[26] Therefore, he argued, "there ought to be a principle in

---

[24] January 6, 1799, *Works*, ed. Lodge, X, 337.

[25] "Tully," No. III, August 28, 1794, *ibid.*, VI, 418–19.

[26] "Phocion," Letter I (1784), *ibid.*, IV, 232–33.

government capable of resisting the popular current,"[27] and that principle ought to be a permanent will, embodied in the executive arm of the Constitution.

Hamilton believed that constitutions should consist only of general and fundamental provisions, since, intended for permanence, they could not calculate in detail for the possible change of things. The content of constitutions might vary with political traditions, but their common purpose was a definition of the objects for which the government was constituted with the grants of authority necessary to the attainment of the ends. A constitution was not a detailed code of law. Hamilton opposed burdening the Constitution of the United States with particular qualifications and restrictions, for he believed that the exigencies of an unpredictable future might lead to the abrogation of the impeding provisions and result in a decline in popular respect for the Constitution itself. Wise politicians, he asserted, "will be cautious about fettering the government with restrictions that cannot be observed, because they know that every breach of the fundamental laws, though dictated by necessity, impairs that sacred reverence which ought to be maintained in the breasts of rulers toward the constitution of a country, and forms a precedent for other breaches where the same plea of necessity does not exist at all, or is less urgent and palpable."[28] And so, explained Hamilton, "the truth is that the general GENIUS of a government is all that can be substantially relied upon for permanent effects."[29]

To the question perplexing the eighteenth-century advocates of a limited state: "How much power ought a government to have?" Hamilton answered simply and directly: As much power as is requisite to accomplish its purpose. He viewed as absurd the erection of a government with broad objectives but with rigidly limited means for effecting their realization. "A Constitution," he wrote, "cannot set bounds to a nation's wants: it ought not therefore to set bounds to its resources."[30] To those who feared to trust power anywhere, Hamilton declared too little power as dangerous as too much, for to deny to society the power to defend its legitimate interests would be to invite anarchy and despotism. "Power must be granted, or civil society cannot exist."[31] He admitted that abuse

---

[27] "Brief of Speech on Submitting His Plan of Constitution" (1787), *ibid.*, I, 375.

[28] *The Federalist*, No. 25, Earle, *op. cit.*, p. 158.

[29] *The Federalist*, No. 83, *ibid.*, p. 554.

[30] "Speech on the Senate of the United States, June 27, 1788," *Works*, ed. Lodge, I, 64.

[31] "Speech in the New York Assembly, January 19, 1787," *ibid.*, VIII, 15.

was a possibility "incident to every species of power, however placed or modified," but contended that this danger was no argument against its proper use. Power was best controlled, not by rigid limitations, but by the provision of channels for its responsible operation.

When Jeffersonian advocates of the minimized state attempted to restrict the powers granted by the Constitution of the United States to the specific means stated in the written document, Hamilton countered with his doctrine of implied powers. In his famous "Opinion as to the Constitutionality of the Bank of the United States," he held that the inflexible limitation of powers short of the objects for which they were given would produce the singular spectacle of a political society without sovereignty, or of a people governed without a government. Nor was this broad construction of constitutional authority merely incidental to the demands of Hamilton's administrative program. For he had earlier written in *The Federalist* that a "government ought to contain in itself every power requisite to the full accomplishment of the objects committed to its care, and to the complete execution of the trusts for which it is responsible, free from every other control but a regard to the public good and to the sense of the people."[32]

In brief, Hamilton's constitutional ideal may be fairly described as "plenary power in the administration, subject to direct and continuous accountability to the people, maintained by a representative assembly, broadly democratic in character."[33] This latter democratic aspect of Hamilton's constitutional theory has been overshadowed by his doctrine of power, but it is essential to an understanding of his theory of the state. He developed his notion of the representative basis of government in a letter to Gouverneur Morris, written in 1777:

That instability is inherent in the nature of popular governments I think very disputable; unstable democracy, is an epithet frequently in the mouths of politicians; but I believe that from a strict examination of the matter—from the records of history, it will be found that the fluctuations of governments in which the popular principle has borne a considerable sway, have proceeded from its being compounded with other principles;—and from its being made to operate in an improper channel. . . . . But a representative democracy, where the right of election is well secured and regulated, and the exercise of the legislative, executive, and judiciary authorities is vested in select persons, chosen really and not nominally by the people, will, in my opinion, be most likely to be happy, regular, and durable.[34]

[32] *The Federalist*, No. 31, Earle, *op. cit.*, p. 190.

[33] Henry Jones Ford, *Figures from American History: Alexander Hamilton* (New York: Charles Scribner's Sons, 1931), pp. 364–65.

[34] May 19, 1777, *Works*, ed. Lodge, IX, 71–72.

Madison noted that, in the Constitutional Convention of 1787, Hamilton, though avowing himself a friend to vigorous government, declared it essential that the popular branch should rest on a broad foundation. In the constitutional scheme that he drafted during the convention, Hamilton proposed that the House of Representatives be elected "by the free male citizens and inhabitants of the several States comprehended in the Union, all of whom, of the age of twenty-one years and upwards, shall be entitled to an equal vote."[35] At a time when the property qualification for electors was almost universally accepted, Hamilton's proposal was drastic indeed. One need only recall that Republicans as orthodox as Madison and Monroe as late as 1830 opposed the abolition of the property qualification for electors in Virginia. Defending the Constitution in the New York Ratifying Convention of 1788, Hamilton again declared that "there should be a broad democratic branch in the National Legislature."[36] Explaining his political principles to Colonel Edward Carrington of Virginia, he maintained that he was "affectionately attached to the republican theory."[37] He expressed a "desire above all things to see the equality of political rights, exclusive of all hereditary distinction, firmly established by a practical demonstration of its being consistent with the order and happiness of society."[38] Yet Hamilton was described by contemporaries as a monarchist who hated republican government and feared democracy. Where lies the truth, and how, in a statesman whose intellectual power and integrity were attested by his bitterest enemies, could so palpable a contradiction survive?

The most reasonable explanation of this paradox may be derived from a statement attributed to Hamilton by his friend, Chancellor Kent. "I presume I shall not be disbelieved," said Hamilton, "when I declare, that the establishment of a republican government, on a safe and solid basis, is an object of all others nearest and most dear to my heart."[39] He differed from Jefferson and the majority of Republicans, not on the issue of the establishment of republican government, but over the question of how republicanism could best be preserved. He distrusted the decentralized, highly democratic regimes with weak executives and rigid constitutions which characterized many of the state governments of the time. His ex-

[35] "Constitution of Government by the People of the United States of America [first draft of Hamilton, 1787]," *ibid.*, I, 351.

[36] "Speech in the New York Ratifying Convention, June 21, 1788," *ibid.*, II, 18.

[37] May 26, 1792, *ibid.*, IX, 533.   [38] *Ibid.*

[39] William Kent, *Memoirs and Letters of James Kent, LL.D., Late Chancellor of the State of New York* (Boston: Little, Brown & Co., 1898), p. 300.

perience during the Revolution and under the Confederation convinced him of the danger to liberty and prosperity in diverse regimes working at cross-purposes, lacking the power and the co-ordination necessary to enforce their laws and covenants—and easily swayed by any temporary outburst of popular violence. He had seen the Congress driven from its sitting by fear of mutinous unpaid soldiery, and he had become convinced that only a strong centralized executive power could preserve the fruits of the American Revolution. He looked to England for the best model of a republican state. Little reason, he believed, to fear the word "king" or "monarchy"; the responsibility of a government to the people was the real test of its republican character.

Here Hamilton was more in the tradition of European political thought than was Jefferson. Hamilton understood a republic in the traditional sense of a state founded on popular consent, its government *of* the people and *for* the people but not necessarily *by* the people. Jefferson understood republicanism in the sense in which the term was coming to be generally accepted in America—government *by* the people: decentralized government in which each man directly participated at some level. In Hamilton's belief in strong executive centralization Jefferson saw only monarchy; and monarchy to Jefferson was the antithesis of personal liberty and self-government. Thus Hamilton's distrust of the species of democratic republicanism which existed in the American states during and immediately following the Revolution won for him the reputation of an opponent of democracy in general. In the course of political history democracy has meant many things; but it has always implied the location of the ultimate political authority in the mass of the people, or in a substantial portion of them. If, therefore, adherence to the doctrine of government in the general welfare based upon popular consent be taken as a test of democratic faith, Hamilton cannot be held an opponent of democracy.

Hamilton's interpretation of society implied a need for energetic government to insure the general welfare. In his concluding remarks in *The Federalist* he declared that "a nation, without a national government, is, in my view, an awful spectacle";[40] and as politician and public administrator he endeavored to give the central government of the Union the form, power, and duration which would enable it to fulfil its proper role as custodian of the social interests. The principles by which Hamilton would organize and administer a truly national government are therefore significant, and it is these principles of administration which now require consideration.

[40] *The Federalist*, No. 85, Earle, *op. cit.*, p. 574.

CHAPTER III

HAMILTONIAN PRINCIPLES OF ADMINISTRATION

BECAUSE Hamilton's administrative ideas were largely developed in response to the needs of a society uncongenial to public controls, his inner convictions concerning public administration are not always evident in his public writing. As much of his private correspondence was of quasi-public character, the more intimate expressions of his administrative theories are disappointingly few. But Hamilton's personal convictions when expressed are fundamental and exact, and when read in the context of his general political philosophy they afford substance adequate to a reasonably rounded interpretation of his administrative thought.

Although Hamilton left no systematic development of his administrative ideas, there is evidence that he planned such a work. According to Chancellor Kent, he contemplated a "full investigation of the history and science of civil government and the practical results of the various modifications of it upon the freedom and happiness of mankind." Hamilton wished, said Kent, "to have the subject treated in reference to past experience and upon the principles of Lord Bacon's inductive philosophy, and to engage the assistance of others in the enterprise."[1]

The science of administration will be ever the poorer for the early death of Hamilton which prevented this ambitious undertaking. If *The Continentalist, The Federalist*, and the great state papers on the public credit, the bank, and manufactures forecast the scope and thoroughness of the work, Hamilton would have given the world a treatise of first magnitude in the literature of politics. One can only guess at the potentialities of such work as an influence on the development of the public service.

Although Hamilton's philosophy of administration cannot be perfectly reconstructed, it is possible to approximate its content and emphasis by synthesizing into certain governing principles the precepts, recommendations, and criticisms relating to the administrative function scattered throughout his writings. These principles, reduced to the few basic generalities which guided his policies as a student and practitioner of administration, may then be applied to the concrete political and administra-

[1] William Kent, *Memoirs and Letters of James Kent* .... (Boston: Little, Brown & Co., 1898), pp. 327–28.

tive problems with which he was concerned. Thus we shall first attempt to understand Hamilton's administrative ideas in terms of theory, and then survey the practical application of those theories to actual administrative situations.

ENERGY

Energy in the Executive is a leading character in the definition of good government.— "THE FEDERALIST," NO. 70.[2]

Assuming with Hamilton that the true test of a good government is its aptitude and tendency to produce good administration, the question logically follows: Of what does good administration consist? To Hamilton it was axiomatic that good administration must be energetic. "There are two objects in forming systems of government," he wrote; "safety for the people, and energy in the administration. When these objects are united, the certain tendency of the system will be to the public welfare. If the latter object be neglected, the people's security will be as certainly sacrificed as by disregarding the former. Good constitutions are formed upon a comparison of the liberty of the individual with the strength of government."[3] But Hamilton did not advocate vigor in the executive carried to oppressive extremes, for he wrote that his plan was ever to combine energy with moderation.[4]

Viewing pure democracy as synonymous with decentralized government, one can understand why Hamilton believed that direct popular rule discouraged energetic national administration. Conceiving public administration to be a unitary process, he insisted that it must be provided with machinery of national scope if it were to function on a national scale. Decentralized government, lacking the unity of a centralized administrative system, would have neither the machinery, the strength, nor very likely the will to pursue any given line of policy with perseverance and dispatch. The executive arm of government was the energetic arm, hence whatever limited the scope of executive action or destroyed the unity of its constitution, reduced the potential energy of the government.

Assuming that all men of sense would agree to the necessity of an energetic executive, Hamilton in *The Federalist*, No. 70, inquired into the ingredients of which this energy is constituted. These he held to be unity, duration, adequate provision for support, and, finally, competent powers; and, of these, he considered unity to be foremost in importance.

[2] Edward Mead Earle (ed.), *The Federalist* (Washington: National Home Library Foundation, 1937), p. 454.

[3] "Speech on the Senate of the United States, June 25, 1788," *Works*, ed. Lodge, II, 51–52.

[4] To William Smith, April 5, 1797, *ibid.*, X, 254.

UNITY

That unity is conducive to energy will not be disputed. Decision, activity, secrecy, and despatch will generally characterize the proceedings of one man in a much more eminent degree than the proceedings of any greater number.—"THE FEDERALIST," No. 70.[5]

Although differences of opinion might promote deliberation and circumspection in legislative bodies, Hamilton believed that "no favorable circumstances palliate or atone for the disadvantages of dissension" in the executive department. "Here," he wrote, "they are pure and unmixed. There is no point at which they cease to operate. They serve to embarrass and weaken the execution of the plan or measure to which they relate, from the first step to the final conclusion of it. They constantly counteract those qualities in the Executive which are the most necessary ingredients in its composition,—vigor and expedition, and this without any counterbalancing good."[6] Thus Hamilton concluded that unity of command lodged in a single executive was indispensable to the pursuance of energetic administration.

Plural executives he considered pernicious and committed to failure; equally self-defeating were executives composed of a chief administrator and council. Colonial experience with an executive combining coequal council and governor testified to the deadlocks, the feebleness, and the want of responsibility inhering in this plan. "The plurality of the Executive," he wrote, "tends to deprive the people of its two greatest securities . . . . *first*, the restraints of public opinion, which lose their efficacy, as well on account of the division of the censure attendant on bad measures among a number, as on account of the uncertainty on whom it ought to fall; and, *secondly*, the opportunity of discovering with facility and clearness the misconduct of the persons they trust."[7] Hamilton deemed the administration of the executive departments by boards and committees a bad policy. "A single man in each department of the administration," he declared, "would be greatly preferable."[8]

Hamilton did not believe that the required concurrence of the Senate in the ratification of treaties and confirmation of presidential appointments of necessity impaired the unity of command vested in the nation's chief executive. In the latter instance the President in all cases possessed the exclusive power of nomination so that whoever was appointed through confirmation by the Senate would represent his choice, although not

[5] Earle, *op. cit.*, p. 455.

[6] *Ibid.*, pp. 458–59.

[7] *Ibid.*, pp. 460–61.   [8] To James Duane, September 3, 1780, *Works*, ed. Lodge, I, 219.

necessarily his first choice. The making of treaties Hamilton adjudged a quasi-legislative function in which the President as the single representative of the nation in foreign affairs and the sole negotiator of treaties must take part. But, as treaties represented a species of law-making, the participation of a legislative body was appropriate.

In the direction of war, the principle of unity of command was of greatest importance. "Of all the cares or concerns of government," wrote Hamilton, "the direction of war most peculiarly demands those qualities which distinguish the exercise of power by a single hand."[9] In his observations on the difficulties of America and her allies during the Revolutionary War, he noted a failure to make sufficient allowance for the want of concert which characterizes the operations of allies, or for the immense advantage to the enemy of having their forces, although inferior, under a single direction. And in the planning of the new American army in 1798, Hamilton repeatedly urged that the principle of unified command be observed so that harmony, system, and vigor might follow.

The Hamiltonian principle of unity may be developed in deductive form: energy, the essence of good administration, implies effective action; action to be effective must have direction; unity of action insures specific direction and provides the outlet for executive energy. But unity of action cannot be obtained without a unity of command. This unity of command is probable only where there is a single commander, for plural commanders tend to disunity. However, if a commander is to execute a unified policy, he must have a unified organization through which to operate. Hence, the unity principle calls for a government in which lines of authority and responsibility are well defined and unimpeded. Thus Hamilton tended to favor a centralized as opposed to a decentralized federal state and did not value highly the contributions of the town meeting and the county court to the energy of government. For he felt that the best safeguard to the people's liberty was not in independent local administrations, potentially obstructive but otherwise ineffective as to national purposes, but in the clear and unmistakable responsibility of a unified national government and unitary executive to the whole people.

DURATION

Duration in office has been mentioned as the second requisite to energy of the Executive authority. This has relation to two objects: to the personal firmness of the executive magistrate . . . . and to the stability of the system of administration which may have been adopted under his auspices.—"THE FEDERALIST," No. 71.[10]

[9] *The Federalist*, No. 74, Earle, *op. cit.*, p. 482.   [10] *Ibid.*, p. 463.

"It is a general principle of human nature," declared Hamilton, "that a man will be interested in whatever he possesses, in proportion to the firmness or precariousness of tenure by which he holds it."[11] Thus he observed that a magistrate subject to brief tenure of office would be condemned to feebleness and irresolution in his administration. He would be unwilling to hazard censure and opposition by the pursuit of independent policies when the time necessary for the consummation of plans was too brief. If the magistrate should be eligible to be continued in his office by the legislature or by the people, "his wishes, conspiring with his fears would tend still more powerfully to corrupt his integrity, or debase his fortitude."[12] However inclined one might be to insist upon executive complaisance to the wishes of the people, Hamilton held that one could with no propriety contend for a like complaisance with the humors of the legislature, for the legislative branch was not the repository of political sovereignty and might sometimes stand in opposition to the general welfare and the public will. The executive had an independent responsibility to the people for his conduct and therefore should be in a situation to dare to act his own opinion with vigor and decision.

Adequate duration of tenure was the only method by which an administration could produce desirable results. This, Hamilton declared, "is necessary to give to the officer himself the inclination and the resolution to act his part well, and to the community time and leisure to observe the tendency of his measures, and thence to form an experimental estimate of their merits."[13] With adequate tenure, the principle of re-eligibility for office would become beneficial, for it would permit the people when they approved his conduct to continue the administrator in office, thereby "to prolong the utility of his talents and virtues, and to secure to the government the advantage of permanency in a wise system of administration."[14]

POWER

Not to confer in each case a degree of power commensurate to the end, would be to violate the most obvious rules of prudence and propriety, and improvidently to trust the great interests of the nation to hands which are disabled from managing them with vigor and success.— "THE FEDERALIST," NO. 23.[15]

Hamilton's theory of administrative power flows directly from his thesis that the powers of a government must be adequate to the ends for

[11] *Ibid.*, pp. 463–64.

[12] *Ibid.*, p. 464.

[13] *The Federalist*, No. 72, *ibid.*, p. 469.

[14] *Ibid.*, pp. 469–70. [15] *Ibid.*, p. 144.

which it was instituted. "A government," he held, "the constitution of which renders it unfit to be trusted with all the powers which a free people *ought to delegate to any government*, would be an unsafe depository of the NATIONAL INTERESTS."[16] Where these can properly be confided, he held that the coincident powers might safely accompany them. He thought it absurd to confer upon government responsibility for the most essential national interests, without daring to intrust it with the authority indispensable to their proper and efficient management. To the administrator charged with the energetic promotion of the public good as defined by the Constitution and the statutes of the Republic, want of adequate powers would condemn him to fail in his responsibility or to exceed his trust. He could only choose whether to be figurehead or usurper. Either alternative Hamilton saw as destructive to constitutional government. Only a powerful executive could be responsible for the promotion of great interests. Those who, fearing despotism, would bind the executive power by rules and regulations designed to limit and retard the responsible exercise of authority, were inviting the disaster which they sought to prevent. For an ambitious executive with popular support would ultimately demand a free hand to act in pursuit of the public good and, overriding the restrictions prescribed on parchment, would establish a personal rule which would complete the destruction of responsible government.

Of importance equal to competent powers was provision for the adequate financial support of executive authority. Hamilton saw that, without a basis for compensation protected from legislative manipulation, the independence of the executive branch would be merely nominal. Thus he considered stabilizing the President's compensation during the term for which he was elected as necessary to vigorous administration. Hamilton, indeed, appears to have considered the provision of adequate compensation a major administrative principle, but one so closely related to the more comprehensive principle of competent powers as to justify joint treatment. In the instances both of judicial and of executive compensation it was the issue of power which seemed uppermost in Hamilton's mind. The independence of the courts and administration from legislative domination was the end in view.

RESPONSIBILITY

The ingredients which constitute safety in the republican sense are, first, a due dependence on the people; secondly, a due responsibility.—"THE FEDERALIST," No. 70.[17]

[16] *Ibid.*, p. 145.   [17] *Ibid.*, p. 455.

Hamilton contended that every magistrate in a republic ought to be personally responsible for his behavior in office. Responsibility, intended both to encourage an energetic performance of duties and to restrain neglectful or usurping practices, moved upward through the administrative hierarchy to the chief executive and outward to the people and to their representatives in Congress. The responsibility of administrators Hamilton understood as twofold in character. "Due dependence on the people" implied conformity to the legal requirements of office, including accountability to the people through their representatives. The other and more characteristically Hamiltonian notion of responsibility was that each administrator must be prepared to act according to the public need to accomplish fully and effectively the tasks which lay within the province of his office. This might require an officer to undertake more than his enumerated duties required. It implied that expansive interpretation of the administrative function which Hamilton's Treasury career came to exemplify. But administrators were not, in Hamilton's thinking, empowered themselves to constitute the law. Where administrators exceeded their powers without regard to their responsibilities, the sanctions of censure and punishment awaited.

Hamilton cited with approval the contention of Delolme that "the executive power is more easily confined when it is *one*" and argued that the principle of unity was calculated best to insure executive responsibility.[18] "The sole and undivided responsibility of one man will naturally beget a livelier sense of duty and a more exact regard to reputation," he explained.[19] Divided responsibility would destroy the efficacy of sanctions because of the uncertainty upon whom the censure ought to fall. "Regard to reputation," he wrote, "has a less active influence, when the infamy of a bad action is to be divided among a number, than when it is to fall singly upon one."[20]

One method of preventing the evasion of administrative responsibility was by clearly separating the executive branch from the other great divisions of government. Hamilton feared particularly the encroachment of the legislature upon the executive, believing not only that the power and energy of the executive would be thereby weakened but that he would be rendered irresponsible. Controlled by the legislature, the executive would merely be its tool and could not be held personally account-

[18] *Ibid.*, p. 462.

[19] *The Federalist*, No. 76, *ibid.*, p. 492.   [20] *The Federalist*, No. 15, *ibid.*, p. 92.

able for administrative policy. Should the executive power overawe the legislature, an equally pernicious irresponsibility would obtain. Hamilton agreed with Madison's argument in *The Federalist*, Nos. 47 and 48, that the mere parchment demarcations of the three great divisions of government were insufficient to restrain a republican legislature from gathering all power into its hands. The only effective method by which the authors of *The Federalist* believed that a true separation of powers could be enforced was by a system of checks and balances to provide each branch, and particularly the executive, with instruments of defense.

The safest guaranty of responsible conduct, however, was the ultimate dependence of the executive upon the people. Although the degree of dependence which Hamilton felt sufficient to insure responsibility did not satisfy the more fervent disciples of democracy, he nevertheless accepted the elective principle and the doctrine of popular will. "The republican principle," he explained, "demands that the deliberate sense of the community should govern the conduct of those to whom they intrust the management of their affairs; but it does not require an unqualified complaisance to every sudden breeze of passion, or to every transient impulse which the people may receive from the arts of men."[21] He declared that in a government "framed for durable liberty, not less regard must be paid to giving the magistrate a proper degree of authority to make and execute the laws with rigor, than to guard against encroachments upon the rights of the community. As too much power leads to despotism, too little leads to anarchy, and both, eventually, to the ruin of the people."[22] Responsibility, he believed, demanded powers adequate to the fulfilment of the tasks imposed upon the executive.

In summary, then, one may distinguish five major principles which Hamilton believed to be the indispensable components of good administration. Briefly they were: energy, unity, duration, power, and responsibility. Derived from his interpretation of social psychology and his theory of constitutional government, they appear singly or in combination in each of his proposals concerning the structure and function of the federal administrative system. To this practical application of Hamiltonian principles of administration we now turn.

[21] *The Federalist*, No. 71, *ibid.*, p. 464.

[22] *The Continentalist*, No. I, July 12, 1781, *Works*, ed. Lodge, I, 246.

CHAPTER IV

THE ORGANIZATION OF PUBLIC ADMINISTRATION

A UNIFIED national system of public administration was the object of Hamilton's constructive genius. To secure that union on solid foundations required sweeping changes in the decentralized government of the Confederation which Hamilton advocated in *The Continentalist* and defended in *The Federalist;* but the task of constitutional change and administrative reconstruction was one which even Hamilton conceived as "herculean." His efforts to secure a constitution that would provide the unified administrative system he believed necessary to national welfare fell short of his objective, and therefore, as first Secretary of the Treasury, he attempted to realize through administrative practice what he had been unable to accomplish through constitutional reform.

Hamilton understood beyond any of his contemporaries that the success of the Union lay in the administration of its affairs and that the success of the administration required an organization adequate to its objectives. He conceived the administration of national policy as a unity, holding, as we have seen, that a mere compound of thirteen distinct units would be incapable of the energy which he deemed an indispensable attribute of good government. His theories of national organization were therefore designed to create a structure through which a unified program of public administration might operate.

THE UNION AND THE STATES

The true principle of government is this—make the system complete in its structure; give a perfect proportion and balance to its parts, and the powers you give it will never affect your security. The question, then, of the division of powers between the General and State governments, is a question of convenience.—"SPEECH ON THE SENATE OF THE UNITED STATES."[1]

The fundamental and incurable defect of the Confederation as diagnosed by Hamilton was "in the principle of LEGISLATION for STATES or GOVERNMENTS, in their CORPORATE or COLLECTIVE CAPACITIES"[2] in contradistinction to the individuals of which they consisted. The Confedera-

[1] June 27, 1788, *Works*, ed. Lodge, II, 63.

[2] *The Federalist*, No. 15, Edward Mead Earle (ed.), *The Federalist* (Washington: National Home Library Foundation, 1937), p. 89.

tion was a league, and the needs of America required a general government. The remedy, wrote Hamilton, was "to incorporate into our plan those ingredients which may be considered as forming the characteristic difference between a league and a government; we must extend the authority of the Union to the persons of citizens, the only proper objects of government."[3]

Hamilton's insistence upon a government rather than a league to fulfil the objectives of union is a clear illustration of his principle that responsibility must always be accompanied by commensurate power. It was the lack of power to enforce its responsibilities that rendered the Confederation contemptible. Without sanctions of law to sustain its administration against the opposition of the states, and without authority to administer directly to individuals, the Confederation faced the dilemma of irresponsibility or resort to war against recalcitrant members. As the component states retained individual sovereignty, they were privileged to choose whether to comply or deny when requests were made upon them. Should the Confederation attempt to fulfil its responsibilities by exceeding its powers and resorting to force, the result could only be civil war.[4]

Not only did the power of the Confederation fail to equal its responsibility but it represented an additional violation of Hamilton's administrative principles in its lack of unity in organization, in command, and hence in action. Government as conceived by Hamilton could not operate without a united structure; no national government could operate through thirteen disunited entities. Public administration was a unitary process which must cut through all layers of governmental organization in pursuit of its objectives. Hence some integrating principle must be introduced into the national constitution.

Hamilton rejected the doctrine of so-called "dual federalism." The general power, he asserted, "whatever be its form, if it preserves itself, must swallow up the State powers. Otherwise, it will be swallowed up by them. . . . . Two sovereignties cannot coexist within the same limits."[5] But he feared that the states, with a traditional first claim upon the loyalties of the people and a more intimate contact with their daily concerns, would outweigh the Union in the balance of power. Accordingly, he favored some device to insure the independence of the national government,

---

[3] *Ibid.*, p. 91.

[4] For an application of Hamilton's theories of organization to the international sphere see L. P. Jacks, "Alexander Hamilton and the Reform of the League: An Historical Parallel," *International Conciliation*, No. 325, December, 1936, pp. 605–21.

[5] "Speech in the Federal Convention, June 18, 1787," *Works*, ed. Lodge, I, 387.

and the plan which he proposed in the Constitutional Convention of 1787 gave to the central government power to appoint state governors and to the governors a veto over state legislation[6] subject only to federal qualification.

Hamilton's insistence upon a unified system of public administration led to the charge that he favored a completely centralized constitution in which the states would be hardly more than administrative units. In a carefully worded letter to Colonel Edward Carrington of Virginia on May 26, 1792, Hamilton attempted to refute the charge and to clarify his position on the place of the states in the Union:

> If the States were all of the size of Connecticut, Maryland, or New Jersey, I should decidedly regard the local governments as both safe and useful. As the thing now is, however, I acknowledge the most serious apprehensions, that the government of the United States will not be able to maintain itself against their influence. I see that influence already penetrating into the national councils and preventing their directions. Hence, a disposition on my part towards a liberal construction of the powers of the national government, and to erect every fence, to guard it from depredations which is, in my opinion, consistent with constitutional propriety. As to any combination to prostrate the State governments, I disavow and deny it.[7]

Because Hamilton's letter to Carrington was written with a view to assuage the fears of the Virginia Federalists concerning his centralizing tendencies, it somewhat understated his case. Writing to Jonathan Dayton of New Jersey in 1799, he expressed himself in stronger terms:

> Great States will always feel a rivalship with the common head; will often be supposed to machinate against it, and in certain situations will be able to do it with decisive effect. The subdivision of such States ought to be a cardinal point in the federal policy, and small States are doubtless best adapted to the purposes of local regulation and to the preservation of the republican spirit.[8]

Hamilton thus pictured a union composed of small states approximately equal in power, each with a representative legislature and with a governor appointed on tenure of good behavior by the national government. State legislation would be held in line with national objectives by two devices: a veto power in the governor, who held his office by federal appointment, and a national judicial system with jurisdiction over all federal questions. In his proposals in the Philadelphia Convention, Hamilton urged election of senators "by electors chosen for that purpose by the people" and the division of the states into electoral districts. It would

---

[6] "Constitution of Government by the People of the United States [first draft of Hamilton]," *ibid.*, p. 366.

[7] *Ibid.*, IX, 533–34.   [8] *Ibid.*, X, 335.

seem that he wished to reduce the influence of the states as such even in the Senate.

Hamilton viewed the problem of national organization in terms of administrative utility, thereby differing from Madison, who viewed the problem primarily in terms of constitutional theory. It was this difference in approach to the interpretation of the Constitution that Madison alleged as the reason for his opposition to Hamilton after 1789: "I deserted Col. Hamilton, or rather Col. Hamilton deserted me; in a word, the divergence between us took place from his wishing . . . . to administer the Government, into what he thought it ought to be; while on my part I endeavored to make it conform to the Constitution as understood by the Convention that produced and recommended it, and particularly by the State conventions that *adopted* it."[9]

Constitutional and administrative aspects of politics were inseparably intertwined in Hamilton's theory, but the needs of effective administration dictated the constitutional arrangements which he proposed, whereas Madison and the Virginia school of politics inclined to conform administrative machinery to a preconceived constitutional ideal. Under the jurisprudence of John Marshall, Hamilton's administrative theory was in large measure embodied in American constitutional law. But the theories of Hamilton regarding the organization of government remain in their own right a major contribution to thought on public administration.

THE LEGISLATURE AND THE EXECUTIVE

The administration of government, in its largest sense, comprehends all the operations of the body politic, whether legislative, executive, or judiciary; but in its most usual and perhaps in its most precise signification, it is limited to executive details, and falls peculiarly within the province of the executive department.—"THE FEDERALIST," NO. 72.[10]

The task of reconciling freedom with order was not ended with the creation of a general government of adequate scope and authority. The internal structure of that government must be so constituted as to guarantee that the powers granted it would not be perverted from their proper ends. Yet if the powers of government were divided in a manner to make their abuse difficult, would not that energetic unity of action essential to effective government be defeated? Hamilton did not believe that divided power would impede energetic government provided the division were

---

[9] Cited in Henry S. Randall, *The Life of Thomas Jefferson* (3 vols.; New York: Derby & Jackson, 1858), Vol. III, Appendix IX, pp. 594–95.

[10] Earle, *op. cit.*, p. 468.

properly apportioned. Indeed, the old Continental Congress represented the prototype of maladministration, although almost all the limited power of the Confederation was placed in its hands. Hamilton declared that the power of the Confederation did not flow through appropriate channels because of the want of a proper executive. He explained that "Congress have kept the power too much in their own hands, and have meddled too much with details of every sort. Congress is, properly, a deliberative corps, and it forgets itself when it attempts to play the executive."[11]

Hamilton believed the functional separation of powers indispensable to orderly and energetic government. But he did not pursue the separation-of-powers doctrine to logical absurdity, for he did not think that functions could be or should be rigidly separated; he knew that the executive must sometimes legislate, that the legislature might best perform the high judicial function of impeachment, and that the duties of judges might require them occasionally to act in an executive character.[12] The essential principle was that each major branch of government be allotted the functions it could best fulfil. This was the principle that governed Hamilton's theory of the separation of powers, and, because he believed that power must be commensurate with responsibility and because he would vest responsibility for the initiation of measures on behalf of the commonwealth in the executive, he was compelled to dissent from the prevalent opinion concerning the separation of powers which favored a preponderance of power in the legislative branch.

On the contrary, he would give the greater authority and responsibility to the executive arm of government. He favored the establishment of a close, direct working relationship between the administration and the Congress, the administration to furnish the expert opinion and information necessary to the intelligent deliberation of the legislative body.[13] This relationship he felt essential to insure an energetic unity of administrative action. Accordingly, he believed that the administration must supply the leadership which effective legislative procedure requires but does not al-

[11] To James Duane, September 3, 1780, *Works*, ed. Lodge, I, 219.

[12] Madison in *The Federalist*, No. 37, expressed the same idea: "Experience has instructed us that no skill in the science of government has yet been able to discriminate and define, with sufficient certainty, its three great provinces . . . ." (Earle, *op. cit.*, p. 229).

[13] In his *Congressional Government* (2d ed.; Boston: Houghton Mifflin Co., 1885), Introd., and in his *Constitutional Government in the United States* (New York: Columbia University Press, 1908), p. 200, Woodrow Wilson emphasizes Hamilton's theory of government as "an affair of cooperative and harmonious forces," contrasting with Madison's theory of co-ordinate and coequal powers, observing the danger of the latter arrangement leading to a deadlock between the executive and legislative branches.

ways possess. By administrative guidance Hamilton hoped to insure a legislature friendly toward administration objectives. Administration policies could be defended directly in the legislative chambers by the ministers who possessed the fullest knowledge of proposed measures. Opposition would have opportunity for pointed and constructive criticism and questioning. Administrative responsibility could be publicly defined by the administrators themselves rather than indirectly by legislative spokesmen for the administration who could readily be repudiated if public reaction to a particular policy should prove embarrassing.

Yet Hamilton's theory of executive-legislative co-operation was to be distinguished from the parliamentary system as it was developing in Great Britain, for Hamilton was a firm believer in executive independence. The Constitutional Convention, influenced by the theory of the separation of powers, had created a separate, independent, initiating executive, modeled, so some thought, after the constitution of Great Britain. Hamilton appears to have shared in the general misconception of the British executive-legislative relationship, for, although he praised the British system of ministerial responsibility and promoted its adoption in the Washington administration, he opposed legislative encroachment on executive independence, unaware of the transformation by which Parliament was becoming the controlling agency in the British constitution and making the executive branch dependent upon its will. Yet Hamilton can hardly be expected to have perceived a change which Britons of his day scarcely sensed. The British constitution was in transition, its trend obscure even to its makers.

Hamilton attempted from the very beginning of his association with Washington's administration to insure the leadership and independence of the executive branch. Advising Washington on presidential etiquette, he observed that the public good required that the dignity of office should be supported. Confessing that notions of equality were yet too strong to admit of great distance being placed between the President and other branches of the government, he held, however, that the dignity, independence, and efficiency of the chief executive required that relations with the legislative branch in particular be formalized. Direct access to the President, he believed, should be permitted only to the heads of departments, the plenipotentiaries of the great powers, and to members of the Senate as individuals "on matters relative to the *public administration*."[14] This privilege he would not grant the representatives, explaining that "the Senate are coupled with the President in certain executive functions,

14 To Washington, May 5, 1789, *Works*, ed. Lodge, VIII, 86.

treaties, and appointments. This makes them in a degree his constitutional counsellors, and gives them a *peculiar* claim to the right of access."[15]

In defining the scope of the executive branch, Hamilton observed that a narrow interpretation of the legislative power of the purse operated to deprive the executive of independence and responsibility in the important area of financial administration. As early as 1783 he intimated that the determination of the budget was an executive rather than a legislative function,[16] and in *The Federalist*, No. 36, he explained that "nations in general, even under governments of the more popular kind, usually commit the administration of their finances to single men or to boards composed of a few individuals, who digest and prepare, in the first instance, the plans of taxation, which are afterwards passed into laws by the authority of the sovereign or legislature."[17]

The determination of the numbers and disposition of the armed forces Hamilton held an executive function, although the Congresses of the era of revolution and confederation would by no means agree with this delineation of authority. The civil employees of the executive branch Hamilton accounted responsible through their department heads to the President. He was against congressional attempts to interpose in matters of discipline and policy determination involving either the civil or the military services. The administration of government personnel he considered an executive function not proper to legislative cognizance.

The independent initiative of the executive branch in public planning was fundamental to Hamilton's conception of executive leadership. In 1794 he declared to Washington that "many persons look to the President for the suggestion of measures corresponding with the exigency of affairs,"[18] and proposed that the executive formulate a plan of national defense to include extensive military preparations, commercial regulations, and perhaps an alliance with other neutral powers. He declared that the executive branch ought to have prepared a *"well-digested* plan" before the meeting of Congress and ought to *"cooperate* in getting it adopted."[19] Deploring the reluctance of the administrations of Washington and Adams to undertake this responsibility, he considered it a pity and a reproach that the administration had no general plan. To Secretary of War Mc-

---

[15] *Ibid.*

[16] "Resolutions for a General Convention, June 30, 1783," *ibid.*, I, 305.

[17] Earle, *op. cit.*, p. 218.

[18] To Washington, March 8, 1794, *Works*, ed. Lodge, X, 65.

[19] To Timothy Pickering, March 22, 1797, *ibid.*, p. 246.

Henry he promised that, should there be any disposition to "concert a rational plan," he would be glad to assist in it.[20]

That Hamilton's theory of executive leadership depended upon the independence of the executive is evident from his prediction in the New York Ratifying Convention of 1788, where he declared that "the President of the United States will himself be the representative of the people. From the competition that ever subsists between the branches of the government, the President will be induced to protect their rights, whenever they are invaded by either branch."[21] This idea of separate legislative and executive representatives of the people he considered a major characteristic of the representative democracy created by the Constitution, and he opposed legislative interference with executive affairs as contrary to the organic law. He advised Washington to reject the demand of the House of Representatives for the submission of papers relating to the Jay Treaty, declaring that "a discretion in the executive department how far and when to comply in such cases is essential to the due conduct of foreign negotiations and is essential to preserve the limits between the legislative and executive departments."[22] Nor did he believe that the representatives could control the executive in foreign affairs by presuming a discretionary power to provide or withhold means for the execution of treaties, for he held that, as in the case of the fixed salaries of judges, "they cannot deliberate whether they will appropriate and pay the money . . . . the *mode* of raising and appropriating the money only remains matter of deliberation."[23]

Although he recognized the constitutional independence of the Congress, Hamilton viewed with dismay the revival in the new legislature of the committee system of the old Confederation which he believed had acted to frustrate executive leadership. The committees, he thought, tended to usurp the executive role of policy formulation and to verge from their proper deliberative and investigative function to the independent promotion of an administrative program and to dictation of departmental policy and procedure. With the retirement of Hamilton from the Treasury Department the power of the executive in matters of finance rapidly gave way before the pretensions of the representatives, led by Albert Gallatin. Rivalry between the executive and legislature in the formulation of public policy defeated his theory of intergovernmental

---

[20] June 27, 1799, *ibid.*, VII, 98.

[21] "Speech on the Constitution Resumed, June 21, 1788," *ibid.*, II, 21.

[22] To Washington, March 7, 1796, *ibid.*, X, 146.

[23] To William Smith, March 10, 1796, *ibid.*, pp. 147–48.

co-operation, yet Hamilton did not wholly despair, for he wrote to Gouverneur Morris that "the time may erelong arrive when the minds of men will be prepared to make an effort to *recover* the Constitution, but the many cannot now be brought to make a stand for its preservation. We must wait awhile."[24]

In defining the constitutional grant of power to the national chief executive, Hamilton stated that the executive functions listed under Article II, Section 2, of the Constitution of the United States served to illustrate and interpret the general grant of power in Section 1 rather than to limit the executive functions to those expressly enumerated:

> The enumeration ought therefore to be considered as intended merely to specify the principal articles implied in the definition of executive power; leaving the rest to flow from the general grant of that power, interpreted in conformity with other parts of the Constitution, and with the principles of free government.
>
> The general doctrine of our Constitution, then, is that the *executive power* of the nation is vested in the President; subject only to the *exceptions* and *qualifications* which are expressed in the instrument.[25]

Here was power of indefinite scope and flexible method; a general grant of power limited only by a few specific qualifications, by interpretation in conformity with the Constitution as a whole and with the principles of free government. Who would judge of the conformity of executive acts to these latter principles? Hamilton did not explain, but one may safely infer that he would make the executive judge of his own powers within the vast area of executive responsibility. Writing to the Secretary of War in 1800, he declared: "Nor do I see why the Executive may not claim the exercise of implied powers, as well as the legislative . . . . there is no public function which does not include the exercise of implied as well as express authority."[26] Limitation on executive authority would be provided by the adjacent areas of legislative and judicial power, by the jurisdiction of the states, and by public opinion.

Adaptability was the essence of executive power as understood by Hamilton. The executive function was active, contrasting with the relatively inactive functions of deliberation and adjudication. The executive among other responsibilities, must translate the decisions of courts and legislature into concrete action and must accordingly be vested with powers adequate to the duties which he might be obliged to perform. Efficacy was therefore a primary requisite of executive power. Power was justi-

---

[24] February 27, 1802, *ibid.*, p. 426.

[25] "Pacificus," No. I, June 29, 1793, *ibid.*, IV, 439.

[26] To McHenry, March 21, 1800, *ibid.*, VII, 205.

fiable if necessary to the accomplishment of a task assigned. But this was not to confess that mere might can make right, for his theory of executive power was predicated on the assumption that the general welfare was the fundamental object of states. Thus public power, to be justifiable, not only must be adequate to meet a public need but the need and the measures proposed to satisfy it must also be consonant with the general good.

The single chief executive exemplified the principle of unity of command, but to insure the effectiveness of that unified energy it must be given time to develop and execute plans. Thus the principle of adequate duration must be applied to public administration. Hamilton favored a lengthy tenure for the chief magistrate and held that, because the American President was elected to a tenure fixed at relatively few years, he should be re-eligible as often as the people should think him worthy of their confidence. The advantages of adequate tenure Hamilton held to be twofold: that it would enhance the personal firmness of the magistrate in the employment of his constitutional powers and that it would make for stability in the system of administration adopted under his auspices. Indeed, the principle that power must be commensurate with responsibility required that presidential tenure be long enough to permit the fulfilment of presidential duties. When, as Hamilton believed, these duties involved the maturation of a complex program of national development, the factor of duration of tenure became doubly important.

A fixed tenure of adequate length reflected the principle that due responsibility must be exacted of a public officer in that, by protecting his tenure from congressional manipulation, he could not easily be controlled by that body and so rendered irresponsible. The provision for fixed presidential compensation operated to the same end. The elective requirement further insured responsibility, for the President must periodically submit to public pronouncement upon his administration.

Turning to Hamilton's interpretation of the actual powers of the President relative to the Congress, one recalls that he held the executive power not susceptible of precise delineation. The President was vested with the whole of this most flexible of political powers except where expressly limited by the Constitution. But in three vital instances the executive authority of the President was subject to constitutional qualifications involving congressional co-operation. These—the appointive power, the treaty power, and the war power—were so indispensable to the executive authority that Hamilton was concerned that their qualifications be interpreted so as to preserve to the executive the maximum freedom which the Constitution could be construed to allow.

The appointive power, Hamilton explained, was really the sum of two distinct processes—those of nomination and of confirmation.[27] The former he deemed wisely vested in the President, thus observing the principles of unity in command and responsibility for action. To the objection that confirmation by the Senate would destroy unity and responsibility, Hamilton replied that the constitutional method possessed every advantage of concentrating the nominative power in the President while avoiding certain dangers involved in his exclusive exercise of the appointive function.[28]

The charge that senatorial confirmation of appointments would open the Senate to presidential influence and corruption, Hamilton branded an absurdity. The contrary was more likely to be true, and this, he explained, so far as the Senate merely exercised a restraining influence on the executive, was precisely what the Constitution intended. Could Hamilton have foreseen the potentialities of senatorial courtesy under a weak executive, he might have had less optimism about the advantages of the constitutional arrangement over the council-of-appointment system established in the state of New York.[29] But Hamilton, discussing the presidency in relation to the power of appointment, assumed that "there would always be great probability of having the place supplied by a man of abilities, at least respectable."[30] His interpretation of the appointive power implied a President with the judgment, the independence, and the impartiality of a Washington. The rise of the party system rendered the two latter qualities impolitic, and even Washington in his second administration discovered that he could no longer remain unpartisan and maintain an effective administration.

Hamilton's appraisal of the appointive power as a phase of the congressional-executive relationship was obviously incomplete; his known writings on this significant phase of administration fall short of the potentialities of the subject. The explanation probably lies in the absence of occasion for a searching analysis comparable to the exigencies of foreign relations and financial reconstruction which characterized the post-Independence era of United States history.

[27] A third, conclusive phase of appointment—that of commissioning— may be distinguished (see Edward S. Corwin, *The President, Office and Powers* [New York: New York University Press, 1940], p. 345, n. 13). Hamilton does not treat this distinction, but as it succeeds senatorial consent it would seldom involve the legislative-executive relationship.

[28] *The Federalist*, No. 76, Earle, *op. cit.*, pp. 493–94.

[29] *The Federalist*, No. 77, *ibid.*, pp. 496 ff. The practice of senatorial courtesy developed as early as Washington's first administration (Corwin, *op. cit.*, p. 69).

[30] *The Federalist*, No. 76, Earle, *op. cit.*, p. 492; *The Federalist*, No. 75, *ibid.*, p. 488.

The advent of the French Revolution in 1789 gave rise to a series of circumstances that brought into sharp focus the relationship between Congress and the President in the field of foreign policy. The outbreak of war between France and Great Britain in 1793 occasioned a controversy over the respective division of the power of war- and treaty-making in which Hamilton, as "Pacificus," became the protagonist of the executive authority. Instigated by Jefferson, Madison, under the pseudonym of "Helvidius," attempted a refutation of Hamilton's constitutional interpretation of the executive as the sole organ of external relations. The essential point in dispute was whether the President by his so-called "proclamation of neutrality" had infringed upon the congressional power to declare the nation in a state of war. The respective arguments and their merits have received comprehensive treatment elsewhere and need not be retold here. The substance of Hamilton's argument was that the Constitution granted plenary executive power to the President and that the specific grants of authority in Article II, except when joined with express restrictions or limitations, specified the principal articles implied in the general grant and served to interpret it. Hamilton, considering the direction of foreign policy as constitutionally and inherently an executive function, held that any incidental effect of presidential action in foreign affairs upon exercise of the congressional power to declare war should not operate to restrain executive action.

Although in the "Pacificus" series Hamilton's constitutional interpretation of the executive power in foreign relations was complete, the implications of his argument were not pushed to their ultimate conclusion until, in the "Lucius Crassus" criticism of Jefferson's message to Congress of December 8, 1801, he delivered his final blow to the theory of exclusive congressional power to recognize the existence of a state of war:

Our Constitution . . . . has only provided affirmatively, that, "The Congress shall have power to declare war"; the plain meaning of which is, that it is the peculiar and exclusive province of Congress, *when the nation is at peace*, to change that state into a state of war; whether from calculations of policy, or from provocations or injuries received; in other words, it belongs to Congress only, *to go to war*. But when a foreign nation declares or openly and avowedly makes war upon the United States, they are then by the very fact *already at war*, and any declaration on the part of Congress is nugatory; it is at least unnecessary . . . . it is self-evident, that a declaration by one nation against another, produces at once a complete state of war between both, and that no declaration on the other side can at all vary their relative situation; and in practice, it is well known that nothing is more common than when war is declared by one party, to prosecute mutual hostilities without a declaration by the other.[31]

[31] No. I, December 17, 1801, *Works*, ed. Lodge, VIII, 249–50.

The latitude which "Lucius Crassus" would allow the President in determining the state of the nation could hardly be exceeded without abrogating the specific provision of the Constitution that only Congress may declare a state of war. Hamilton would allow the President to find a state of war existing between the United States and another power when that power had taken the initiative in hostilities. Although Hamilton observed that Tripoli, the offending state in question, had declared war in form against the United States, one concludes from the context of his remarks that the mere commencement of hostilities would be sufficient to justify reprisals under the authority of the President. However, in his letter to McHenry of May 17, 1798, Hamilton had taken a distinctly cautious position concerning the powers of the President as commander-in-chief in the absence of a congressional declaration of war. Whether Hamilton's restraint resulted from a feeling of personal responsibility in advising the Secretary of War, whether from a desire to maneuver John Adams into appearing to recommend a declaration of war, or whether Hamilton changed his mind between 1798 and 1802 remains undetermined.[32]

A second major aspect of the President's authority in the direction of foreign policy was the power to negotiate treaties. Here also as in the appointive power and in the exercise of the so-called "war powers," the respective authorities of Congress and the executive lacked precise definition. But this aspect of constitutional law received more comprehensive treatment by Hamilton than did the appointive power, and without the contradiction which confused the President's authority to determine a state of war or peace. In *The Federalist*, No. 75, Hamilton expounded the treaty power of the President and the Senate, and in the controversy concerning the ratification of the Jay Treaty, he completed the definition of his earlier contentions.

In *The Federalist*, No. 75, Hamilton described the making of treaties as partaking of both legislative and executive functions, although, strictly construed, he held it an executive power. He explained that "the qualities elsewhere detailed as indispensable in the management of foreign negotiations [decision, secrecy, despatch], point out the Executive as the most fit agent in those transactions; while the vast importance of the trust, and the operation of treaties as laws, plead strongly for the participation of the whole or a portion of the legislative body in the office of making them."[33] But Hamilton deemed the House of Representatives too numerous and too fluctuating in membership to develop the "accurate and com-

[32] *Ibid.*, X, 281–82.   [33] Earle, *op. cit.*, p. 486.

prehensive knowledge of foreign politics; a steady and systematic adherence to the same views; a nice and uniform sensibility to national character"[34] essential to the proper consideration of treaties. The Constitution therefore wisely confined the treaty power to the President and to the smaller, more stable Senate.

In thus defining by theory and example the structural relationship between the Congress and the chief executive, Hamilton was applying those principles of organization and administration which seemed to him indispensable to the practice of good government. Energy, unity, responsibility, power, and duration were the conditions he sought to insure by maintaining the executive independence from congressional domination and in promoting his theory of executive leadership in the formulation of national policy. Accordingly, he turned to account the opportunities which the exigencies of the times afforded for strengthening the executive power and encouraging congressional reliance upon executive leadership. It was therefore the congressional-executive relationship in exercise of the war and treaty powers that afforded Hamilton opportunity for advancing his theories after 1793. This also is why potentially fertile areas of executive leadership implied in the appointive power were neglected by Hamilton—the occasions for their development being relatively less promising during his political career. This circumstance explains as well the fact that Hamilton's political writings, including *The Federalist*, do not cover all areas of American politics and administration with equal thoroughness. The contemporaneous nature of his writings deprived his work of the more comprehensive scope possible to one less involved in the immediate current of political life.

Although the principle of administrative unity was symbolized by the person of the chief executive, Hamilton conceived "the executive" as more than a single personality. The executive was a composite individual and, like the British crown, functioned through diverse ministers acting in its name and under its authority. As early as 1780 Hamilton recommended that the Continental Congress create a true executive branch by the appointment of the following great officers of state: "A Secretary of Foreign Affairs, a President of War, a President of Marine, a Financier, a President of Trade." Instead of this last, he observed, "a Board of Trade may be preferable, as the regulations of trade are slow and gradual, and require prudence and experience more than other qualities, for which Boards are very well adapted."[35] One may conclude that the status of the

34 *Ibid.*, p. 488.

35 To James Duane, September 3, 1780, *Works*, ed. Lodge, I, 225–26.

ministry which Hamilton proposed was pitched at a level higher than the cabinet was subsequently to enjoy, for he maintained that they "should have nearly the same powers and functions as those in France analogous to them; and each should be chief in his department, with subordinate Boards, composed of assistants, clerks, etc. to execute his orders."[36]

In the administration of each of the several departments of the government, Hamilton strongly recommended a single man at the helm. Observing a tendency in the Continental Congress to resort to boards rather than to individual administrators to direct the executive business, he protested that

a single man in each department of the administration would be greatly preferable. It would give us a chance of more knowledge, more activity, more responsibility, and, of course, more zeal and attention. Boards partake of a part of the inconveniences of larger assemblies. Their decisions are slower, their energy less, their responsibility more diffused. They will not have the same abilities and knowledge as an administration by single men. Men of the first pretensions will not so readily engage in them, because they will be less conspicuous, of less importance, have less opportunity of distinguishing themselves. The members of Boards will take less pains to inform themselves and arrive to eminence, because they have fewer motives to do it. All these reasons conspire to give a preference to the plan of vesting the great executive departments óf the State in the hands of individuals.[37]

The relationship which Hamilton believed necessary between the executive chief and his ministers will be developed in a following chapter, but it was in keeping with his administrative principles that Hamilton insisted that a sense of common purpose and mutual responsibility should govern interexecutive relations. The organization of the executive department under single administrators responsible to a single chief executive facilitated this relationship and thus promoted that unified energy in the executive which Hamilton admired.

But the administrative structure of the federal Union, as Hamilton would have it, embraced even more than the presidency and the great executive departments. He wrote to Washington in 1796 that he had completed a rough draft on the establishment of a national university, a military academy, a board of agriculture, and "the establishment of such manufactories on *public account* as are relative to the equipment of army and navy."[38] The forms and functions of these agencies may be reserved for later inquiry. The essential point is that Hamilton believed that the government of the United States had the power to create and manage public corporations in all areas wherein it had authority to legislate. "For," he said, "it is unquestionably incident to *sovereign power* to erect corpora-

[36] *Ibid.*   [37] *Ibid.*, pp. 219–20.   [38] *Ibid.*, X, 204–5.

tions, and consequently to *that* of the United States, in *relation* to the *objects* intrusted to the management of the government. The difference is this: where the authority of the government is general, it can create corporations in *all cases;* where it is confined to certain branches of legislation, it can create corporations *only* in those cases."[39]

The first United States Bank, alone of Hamilton's several projected nondepartmental government agencies, was actually established under his direction. Its immediate utility to the Union and value in supporting the financial program which Hamilton was developing account for its success. But popular antagonism to the bank whipped up by the Republican press was unquestionably a factor in retarding the establishment of the other agencies which Hamilton contemplated. Although Jefferson was not altogether opposed to the ends which these agencies were designed to serve, he was committed to the doctrine that the Constitution as it stood did not permit the establishment of government corporations, nor did it provide for the broad objectives which Hamilton believed were implied in the necessary and proper and general welfare clauses.[40] Although a gradual broadening of the Jeffersonian interpretation occurred in the decades following 1801, with several nondepartmental agencies being established, including a second United States Bank, it was not until after the Civil War that the implied power and incorporation theories which Hamilton had developed gained ascendancy in American constitutional law.

The leaven of Alexander Hamilton's contentions and John Marshall's opinions gradually permeated constitutional doctrine, and the defeat of the Confederacy, combined with the demands of civil war upon the Lincoln administration, established the Hamiltonian thesis as the more widely accepted meaning of the Constitution. As to whether the framers of the Constitution intended the broad interpretation of Hamilton or the more literal construction of Jefferson, opinions differ; and probably differences of opinion among the framers themselves preclude a definite conclusion. However that may be, the fact remains that circumstances have favored the Hamiltonian interpretation, and it has generally prevailed.

THE JUDICIARY AND PUBLIC ADMINISTRATION

The complete independence of the courts of justice is peculiarly essential in a limited Constitution.—"THE FEDERALIST," NO. 78.[41]

[39] "Opinion as to the Constitutionality of the Bank of the United States," *ibid.*, III, 448.

[40] *The Works of Thomas Jefferson*, ed. Paul Leicester Ford (12 vols.; Federal ed.; New York: G. P. Putnam's Sons, 1904), I, 197.

[41] Earle, *op. cit.*, p. 505.

Although outside the main current of Hamilton's administrative philosophy, his ideas concerning the place of the judiciary in the structure of government serve in several respects to clarify his conception of the scope and nature of the public service as a whole. We have already observed that Hamilton believed that the executive should enjoy substantial independence of the legislature but that the legislature should accept a considerable degree of guidance by the executive. The judiciary, however, he would isolate from the two more active branches. "It is impossible," he asserted in *The Federalist*, "to keep the judges too distinct from every other avocation than that of expounding the laws."[42] Not only was legislative dictatorship a threat to judicial independence, but Hamilton deemed it "peculiarly dangerous" to place judges in a situation where they might be subject to influence on behalf of the political views of the magistrate, thus cementing an improper connection between the executive and the judiciary departments.[43] Under the pressure of political opposition, however, Hamilton seems to have favored mutual co-operation between the federal courts and the policy-forming branches, for, referring to the resolutions of the Virginia legislature of 1790 which opposed his assumption policy, he wrote to Chief Justice John Jay, asking, "Ought not the collective weight of the different parts of the government be employed in exploding the principles they contain?"[44]

The provisions of the federal Constitution governing the judiciary conformed to Hamilton's principles of good administrative organization, particularly in that judges were to hold office during good behavior. "The standard of good behavior for the continuance in office of the judicial magistracy, is certainly one of the most valuable of the modern improvements in the practice of government," Hamilton explained, "and it is the best expedient which can be devised in any government, to secure a steady, upright, and impartial administration of the laws."[45] He observed that "the judiciary is beyond comparison the weakest of the three departments of power; that it can never attack with success either of the other two; and that all possible care is requisite to enable it to defend itself against their attacks."[46] Permanency in office was the quality deemed by Hamilton as indispensable to judicial independence and the preservation of popular liberties.

[42] *The Federalist*, No. 73, *ibid.*, p. 481.

[43] *The Federalist*, No. 78, *ibid.*, pp. 503 ff.

[44] *Correspondence and Public Papers of John Jay*, ed. Henry Phelps Johnston (4 vols.; New York: G. P. Putnam's Sons, 1890–93), III, 405.

[45] *The Federalist*, No. 78, Earle, *op. cit.*, p. 503.   [46] *Ibid.*, p. 504.

In *The Federalist*, No. 79, Hamilton asserted that "next to permanency in office, nothing can contribute more to the independence of the judges than a fixed provision for their support."[47] The constitutional provision that the judges of the United States "shall at *stated times* receive for their services a compensation which shall not be *diminished* during their continuation in office" he deemed one of the most effective safeguards of judicial independence that could be devised.[48]

The permanence of tenure and the restrictive provisions governing the compensation of judges gave rise to an interesting interpretation by Hamilton of the nature of judicial office. The attempt of the Jefferson administration to diminish the power of the Federalist judiciary and reduce its numbers by the abolition of certain federal courts was opposed by Hamilton on the ground that the office of a judge was distinct from the court in which he might happen to preside. Congress was at liberty to abolish such inferior courts as it created, but it was powerless to abolish the judges by the same process. Hamilton's reasoning to this end is of sufficient interest to the law of public offices to justify quotation at some length:

> . . . . *Congress have a right to change or abolish inferior courts, but not to abolish the actual judges.*
>
> Towards the support of this construction, it has been shown in another place, that the courts and the judges are distinct legal *entities*, which, in contemplation of law, may exist, independently the one of the other—mutually related, but not inseparable. The act proposed to be repealed exemplifies this idea in practice. It abolishes the District Courts of Tennessee and Kentucky, and transfers their judges to one of the Circuit Courts. Though the authorities and jurisdiction of those courts are vested in the Circuit Court, to which the judges are transferred; yet the *identity of the courts ceases*. It cannot be maintained that courts, so different in their organization and jurisdiction, are the same; nor could a legislative transfer of the judges have been constitutional but upon the hypothesis, that the office of a judge may survive the court of which he is a member. A *new appointment* by the Executive, of two additional judges, for the Circuit Court, *would otherwise have been necessary.* . . . .
>
> . . . .
>
> It will not be disputed, that the Constitution *might* have provided *in terms*, and with effect, that an inferior court which had been *established by law* might by law be abolished, so, nevertheless, that the judges of such court should retain the offices of judges of the United States with the emoluments before attached to their offices. The operation of such a provision would be, that when the court was abolished, all the functions to be executed in that court would be suspended, and the judge could only continue to exert the authorities and perform the duties, which might before have been performed, without reference to causes *pending in court;* but he would have the capacity

---

[47] *Ibid.*, p. 512.   [48] *Ibid.*

to be annexed to another court, without the intervention of a new appointment, and by that annexation, simply to *renew* the exercise of the authorities and duties which had been *suspended*.

If this might have been the effect of positive and explicit provision, why may it not likewise be the *result* of provisions which, presenting opposite considerations, point to the same conclusion: as a compromise calculated to reconcile those considerations with each other and to unite different objects of public utility? Surely the affirmative infringes no principle of legal construction; transgresses no rule of good sense.

Let us then inquire, whether there are not in this case opposite and conflicting considerations, *demanding* a compromise of this nature? On the one hand, it is evident, that if an inferior court once instituted, though found inconvenient, cannot be abolished, this is to entail upon the community the mischief, be it more or less, of a first error in the administration of the government; on the other hand, it is no less evident, that if the judges hold their offices at the discretion of the Legislature, they cease to be co-ordinate, and become a dependent branch of the government; from which *dependence*, mischiefs infinitely greater are to be expected.

All these mischiefs, the lesser as well as the greater, are avoided by saying: "*Congress may abolish the courts, but the judges shall retain their offices with the appertinent emoluments.*"[49]

If judges, once appointed, must be continued at a minimum compensation during good behavior, even though they have no courts in which to preside, how could their responsibility to the people be enforced? Hamilton believed that the process of impeachment was the only lawful method of removing judges in the course of their tenure. Want of ability he did not deem a valid occasion for impeachment, as he believed that the vagueness of the criteria of judicial ability would afford a handle to partisan abuse of the judicial system. Nor did he agree that limitations of age should restrict the tenure of judges, for he held the deliberating and comparing faculties generally to preserve their strength beyond the life-span enjoyed by most men. "In a Republic," he maintained, "where fortunes are not affluent, and pensions not expedient, the dismission of men from stations in which they have served their country long and usefully, on which they depend for subsistence, and from which it will be too late to resort to any other occupation for a livelihood, ought to have some better apology to humanity than is to be found in the imaginary danger of a superannuated bench."[50]

Hamilton's conception of the organization and jurisdiction of the judicial system treated in *The Federalist*, Nos. 79-82, describes quite accurately the way in which the new judiciary was to function under the Constitution. But his interpretation did not pass without challenge. The

---

[49] "Lucius Crassus," No. XVI, March 19, 1802, *Works*, ed. Lodge, VIII, 350-52.

[50] *The Federalist*, No. 79, Earle, *op. cit.*, pp. 514-15.

right of appeal to the federal courts from the highest courts of the states was resisted, and the authority of the Supreme Court to review acts of Congress was widely questioned. Hamilton's contention that all cases involving federal questions arising in state courts could be appealed to the courts of the United States was confirmed in the constitutional law of the nation by Justice Story in *Martin* v. *Hunters Lessee*[51] and by Chief Justice Marshall in *Cohens* v. *The State of Virginia*.[52] Remaining doubts as to the respective authority of the Union and the states were largely settled at Appomattox Court House. Although the right of the federal judiciary to hold acts of Congress unconstitutional has never secured unanimous acquiescence, the preponderance of opinion and certainly the consistent practice of the courts have established this aspect of judicial review as forecast by Hamilton.

Although Hamilton did not explore the administrative aspects of the judiciary, he expounded one of the earliest arguments on behalf of administrative adjudication. In his "Treasury Circular" of July 20, 1792, Hamilton declared the Secretary of the Treasury impowered to settle for the customs officers in the first instance the construction of the laws pertaining to revenue. This authority he held necessary to uniformity of execution and to forestall disputes between the collectors and the public which encouraged contempt for the laws. Discounting the benefit of resort to the courts for a judicial interpretation of the revenue measures, Hamilton declared "the vexatious course of tedious law suits . . . . very unsatisfactory to the suffering parties,—and very ill suited, as an ordinary expedient, to the exigencies and convenience of trade."[53]

Hamilton appears to have underestimated the power which the judiciary was capable of developing and to have overestimated the degree of restraint which it would exercise in separating bias from considered judgment. But a crucial issue in the infancy of the Republic was the safeguarding of judicial independence; accordingly, Hamilton, responding to the exigencies of the times, devoted his efforts to this end, leaving the problem of judicial responsibility and its enforcement to men of later decades. His analysis of the nature of judicial office affords a valuable commentary upon his notion of the tenure of public office generally and represents a defense of order and stability in the public service. The significance of his contribution to the public service in this respect is scarcely lessened by its indirect bearing on the administrative arm. That the judiciary suffered

[51] 1 Wheat. 304, 4L. Ed. 97 (1816).

[52] 6 Wheat. 264, 5L. Ed. 257 (1821).

[53] "Treasury Circulars, 1789–96," MSS, Library of Congress, July 20, 1792.

least of the great national departments from the infection of spoils politics is in no small measure due to the general acceptance of the attitude toward the courts which Hamilton defended. Thus a conception of public office separated from direct control in the partisan interest was maintained as a present example that continuity of tenure during good behavior was compatible with republican government.

CHAPTER V

PUBLIC ADMINISTRATION AND PUBLIC POLICY

IN THE preceding chapter it was observed that Hamilton held the executive responsible for the formulation of public policy. The legislative branch was primarily responsible for the final determination of proposed policy, but it might be properly subject to administrative guidance. The execution of policy was an executive function in which the judiciary participated. But only the executive was concerned from first to last with the evolution of public policy.

Hamilton's sweeping conception of the scope of executive policy-forming is evident from the extent of his own comprehensive administrative program. Because he believed the various aspects of public concern—finance, taxation, the regulation of commerce and industry, public works, education, agriculture, foreign affairs, and national defense—to relate closely to one another, he held that public administration should develop a unified plan of action, the several parts of which would contribute to the success of the whole. The principle by which he proposed to test the relevance of a particular policy to the general objective of the national administration was its tendency to promote the strength and prosperity of the nation. As the consolidation of the American Confederation into a true national state was the governing purpose of Hamilton's administrative program whatever enhanced the status of the Union was likely to be good policy, while measures which retarded the unifying process were undesirable.

In the following sections the relation of specific measures to the general purpose of consolidation will be developed. Secondary considerations obviously influenced Hamilton's opinion on many issues, and it would be misleading to suggest that each of his policies was designed with the nationalizing of the Union as its single purpose. Rather it was the integration of diverse policies and purposes to serve a general end which character-ized Hamilton's administrative thought.

PUBLIC CREDIT AND TAXATION

To justify and preserve . . . . confidence; to promote the increasing respectability of the American name; to answer the calls of justice; to restore landed property to its due value; to furnish new resources, both to agriculture and commerce; to cement more closely the union of the States; to add to their security against foreign attack; to establish public order on the basis of an upright and liberal policy;—these are the great and invaluable ends to be secured by a proper and adequate provision, at the present period, for the support of public credit.—"First Report on the Public Credit."[1]

Hamilton understood that only a true government—one that operated directly upon real persons—was capable of creating the necessary conditions for national unity and stability. But he also understood that merely to set up a national government was insufficient; for, to endure, a government must be united with its people in bonds of interest. To forge these common bonds was the work of statesmanship and the task to which Hamilton set himself. The interests subsisting between a people and its government were several, chief among them being order, stability, and security. But each of these required that adequate support for government be provided and that the resources of government be sufficient to realize all that these major interests implied.

Neither order, stability, nor security could exist under a regime incapable of fulfilling its most solemn promises, or scarce willing to make the effort; and Hamilton, therefore, was inflexible in his opposition to those who would take advantage of the weakness of the general government and the confusion of its finances to scale down or abolish the common debt. Nor did he believe that the provisions for payment promised when the debt was contracted should be altered to compensate for the misfortunes of some individuals at the cost of destroying the confidence which the people generally ought to have in the integrity of the government. Thus the cornerstone of Hamilton's public policy was the prompt provision for the payment of the public debt of the United States as it had been promised.

Two major operations were necessary, he believed, to effect this policy: the assumption by the new Union of the war debts contracted by the states and the funding of the entire debt of the nation—state and confederation, domestic and foreign. The immediate and ostensible object of Hamilton's funding scheme was to provide for the redemption of the en-

[1] January 9, 1790, *Works*, ed. Lodge, II, 232.

tire public debt, interest and principal. With the details of funding we need not be concerned beyond the observation that they were designed to conform to the interests of all classes of creditors.[2] To provide for immediate payment of the principal of the debt was obviously beyond the financial strength of the country, and the redemption would accordingly have to be spread over a number of years at the cost of increased interest obligations. In justification of this policy Hamilton had earlier declared: "We ought not to run in debt to avoid present expense, so far as our faculties extend, yet the propriety of doing it cannot be disputed when it is apparent that these are incompetent to the public necessities. Efforts beyond our abilities can only tend to individual distress and national disappointment."[3] Believing that the current rates of interest were beyond the ability of the government to meet, Hamilton proposed that the public creditors exchange their certificates of indebtedness for long-term bonds at relatively low interest rates. Short-term bonds bearing 6 per cent interest were to be optional, and a final portion of the debt was to be redeemable in land or in bonds with interest deferred for ten years. A sinking fund was to be created from which the Treasury could purchase its securities in the market at opportune times to retire the debt and to support the structure of credit erected upon it.[4] Finally, a national bank was to be incorporated, a quasi-private institution over which the government would exercise supervision but abstain from direct control.

It is difficult to appraise the merit of the funding scheme as a plan solely for debt redemption. Viewing it in this restricted sense, Jefferson and his allies believed it overly complicated, and even Hamilton's friend and Treasury successor, Oliver Wolcott, thought the plan unnecessarily complex.[5] But Hamilton conceived the funding scheme not merely as a method for debt redemption but as the foundation of a national credit structure wherein commerce, industry, and finance might flourish.

The bonds issued by the Treasury would circulate as currency and would serve as capital upon which additional loans between private groups might be negotiated. To the charge that this policy meant the perversion

---

[2] Hamilton's plan was outlined in detail in the *First Report on the Public Credit, ibid.*, pp. 227–89.

[3] *The Continentalist*, No. VI, July 4, 1782, *ibid.*, I, 285.

[4] For a discussion of the origin and operation of Hamilton's sinking fund see Edward A. Ross, "Sinking Funds," *Publications of the American Economic Association*, VII (July and September, 1892), 9–106.

[5] *The Works of Thomas Jefferson*, ed. Paul Leicester Ford (12 vols.; Federal ed.; New York: G. P. Putnam's Sons, 1904), IX, 358–59; George Gibbs (ed.), *Memoirs of the Administration of Washington and John Adams* (New York: Printed for the subscribers, 1846), I, 50, 55.

of the public trust on behalf of moneyed interests Hamilton declared that the creation of a workable monetary system was necessary to the great public purposes of the nation. Funding systems, he asserted, reduced the dangers attendant upon large-scale borrowing by the national government, enabling it readily to obtain the money "of which it stands in need for its defence, safety and the preservation or advancement of its interests . . . . without crushing the people beneath the weight of intolerable taxes; without taking from industry the resources necessary for its vigorous prosecution; without emptying all the property of individuals into the public lap; without subverting the foundation of social order."[6]

This plan to use the funded debt as a base for credit expansion explains Hamilton's opposition to proposals for redemption which would reduce the transfer value of federal securities. Because thé old certificates of indebtedness had been transferable, Hamilton believed that the good faith of the government required redemption without regard to whether the holders of the debt were original subscribers or more recent purchasers. Madison argued that it was a matter of simple justice to allow some return to those who, having originally supported the government, had since sold their certificates at a depreciated price to others who now stood to profit by Hamilton's funding scheme. But Hamilton contended that to discriminate between original and secondary creditors would produce as many inequities as it would cure and would ultimately threaten the prosperity and security of all by undermining the credit value of government borrowing.[7] "We seem not to reflect," he had declared in *The Continentalist*, "that in human society there is scarcely any plan, however salutary to the whole and to every part . . . . but in one way or another . . . . will operate more to the benefit of some parts than of others."[8]

Hamilton believed the national bank was necessary to the full realization of the benefits of the funded debt as a basis for an expanded public credit. Although he developed the constitutional theory of government corporations in his "Opinion as to the Constitutionality of the Bank of the United States," the institution which he proposed was a government-

[6] *Defence of the Funding System, Works*, ed. Lodge, VIII, 439.

[7] *Vindication of the Funding System* (1791[?]), *ibid.*, III, 17–24. See also Hamilton's views on the arrears of pay originally due certain Virginia and North Carolina soldiers, but which they had assigned. Hamilton opposed the congressional plan for payment to the soldiers rather than to the assignees, holding that the relief enjoyed by the soldiers would be more than offset by the resulting loss of confidence in the ability of the government to follow a consistent policy in relation to public credit and private property ("Arrears of Pay," Hamilton to Washington, May 28, 1790, *ibid.*, II, 334–36).

[8] No. V, April 18, 1782, *ibid.*, I, 277.

chartered rather than a publicly owned or operated agency. Declaring that "considerations of public advantage suggest . . . . that the bank . . . . be established upon principles that would cause the profits of it to redound to the immediate benefit of the State," he nevertheless held this idea liable to "insuperable objections."[9]

Opposing direct public management of the bank, Hamilton maintained that public policy required the government "to reserve to itself a right of ascertaining, as often as may be necessary, the state of the bank; excluding, however, all pretension to control."[10] That the government might exercise a compelling influence on bank policy although ostensibly lacking control was, of course, obvious. Hamilton observed that as the institution "must depend for its renovation, from time to time, on the pleasure of the government, it will not be likely . . . . to render itself . . . . unworthy of public patronage."[11] He pointed out that, in the administration of its finances, the government possessed the power to confer benefits upon the bank for which reciprocal co-operation might be expected; and, independent of these more particular considerations, he believed that "the natural weight and influence of a government will always go far towards procuring a compliance with its desires."[12]

In view of Hamilton's willingness to utilize direct governmental controls in other vital areas of economic life, it is possible that his fear of what he deemed the financial heresies of the times and the proclivity of legislative assemblies for cheap-money schemes induced him to limit the scope of public administration in the area of currency and banking. Evidently, he did not contemplate the future with sufficient equanimity to propose an institution capable of destroying as well as supporting the system of public finance which he believed the commonwealth required.[13]

It was, however, in Hamilton's proposal that the federal government assume the Revolutionary War debt of the states that the political-administrative significance of his financial system was most apparent. In a letter to Washington written in defense of his funding policy, Hamilton outlined three reasons, all of them essentially administrative, which induced him to favor the assumption of state debts:

[9] *Report on a National Bank, ibid.*, III, 427. [11] *Ibid.*, p. 429.

[10] *Ibid.*, p. 430. [12] *Ibid.*, pp. 429–30.

[13] For accounts of the establishment of the bank see John Holdsworth and Davis R. Dewey, *The First and Second Banks of the United States* (National Monetary Commission, 61st Cong., 2d sess.; Senate Document No. 571 [Washington: Government Printing Office, 1910]); and J. S. Davis, *Essays on the Earlier History of American Corporations* (Cambridge, Mass.: Harvard University Press, 1917), Vol. II, Essay IV, chap. ii.

1. To consolidate the finances of the country, and give an assurance of permanent order in them; avoiding the collision of thirteen different and independent systems of finance under concurrent and coequal authorities, and the scramblings for revenue which would have been incident to so many different systems.

2. To secure to the government of the Union, by avoiding those entanglements, an effectual command of the resources of the Union for present and future exigencies.

3. To *equalize the condition* of the citizens of the several States in the important article of taxation; rescuing a part of them from being oppressed with burdens beyond their strength, on account of extraordinary exertions in the war, and through the want of certain adventitious resources which it was the good fortune of others to possess.[14]

In his speech of June 28 in the New York Ratifying Convention of 1788 Hamilton had argued that there was no essential conflict between the Union and the states concerning the sources of taxable wealth and that, aside from constitutional prohibitions, each would enjoy concurrent powers of taxation. Wisdom dictated that potential federal-state conflicts in this sphere be minimized when the ratification of the Constitution hung in the balance. But in the organization of the new federal government the conflict inherent in federal-state competition for control of the available sources of revenue could not be denied. In his *Defence of the Funding System* Hamilton declared that the way to cut the Gordian knot of concurrent federal-state taxation was "to leave the States under as little necessity as possible of exercising the power of taxation."[15] He asserted that "to give a clear field to the Government of the United States was so manifestly founded in good policy that the time must come when a man of sense would blush to dispute it."[16] By a consolidation of the finances of the country in the central government, occasion could be avoided for the extension of state revenue systems into territory which the federal government might wish to enter. Conversely, the vesting in the federal government of responsibility for the debt would furnish occasion for extending its command over the financial resources of the Union.

The equalization of the tax burden of the citizens of the several states was also political and administrative in purpose, for Hamilton understood that fiscal policy need not be circumscribed by limitations of fiscal necessity, and it was the creation of a strong centrally controlled system of public finance supporting the national government rather than merely the redemption of the public debt which was the underlying purpose of his financial system.

[14] "Objections and Answers Respecting the Administration of the Government," *Works,* ed. Lodge, II, 436–37.

[15] *Ibid.,* IX, 5.   [16] *Ibid.*

That Hamilton believed a national debt to be a national blessing was an allegation as untrue as it was persistent. Under the circumstances confronting the new nation in 1789, Hamilton did believe that the debt, properly funded, could confer positive benefits upon the community. Its utility as a base for credit and as a device for consolidating the Union represented advantages which under other circumstances might not obtain. An accumulation of debt was not desirable merely because a certain amount of it operated as capital, for he argued that the utility of "such artificial capital" depended upon the need for it in the community. Because America in 1789 was deficient in circulating media and easily negotiable capital, Hamilton held the credit potentialities of the debt a public benefit. But he recognized that there was danger that the public debt "may be swelled to such a size as that the greatest part of it may cease to be useful as a capital . . . . as that the sums required to pay the interest upon it may become oppressive and beyond the means which a government can employ, consistently with its tranquillity, to raise them; as that the resources of taxation to face the debt may have been strained too far to admit of extensions adequate to exigencies which regard the public safety."[17]

Where this critical point in the expansion of debt was attained, Hamilton could not say, but he declared it impossible to believe that there was not such a point. Accordingly, he held it a principle of public finance that, "as the vicissitudes of nations beget a perpetual tendency to the accumulation of debt, there ought to be, in every government, a perpetual, anxious, and unceasing effort to reduce that which at any time exists, as fast as shall be practicable, consistently with integrity and good faith."[18] It therefore appears that in the management of debt the true role of public finance was to serve the larger ends of general public policy. The general welfare required that public debt be so controlled as to derive its benefits without incurring its dangers, and it was this requisite which Hamilton believed his funding scheme answered.

Hamilton's theory of funded debt as a basis for public credit implied a collateral theory of taxation, and in his *First Report on the Public Credit* he declared:

Persuaded, as the Secretary is, that the proper funding of the present debt will render it a national blessing, yet he is so far from acceding to the position, in the latitude in which it is sometimes laid down, that "public debts are public benefits"— a position inviting to prodigality, and liable to dangerous abuse—that he ardently wishes to see it incorporated as a fundamental maxim in the system of public credit

[17] *Report on Manufactures, ibid.,* IV, 125–26.

[18] *Ibid.,* p. 126.

of the United States, that the creation of debt should always be accompanied with the means of extinguishment. This he regards as the true secret for rendering public credit immortal.[19]

Hamilton required of a tax system that it yield revenue to meet the purpose of its levy, that it be equitable in its weight upon the taxpayers, and that it be unobstructive of national development and indiscriminatory in its application. "Equality and certainty are the two great objects to be aimed at in taxation,"[20] he declared. He favored a revenue system wherein "the passions and prejudices of the revenue officers" would be confined to the narrowest limits[21] and declared that "all revenue laws which are so constructed as to involve a lax and defective execution, are instruments of oppression to the most meritorious."[22] He lauded the English system of taxation "because little or nothing is left to the discretion of the officers of the revenue"[23] and observed that the great French authority on public finance, M. Necker, shared this opinion.[24] "The great art," he declared, "is to distribute the public burthens well, and not suffer them, either first or last, to fall too heavily on parts of the community, else distress and disorder must ensue; a shock given to any part of the political machine vibrates through the whole."[25] Yet the contention has been advanced that Hamilton wished to favor certain economic classes in the administration of federal taxation. It is more correct to say that he wished to encourage and protect certain aspects of American economic life which he felt must be strengthened if the nation was to become economically strong and independent. It was not a manufacturing class but manufacturing as such that Hamilton wished to favor. The lifeblood of capitalist economy was the fluid wealth available for investment. This Hamilton wished to increase, and accordingly he was opposed to any form of taxation which would reduce the incentives and opportunities for investment.

[19] *Ibid.*, II, 283.

[20] "Speech in the New York Assembly," February 17, 1787, *ibid.*, VIII, 35.

[21] *Report on Manufactures, ibid.*, IV, 162.

[22] See *Public Credit*, December 13, 1790, *ibid.*, II, 342. Hamilton may be termed the father of the United States Coast Guard, for on April 22, 1790, he urged the establishment of a coastal patrol to enforce the revenue laws. This revenue cutter service, initially designed to enforce the customs regulations, was soon assigned alien duties, e.g., enforcement of American neutrality in the sea war between Great Britain and France after 1793 (see Darrell H. Smith and Fred W. Powell, *The Coast Guard: Its History, Activities and Organization* [Washington: Brookings Institution, 1929], pp. 1–5).

[23] "Speech in the New York Assembly," February 17, 1787, *Works*, ed. Lodge, VIII, 34.

[24] *Ibid.*, p. 35.

[25] *The Continentalist*, No. VI, *ibid.*, I, 279.

Hamilton would tax individuals in proportion to their ability to pay, but, in so doing, he would encourage them to put their money to work in productive rather than in nonproductive expenditures. "The rich must be made to pay for their luxuries," he declared, "which is the only proper way of taxing their superior wealth."[26] In the New York Ratifying Convention of 1788 he predicted that the proposed federal administration would found its tax system on the "most easy and equal principles—to draw as much as possible from direct taxation, to lay the principle burden on the wealthy, etc."[27] But he opposed taxation of federal securities on the ground that "to tax the funds, is manifestly to *take*, or to *keep back*, a portion of the principal or interest stipulated to be paid."[28] Underlying this argument was, of course, his interest in popularizing the purchase of government securities and in building a reservoir of public and private funds for financing the great national improvements which he envisaged.

In view of Hamilton's opposition to the taxation of fluid wealth as such, it is unlikely that he would have favored the taxation of income. Although his contention as counsel for the government in the case of *Hylton* v. *United States*[29] that the only direct taxes contemplated by the Constitution were poll and land taxes would seem to indicate that he would not have viewed unapportioned income taxes as unconstitutional, it seems improbable that he would have viewed them as desirable given the conditions of the time and the nature of his objectives. Personal estate he held an unsatisfactory source of revenue "from the difficulty in tracing it" and believed that it could not be subjected to large contributions "by any other means than by taxes on consumption."[30] This species of tax would bear inequitably on the city dweller, where enforcement would be most effective. Conversely, a land tax would fail to meet the requirement of equity, as it would bear unduly upon the farmers.

Hamilton's opinion regarding poll taxes is not entirely clear. In *The Continentalist*, No. IV, he proposed a national capitation tax but would have exempted "common soldiers, common seamen, day laborers, cottagers, and paupers" from payment.[31] In *The Federalist*, No. 36, he revised

[26] *Ibid.*, pp. 283–84.

[27] *Ibid.*, II, 82.

[28] *Second Report on the Public Credit, ibid.*, III, 282. Hamilton's opposition to state taxation of federal securities was expressed to the Supervisors of Boston, July 27, 1791, *ibid.*, II, 353.

[29] 3 Dall. 171; 1 L. Ed. 556 (1796).

[30] *The Federalist*, No. 12, Edward Mead Earle (ed.), *The Federalist* (Washington: National Home Library Association, 1937), p. 75.

[31] August 30, 1781, *Works*, ed. Lodge, I, 261–62.

his opinion and declared that "as to poll taxes, I, without scruple, confess my disapprobation of them."[32] A reconciliation between his opposition to poll taxes and his advocacy of them in *The Continentalist* can perhaps be derived from his remark in the Poughkeepsie Convention of 1788, that "I am as much opposed to capitation as any man. Yet who can deny that there may exist certain circumstances which will render this tax necessary?"[33] However, in the *Report on Manufactures* he expressed disapproval of "all poll or capitation taxes,"[34] and this seems to have been his final view of the matter, his attitude toward the direct tax on slaves enacted July 14, 1798, being uncertain.[35]

Hamilton proposed customs and excise taxes as those best conforming to the features of yield, equity, and unobstructiveness which he held requisite to a good system of taxation. In *The Federalist*, No. 12, he had declared that "the genius of the people will ill brook the inquisitive and peremptory spirit of excise laws."[36] But, although he held this mode of taxation to be of limited use, the need for revenue in excess of the return from customs duties and the desire to protect all possible sources of federal revenue from state pre-emption led him to incorporate excise taxes into his Treasury policy, although he had intimated in the New York Ratifying Convention of 1788 that the federal government would draw as much as possible upon direct taxation. In practice the so-called "direct taxes" proved objectionable because the constitutional requirement of apportionment rendered them difficult to administer. The indirect taxes possessed the added advantage of a less obtrusive form of levy and were less likely to arouse popular antagonism. But the excise taxes, as he predicted, proved unpopular, and Madison declared that the tax on carriages which Hamilton promoted was in fact a direct tax and therefore unconstitutional because unapportioned among the several states.[37]

In defense of his excise policy Hamilton pleaded that the customs duties were insufficient to meet the demands of the funding system and asserted that some further source of revenue was imperative and that "none equal-

[32] Earle, *op. cit.*, p. 223.

[33] "Speech in the New York Ratifying Convention," June 28, 1788, *Works*, ed. Lodge, II, 81.

[34] *Ibid.*, IV, 161.

[35] For additional views of Hamilton's see *Report on Improvement of the Revenue System* communicated to the House of Representatives, February 2, 1795 (*ibid.*, III, 301–12), and Hamilton's plan for a building tax sent to Oliver Wolcott, June 7, 1797 (*ibid.*, pp. 312–15).

[36] Earle, *op. cit.*, p. 72.

[37] James Madison, *Letters and Other Writings of James Madison, Fourth President of the United States* (4 vols.; New York: R. Worthington, 1884), II, 14.

ly productive would have been so little exceptionable to the mass of the people."[38] But political policy and administrative considerations likewise influenced Hamilton's course, for he "thought it well to lay hold of so valuable a resource of revenue before it was generally preoccupied by the State governments,"[39] and he feared that the nonexercise of the national authority over internal revenue might "beget an impression that it was never to be exercised, and next, that it ought not to be exercised."[40] Thus, fiscal considerations aside, the strengthening of the central administration as against the states was a declared objective of Hamilton's tax program.

Whether the excise of 1791 on whiskey actually strengthened the national government is difficult to determine. In the short run the bitter opposition which the whiskey tax aroused in the settlements of the South and West certainly injured both the federal authority and Hamilton's Treasury administration. But in the long run the successful enforcement of the unpopular measure and the suppression of armed resistance to federal authority probably strengthened the position of the central government in the Union. The tax itself appears to have been relatively unproductive so that the advantage gained from the whiskey excise was primarily of a long-run administrative nature.[41]

Hamilton was aware of the reluctance of a democratically controlled government to tax its constituency, and, although he believed borrowing preferable to taxation so heavy as to weaken the national economy, he knew that resort to loans when taxes ought to be levied was the invariable tendency of popularly elected legislators. His ideas concerning the proper occasions for loans and taxes were developed in a *Report of the Secretary of the Treasury Relative to Additional Supplies for Carrying on the Indian War*, presented to Congress on March 16, 1792:

> Great emergencies might exist in which loans would be indispensable. But the occasions which will justify them must be truly of that description. The present is not of such a nature. The sum to be provided is not of magnitude enough to furnish the plea of necessity. Taxes are never welcome to a community. They seldom fail to excite uneasy sensations more or less extensive; hence a too strong propensity in the Govern-

[38] "Objections and Answers Respecting the Administration of the Government," *Works*, ed. Lodge, II, 438.

[39] *Ibid.*   [40] *Ibid.*

[41] Davis R. Dewey, *Financial History of the United States* (12th ed.; New York: Longmans, Green & Co., 1938), p. 106. Direct taxes proved to be equally unpopular in certain areas. The Fries Rebellion in Pennsylvania resulted in riots against the house and land tax of July 14, 1798.

ment of nations to anticipate and mortgage the resources of posterity, rather than encounter the inconveniences of a present increase of taxes.

But this policy when not dictated by very peculiar circumstances, is of the worst kind. Its obvious tendency is, by enhancing the permanent burthens of the people, to produce lasting distress and its natural issue is in national bankruptcy.[42]

Hamilton therefore opposed government borrowing to meet ordinary and recurrent demands upon the national treasury. Loans were to answer the demands of great emergencies but were not to be employed as a part of the regular system of revenue. The strength and flexibility of the central administration would thereby be enhanced, for, by holding interest charges to a minimum, the government would enjoy greater freedom in the use of obtainable revenue and its borrowing power would stand unimpaired, a reserve for times of crises. Here again political and administrative considerations were as important as fiscal theory in shaping Hamilton's policies of public finance.

The great contribution to administrative theory of Hamilton's financial system was in its effort to integrate the fiscal aspects of public policy into a comprehensive administrative program. Finance served not merely the ends of the national government by providing the revenue to support its operation, but it likewise served Hamilton's greater objective—the national unification under the guidance of national administrators. His fiscal policy was unitary, and no part of it can be properly understood without reference to its entirety. Hamilton conceived and framed it as a whole and promoted it as a whole. Neither in the funding of the debt nor in the creation of the bank was Hamilton working counter to his taxing theory. The unifying, strengthening, and systematic ordering of the Union and its administration was ever the dominating objective.[43]

These were the considerations which shaped Hamilton's system of public finance and furnished the gist of argument in his first and second reports on the public credit, his report on a national bank, and his report on manufactures. These great state papers were therefore components of a single system which exemplified in every particular the Hamiltonian philosophy of unified national public policy. The system was designed to tie the people to the government and to launch the government upon an

---

[42] *Fact* (for the *National Gazette*), September 11, 1792, *Works*, ed. Lodge, III, 44–45.

[43] Hamilton's fiscal measures were not in themselves original, being strongly influenced by the public finance of William Pitt. For discussions of the British origins of Hamilton's financial policy see E. C. Lunt, "Hamilton as a Political Economist," *Journal of Political Economy*, III (June, 1895), 289–310; E. G. Bourne, "Alexander Hamilton and Adam Smith," *Quarterly Journal of Economics*, VIII (April, 1894), 328–44; C. F. Dunbar, "Some Precedents Followed by Alexander Hamilton," *Quarterly Journal of Economics*, III (October, 1888), 32–59.

active program in the public welfare, for which means were supplied by the financial system. Hamilton the statesman stood at the center of the system shaping the conflicting interests of the people into a generally beneficial program and forcing the lifeblood of credit and confidence through the inert administrative structure created by the paper Constitution of 1787. Over the merit of his methods economists may dispute, but in his conception of the role of public finance in the national economy and of the responsibility of administration for the integration of finance into a comprehensive nationalizing program, his contribution to thought on public administration is large indeed.[44]

COMMERCE AND INDUSTRY

There are some who maintain that trade will regulate itself, and is not to be benefited by the encouragements or restraints of government. Such persons will imagine that there is no need of a common directing power. This is one of those wild speculative paradoxes, which have grown into credit among us, contrary to the uniform practice and sense of the most enlightened nations.—"THE CONTINENTALIST," No. V.[45]

The need of "a common directing power" Hamilton believed no less evident in commerce and industry than it was in public finance. Since the directive authority in government was of executive character, the comprehensive superintendence of commerce and industry became a province of public administration. In *The Continentalist* Hamilton first developed his theories of government and business, contending that Hume's essay on "Jealousy of Trade" did not "insinuate that the regulatory hand of government was either useless or harmful," and he cited with approval mercantilist control of business enterprise in Holland, France, and Great Britain.[46] But it was the *Report on Manufactures* presented to Congress in December, 1791, that provided his notable exposition of the directive role of government in economic affairs.

The purpose of the report was defined by a congressional resolution adopted early in 1790, requesting the Secretary of the Treasury to give attention "to the subject of Manufactures, and particularly to the means for promoting such as will tend to render the United States independent on

[44] No account of Hamilton's fiscal system would be complete without reference to his reports on coinage and the mint. The Mint Act of April 2, 1792, followed Hamilton's suggestions in the main, but the administration of the Mint became a source of contention between Jefferson and Hamilton, for it was first placed under the control of the Secretary of State and only later transferred to the Treasury upon the strong recommendation of Hamilton (see *Works*, ed. Lodge, IV, 3 ff.; Dewey, *op. cit.*, pp. 102–4).

[45] *Works*, ed. Lodge, I, 267–68.

[46] *Ibid.*, pp. 269–70.

foreign nations."[47] Although Hamilton took the occasion to expound his philosophy of the relation of government to commerce, the underlying theory of the report ought not be confused with the specific proposals which, given the conditions of 1791, seemed to Hamilton best calculated to promote the public welfare.

The report was based upon a comprehensive survey of domestic and commercial manufacturing throughout the Union. Hamilton supplemented his own great fund of knowledge and that of his immediate friends with letters of inquiry addressed to leading citizens in several of the states, who in turn sought from their acquaintances in the towns and counties the information requested by the Secretary. Hamilton also utilized the officers of the internal revenue as collectors of information, thus foreshadowing the future comprehensive fact-finding activities of administrative personnel;[48] and, writing to Jefferson in June, 1791, he suggested that diplomatic representatives abroad might supply the administration with reports on foreign economic affairs.[49]

The argument of the *Report on Manufactures* was that the general welfare required the encouragement of manufactures in the United States and that the direction of the national economic life to effect this end was the business of the federal government. From the development of domestic industry and the diversification of American economic life, Hamilton foresaw a strengthened political union in place of a divisive sectionalism. The interdependence of all parts of the Union he believed to be the best guaranty of a strong, enduring nation. A purely agricultural country could never achieve the wealth and security which followed a conjunction of agriculture and industry as complementary phases of the national economy. Diversified economics promised strength and mutual prosperity, but purely agricultural countries he believed to have always been poor, weak, and difficult to defend against aggression. The defense of the Union was a major consideration in his plan to encourage manufactures, and he favored the government creation of armament industries where private initiative was unable or unwilling to provide essential equipment. Finally, the need for protecting newborn American industries from the rigors of European competition and for an unobjectionable source of revenue was answered

[47] *Ibid.*, IV, 70.

[48] Much of this interesting correspondence has been collected and published under the auspices of the Business Historical Society, Inc., in Arthur Harrison Cole (ed.), *Industrial and Commercial Correspondence of Alexander Hamilton, Anticipating His Report on Manufactures* (Chicago: A. H. Shaw Co., 1928).

[49] *Works*, ed. Lodge, IV, 58.

by a tariff, but the need for revenue premised that the duties would not be so excessive as to defeat their collection and shut off foreign trade.[50] For, although Hamilton indorsed the protection of industry, he did not favor an exclusionist economic policy:

It is a primary object of the policy of nations, to be abe lto supply themselves with subsistence from their own soils; and manufacturing nations, as far as circumstances permit, endeavor to procure from the same source the raw materials necessary for their own fabrics. This disposition, urged by the spirit of monopoly, is sometimes even carried to an injudicious extreme. . . . . Nations who have neither mines nor manufactures can only obtain the manufactured articles of which they stand in need, by an exchange of the products of their soils; . . . . if those who can best furnish them with such articles are unwilling to give a due course to this exchange, they must, of necessity, make every possible effort to manufacture for themselves; the effect of which is, that the manufacturing nations abridge the natural advantages of their situation, through an unwillingness to permit the agricultural countries to enjoy the advantages of theirs, and sacrifice the interests of a mutually beneficial intercourse to the vain project of selling everything and buying nothing.[51]

Hamilton found the constitutional basis for the regulation of commerce and industry in the commerce, taxing, and spending powers of the federal Union. He declared that the Constitution of necessity left to the discretion of the national legislature "to pronounce upon the objects which concern the general welfare," adding that "there seems to be no room for a doubt that whatever concerns the general interests of learning, of agriculture, of manufactures, and of commerce, are within the sphere of the national councils, as far as regards an application of money."[52] Upon the basis of this general welfare power Hamilton proposed a federal agency "for promoting arts, agriculture, manufactures, and commerce."[53]

Let a certain annual sum be set apart, and placed under the management of commissioners, not less than three, to consist of certain officers of the government and their successors in office.

Let these commissioners be empowered to apply the fund confided to them, to defray the expenses of the emigration of artists and manufacturers in particular branches of extraordinary importance; to induce the prosecution and introduction of useful discoveries, inventions, and improvements, by proportionate rewards, judiciously held out and applied; to encourage by premiums, both honorable and lucrative, the exertions of individuals and of classes, in relation to the several objects . . . . as may be generally designated by law.

. . . .

[50] For a discussion of the origins of protectionism see William Hill, "The First Stages of the Tariff Policy of the United States," *Publications of the American Economic Association*, VIII (November, 1893), 9–162.

[51] *Report on Manufactures, Works*, ed. Lodge, IV, 95–96.

[52] *Ibid.*, pp. 151–52.   [53] *Ibid.*, p. 195.

In countries where there is great private wealth, much may be effected by the voluntary contributions of patriotic individuals; but in a community situated like that of the United States, the public purse must supply the deficiency of private resource. In what can it be so useful, as in prompting and improving the efforts of industry?[54]

The implication of Hamilton's proposal was that this board of commissioners would have something of the character of a national planning agency vested with positive administrative power to promote the national welfare. The proposed board and the provision for bounty payments on certain manufactures appear to have been designed to aid such large-scale industrial enterprises as the Society for Establishing Useful Manufactures incorporated in New Jersey with the interest and support of Hamilton.[55]

But Hamilton's proposals were not confined to the extension of direct government aids but extended also to include what he termed "judicious regulations for the inspection of manufactured commodities."[56] In *The Continentalist*, No. VI, Hamilton had favored governmental regulation to check forms of business harmful to the common interest, and in the *Report on Manufactures* he forecast the future activities of the Federal Trade Commission, calling for regulatory inspection to "prevent frauds upon consumers at home and exporters to foreign countries."[57] He held such supervision contributory to improving the quality of American manufactures and certain "to aid the expeditious and advantageous sale of them" in the face of foreign competition. Observing that the reputation of the flour and lumber of some states and of the potash of others had been established in this manner, he suggested that the national inspection of grain for export might be desirable and recommended regulations to improve the quality of iron and gunpowder.[58] Although he favored a wide margin of freedom for private business enterprise, Hamilton clearly did not advocate laissez faire as a principle of public policy.

The notion that government might own and operate certain industries essential to the general welfare did not appear to Hamilton as novel or revolutionary. His interest in government armaments industry has been noted, and in the *Report on Manufactures* he urged that steps be taken to

[54] *Ibid.*, pp. 196–98.

[55] For an account of the S.U.M. see Davis, *op. cit.*, I, 349–518. The Pennsylvania Society for the Encouragement of Manufactures and the Useful Arts and the New York Manufacturing Society also represented attempts to establish large-scale manufacturing and are described by Davis (*ibid.*, Vol. II, Essay IV, chap. v).

[56] *Report on Manufactures, Works*, ed. Lodge, IV, 157.

[57] *Ibid.*, p. 158.   [58] *Ibid.*, pp. 158, 166, 174, 190.

stimulate this field of enterprise by regular government purchasing, adding:

> But it may, hereafter, deserve legislative consideration, whether manufactories of all the necessary weapons of war ought not to be established on account of the government itself. Such establishments are agreeable to the usual practice of nations, and that practice seems founded on sufficient reason.
>
> There appears to be an improvidence in leaving these essential implements of national defence to the casual speculations of individual adventure—a resource which can less be relied upon, in this case, than in most others; the articles in question not being objects of ordinary and indispensable private consumption or use. As a general rule, manufactories on the immediate account of government are to be avoided; but this seems to be one of the few exceptions which that rule admits, depending on very special reasons.[59]

In his draft of Washington's message to Congress of December 7, 1796, Hamilton repeated his recommendation in almost identical language, and in his letter to Jonathan Dayton concerning the future course of Federalist policy he declared that "manufactories of every article, the woolen parts of clothing included, which are essential to the supply of the army, ought to be established."[60] Therefore, although he opposed government manufacturing as a general rule, the standard by which he judged the feasibility of public enterprise was consideration for the general welfare. Expediency rather than economic doctrine was the measure of wisdom in this respect. Government manufacturing was desirable only so far as it could meet a public need which private enterprise was unable or unwilling to undertake properly. But with this limitation the latitude for the extension of public policy into the manufacturing area might still be very considerable.

One should not infer, however, that Hamilton believed that a thoroughgoing governmental regulation of industrial enterprise was desirable, for he declared that "in matters of industry, human enterprize ought, doubtless, to be left free in the main; not fettered by too much regulation."[61] Comprehensive supervision of a general nature, guidance toward the objective of the general welfare, described the proper sphere of public administration.

Obviously, Hamilton's regulations for commerce and industry required continuing administrative supervision and implied a hierarchy of civil officials in whom the supervisory task would be vested. The complexity of the undertaking and the need for predictability in business enterprise required

[59] *Ibid.*, p. 168.   [60] *Ibid.*, X, 334.

[61] "Lucius Crassus," No. III, December 24, 1801, *ibid.*, VIII, 263.

competence and long-term tenure in the civil personnel charged with the regulatory function. Thus Hamilton's system foreshadowed the rise of government career service as well as the demands which a developing industrial order would make upon public administration. Hamilton represented a broad and constructive policy of governmental participation in the commercial and industrial life of the nation; he proposed a liaison between public policy, industrial and scientific progress, and public administration which, had it been accepted, would surely have produced consequences of greatest benefit to the American people.

AGRICULTURE AND CONSERVATION

Mutual wants constitute one of the strongest links of political connection.—"REPORT ON MANUFACTURES."[62]

Hamilton's alleged indifference to agriculture finds no confirmation in his writings. It is, of course, true that his greater concern was for the development of trade and industry, in which the nation was deficient. Agriculture, the overwhelmingly predominant occupation in America, needed little encouragement, and agriculture without industry tended, in Hamilton's opinion, to promote sectionalism in politics. In the *Report on Manufactures* he described the fallacy that agricultural and manufacturing interests were opposed as "the common error of the early periods of every country."[63] Arguing that the aggregate prosperity of manufactures and the aggregate prosperity of agriculture are intimately connected, he saw in the mutual exchange of products of farm and factory a force for national unity. Hamilton's purpose was to create an industrial economy which would complement the nation's agriculture and unite all sections in common prosperity and interdependence.

The proposal of a board to encourage the development of improvements in agriculture and industry was included in the *Report on Manufactures*. In President Washington's address to Congress of December 7, 1796, Hamilton, who prepared the initial draft, elaborated on the benefits of such a foundation to the nation's farmers and significantly observed the harmful effect of the exploitive practice of agriculture on the wealth and stability of the American people. Recognizing that the cultivation of the soil was the basis of national prosperity, Hamilton declared that the general welfare was served by making agriculture an object of public patronage and care. Presaging a national department of agriculture, he pointed out that, as the economy of a nation matures, institutions for the promotion of agriculture "sooner or later grow up, supported by the public purse—

[62] *Ibid.*, IV, 139.   [63] *Ibid.*

and the full fruits of them, when judiciously conceived and directed, have fully justified the undertaking."[64]

Agriculture among us is certainly in a very imperfect state. In much of those parts where there have been early settlements, the soil, impoverished by an unskillful tillage, yields but a scanty reward for the labor bestowed upon it, and leaves its possessors under strong temptation to abandon it, and emigrate to distant regions, more fertile. . . . . Nothing appears to be more unexceptionable, and more likely to be efficacious, than the institution of a Board of Agriculture, with the views I have mentioned, and with a moderate fund towards executing them.[65]

Hamilton's concern over the impoverishment of the nation's soil was shared by Jefferson and the more progressive agrarians, but Hamilton seems most clearly to have understood the responsibility of the government in protecting this basic national resource. Hamilton was no agrarian, yet he saw as few did that farming is not merely a local matter but an industry of vital national concern. Not only would he create a national agency to promote the conservation and development of agricultural resources, but he advocated direct benefits paid from the federal treasury to stimulate branches of husbandry needful to the national economy. In the *Report on Manufactures* he proposed bounties or premiums for the production of flax, hemp, and wool.[66] Not foreseeing the great increase in cotton production which was presently to follow the perfection of ginning, Hamilton recommended a bounty on the fabrication of domestic cotton which, although paid to the manufacturer, was designed to promote the growth and improvement of the natural product.

In the development of the mineral wealth of the nation Hamilton again appears as a true conservationist. He declared that "mines in every country constitute a branch of revenue . . . . and . . . . they require the care and attention of government to bring them to perfection."[67] He believed that this care, and a share in the profits thereof, should devolve upon the national government. All precious metals, he asserted, "should absolutely be the property of the Federal Government, and with respect to the others it should have a discretionary power of reserving, in the nature of a tax, such part of it as it may judge not inconsistent with the encouragement due to so important an object."[68] To stimulate the mining of coal, he favored the judicious use of bounties and premiums, for he believed the

[64] *Ibid.*, VIII, 215.

[65] *Ibid.*, pp. 215–16.   [66] *Ibid.*, pp. 179, 188.

[67] *The Continentalist*, No. VI, *ibid.*, I, 285.

[68] *Ibid.*; see also *The Continentalist*, No. IV, *ibid.*, p. 262.

development of this industry essential to the progress of American manufactures. Given proper federal supervision, it apparently mattered little whether mining was undertaken by private or by public enterprise. Hamilton observed that a Virginia lead mine had yielded well under both public and private management.

In the administration of the timber resources of the nation Hamilton likewise showed unusual foresight. Although America then seemed to have an inexhaustible supply of wealth in wood, Hamilton observed that "the increasing scarcity and growing importance of that article, in the European countries, admonish the United States to commence, and systematically to pursue, measures for the preservation of their stock. Whatever may promote the regular establishment of magazines of ship timber, is in various views desirable."[69]

Thus Alexander Hamilton was among the first American statesmen to advocate the conservation of natural resources under federal legislation, and it reveals the breadth of his conception of public policy that he advocated the essentials of a national conservation system fully a century before the idea of comprehensive federal supervision in this area began to receive serious political consideration.

The unity of purpose underlying Hamilton's theories of conservation, government aid to agriculture, and participation in industry is again illustrated by his public land policy. In a report to the House of Representatives on July 22, 1790, he opposed the rapid settlement of the western lands,[70] favoring a carefully regulated system of gradual sale and settlement in order to develop in the seaboard states a compact, diversified economy. Thus agriculture must be sustained, and the exploitive soil-exhausting methods of the American farmer corrected if the drift to newer, richer lands was to be halted. As early as 1781 Hamilton advanced his theory of a restricted development of western lands to increase the labor supply and encourage manufacturing in the East.[71] He wished to discourage the draining of the eastern labor supply into the West, as he deemed the creation of a domestic industrial economy essential to national safety and prosperity. He would, accordingly, encourage the mechanic arts and reduce the opportunities for a rapid expansion of western agriculture. But such conservative development was not to be, for Hamilton was no more successful than were the ministers of George III in stopping the rush to

[69] *Report on Manufactures, ibid.,* IV, 172.

[70] *Report of a Uniform System for the Disposition of the Lands, the Property of the United States, ibid.,* VIII, 87–94.

[71] *The Continentalist,* No. VI, *ibid.,* I, 279.

the virgin lands.[72] The natural wealth which he would have conserved to insure the continued prosperity of the nation passed quickly into private hands and could be redeemed only in future years by something approaching a social revolution.

INTERNAL IMPROVEMENTS AND PUBLIC EDUCATION

The improvement of the communications between the different parts of our country is an object well worthy of the national purse.—"LUCIUS CRASSUS," No. III.[73]

Having surveyed Hamilton's administrative policies thus far, one would expect him to favor the construction of useful public works by the national government. He was particularly sympathetic to the improvement of the national avenues of communication—highways, bridges, and canals—for those were the arteries through which trade, the lifeblood of the nation, flowed. He declared the provision of roads and bridges within the direct purview of the Constitution and believed aqueducts and canals appropriate subjects for federal financial aid.[74] The benefit derived from an improved transportation system, he insisted, was general, agriculture, labor, and the arts enjoying advantages which would be felt throughout the Union.

Writing to Jonathan Dayton in 1799, Hamilton urged that "the improvement of the roads would be a measure universally popular."[75] For this purpose he held that a regular plan should be adopted, coextensive with the Union, to be successively executed and that a fund should be appropriated sufficient for the basis of a loan of a million dollars.[76] Tolls for use of roads, he believed, would ultimately reimburse the expense, and public utility would be promoted in every direction. Supplementing this system of public highways, Hamilton declared: "An article ought to be proposed, to be added to the Constitution, for empowering Congress to open canals in all cases in which it may be necessary to conduct them through the territory of two or more States, or through the territory of a State and that of the United States."[77] Not only would a comprehensive canal system assist agriculture and commerce, by rendering the transportation of commodities more cheap and expeditious, but, by tying together

---

[72] Hamilton's fiscal policies appear to have had a detrimental effect upon the speculations in Ohio lands, but there appears to be no evidence that this result was foreseen by Hamilton (see Davis, *op. cit.*, I, 142–45, 172–73).

[73] December 24, 1801, *Works*, ed. Lodge, VIII, 262.

[74] *Ibid.*, p. 262.

[75] *Ibid.*, X, 332.

[76] *Ibid.*

[77] *Ibid.*, p. 334.

the distant portions of the Union, he predicted that it would strengthen the attachment of the people to national interests. One of Hamilton's favorite arguments on behalf of public works was that, properly administered, they would ultimately repay their cost. Thus the expenditures for canals, highways, bridges, and harbor improvements were not irrecoverable expenses but actually loans to be repaid, first, by the advantages derived by the public from the resulting improvements and, second, by a possible reduction in taxation or increase in the value received from taxation as the surplus revenue from a public works project offset a portion of the regular expenses of government.[78]

In addition to these instruments of public utility, Hamilton held advisable the erection of proper works pertaining to national security. These included the creation of a navy, arsenals, foundries, dockyards, magazines, and fortifications, all of which must be financed by the public purse. Although the defense and security of the country justified the expenditures required for these undertakings, even they might be so managed as to offset a portion of the expenses of government. In the "Plan for Military Peace Establishment," which he helped to formulate in 1783, he recommended that "as soon as the situation . . . . will permit public manufactories of arms, powder, etc., should be established; and a part of the troops, employed in this way, will furnish those necessary articles to the United States, and defray a considerable part of the expense of supporting themselves."[79]

In the *Report on Manufactures* Hamilton included "whatever concerns the general interests of learning . . . . within the sphere of the national councils, as far as regards an application of money."[80] Not only was the encouragement of learning through the spending power within the purview of public policy, but Hamilton appears to have recognized a general competence upon the part of the federal government to promote public education. In recommending an increase in the duty on imported books, he declared that with regard to books which may be specially imported for the use of particular seminaries of learning, and public libraries, a total exemption of duty would be advisable. Hamilton's interest in the establishment of a national academy for military and naval instruction appears repeatedly in his correspondence and in certain of the recommendations to Congress which he prepared for President Washington. He advocated "an establishment for the maintenance and education of the children of persons in the army and navy" and a corps of invalids organized to reha-

[78] "Lucius Crassus," No. III, *ibid.*, VIII, 262.

[79] *Ibid.*, VI, 467.   [80] *Ibid.*, IV, 151–52.

bilitate, employ, and protect from misery and want men who had spent their best years or acquired infirmities in the service of their country.[81]

In his address to Congress of December 7, 1796, Washington presented the recommendation which Hamilton had drafted concerning the establishment of a national university:

> The extension of science and knowledge is an object primarily interesting to our national welfare. To effect this is most naturally the care of the particular local jurisdictions into which our country is subdivided, as far as regards those branches of instruction which ought to be universally diffused, and it gives pleasure to observe that new progress is continually making in the means employed for this end. But, can it be doubted that the general government would with peculiar propriety occupy itself in affording nutriment to those higher branches of science, which, though not within the reach of general acquisition, are in their consequences and relations productive of general advantage? Or can it be doubted that this great object would be materially advanced by a university erected on that broad basis to which the national resources are most adequate, and so liberally endowed as to command the ablest professors in the several branches of liberal knowledge? It is true, and to the honor of our country, that it offers many colleges and academies highly respectable and useful, but the funds upon which they are established are too narrow to permit any of them to be an adequate substitute for such an institution as is contemplated.[82]

Hamilton's policy of national unification was involved in the plan, for Washington listed "amongst the motives to such an institution, the assimilation of the principles, opinions, manners, and habits of our countrymen, by drawing from all quarters our youth to participate in a common education."[83] Hamilton's interest in public education was nevertheless sincere, for he was a member of the committee in the New York legislature which reported the act of 1787 creating the University of New York. He drafted the report and gave the form to the educational system of the state which still endures. The first act of the regents in exercise of their power to create institutions of learning was to create the Hamilton Oneida Academy, which is now Hamilton College. Thus Hamilton's service to educational administration in his state was considerable. A curious evidence of his interest in public education appears in the plan for political organization which he submitted to James A. Bayard. Intended to effect the regeneration of the Federalist party, the plan included a proposal that the party promote the establishment of "academies, each with one professor, for instructing the different classes of mechanics in the principles of mechanics and the elements of chemistry."[84]

[81] To James McHenry, September 17, 1799, *ibid.*, VII, 136–37.

[82] *Ibid.*, VIII, 217.   [83] *Ibid.*

[84] To James A. Bayard, April, 1802, *ibid.*, X, 436.

FOREIGN POLICY AND NATIONAL DEFENSE

. . . . a policy regulated by their own interest, as far as justice and good faith permit, is, and ought to be, their prevailing one.—"PACIFICUS," No. IV.[85]

The measures taken by a nation in its self-defense will always be determined by its orientation with respect to its own people and the world at large. Hamilton envisaged the statesman as one who, understanding his people and the world of men, used the conditions at his disposal to place his nation in the strongest possible position consonant with freedom at home and good faith abroad. Hamilton's world after 1789 was in the throes of the first of the great revolutionary convulsions that were to rend modern civilization. The effort of France to establish a republic after 1789 had miscarried, and, following an agonizing succession of revolutionary dictatorships, a military despot had placed himself at the head of the state and embarked upon the conquest of Europe.

The issues of the Revolution were far from clear, and neither its friends nor its enemies fully understood its significance. But Hamilton was concerned with the position of the United States rather than with the merit of the contending forces.[86] Participation in war without national ruin required that America have a strong, well-ordered military establishment, a navy, an adequate financial system, and a general adherence to the national government. None of these conditions existed in 1793 when President Washington, with Hamilton's vigorous support, inaugurated an American policy of neutrality.

Hamilton's foreign policy was, indeed, only a facet of his national program, and, although foreign affairs bulk large in his writings, their emphasis is always the same. The Union, he held, must abstain from foreign adventures until its strength gave promise of success. Hamilton and Jefferson both sought to take full advantage of the relatively isolated position of America in their world, but Hamilton relied less on geographic strategy than did his opponent. Both favored the expansion of the United States in continental America and desired particularly the acquisition of Florida and Louisiana. But Hamilton, unlike Jefferson, urged a strong military establishment to reinforce national policy in foreign affairs. Until such an establishment could be created, Hamilton insisted that friendship with Great Britain must be the cornerstone of American foreign policy. For Britain was the one power capable, through her naval might, of attacking

[85] July 10, 1793, *ibid.*, IV, 465.

[86] For a little-known aspect of Hamilton's foreign policy see Samuel Flagg Bemis, "Alexander Hamilton and the Limitation of Armaments," *Pacific Review*, II (March, 1922), 587–602, reviewed in *Review of Reviews*, LXV (June, 1922), 655–56.

America, and the power whose interests were most compatible with those of America.

Contending that the rapid vicissitudes of Europe rendered impractical an American policy which depended upon its fluctuations, he held it obvious to place the national safety beyond the reach of the casualties attendant upon European wars. "The way to effect this," he asserted, "is to pursue a steady system, to organize all our *resources*, and put them in a state of preparation for prompt action."[87] Thus Hamilton again emphasized his conviction that the public welfare and security depended upon a comprehensive plan for national development.

Regarding the overthrow of Europe at large as a matter not entirely chimerical, it will be our prudence to cultivate a spirit of self-dependence and to endeavor by unanimity, vigilance, and exertion, under the blessing of Providence, to hold the scales of our destiny in our own hands. Standing as it were in the midst of falling empires, it should be our aim to assume a station and attitude which will preserve us from being overwhelmed in their ruins.

It has been very properly the policy of our government to cultivate peace. But, in contemplating the possibility of our being driven to unqualified war, it will be wise to anticipate, that frequently the most effectual way to defend is to attack. There may be imagined instances of very great moment to the permanent interests of this country, which would certainly require a disciplined force. To raise and prepare such a force will always be a work of considerable time, and it ought to be ready for the conjuncture whenever it shall arrive. Not to be ready then, may be to lose an opportunity which it may be difficult afterwards to retrieve.[88]

As Washington's secretary, Hamilton was well situated during the Revolutionary War to study problems of military organization, a branch of administration in which he retained a compelling interest. In 1783 he was a member of the congressional committee which prepared "A Plan for a Military Peace Establishment." The report of the committee evidences Hamilton's influence and illustrates his comprehension of national defense in its relation to the consolidation of the Union.[89] Describing defense as a major objective of the Union, the report advocated a unified plan for national security administered by the national government rather than by the states: "The fortifications to be established for the security of the States ought to be constructed with relation to each other on some general and well-digested plan; and the provisions for their defence should be made on the same principles."[90] A unified plan, the committee observed,

[87] Washington to McHenry, Secretary of War, December 13, 1798, draft by Hamilton, *Works*, ed. Lodge, VII, 11.

[88] *Ibid.*, pp. 11–12.

[89] See Hamilton's letter to Governor Clinton, October 3, 1783, *ibid.*, IX, 388–94.

[90] *Ibid.*, VI, 465–66.

was more effective, economical, and equitable than a series of separate state plans.

Hamilton carried his interest in military organization into the Washington administration, where his influence was apparent in the War Department as well as in the Treasury. During the Adams administration, Hamilton contrived to be appointed Inspector-General in the new army which was being formed in expectation of war with France. In this capacity some of his most effective organizing work was done, although the majority of his plans failed of their purpose because of maladministration by Secretary of War McHenry and because Congress and the President did not really intend to fight. Recognizing that the cost and inconvenience of military service were unpopular in America, Hamilton believed that public antipathy might be partially overcome through efficient organization of the armed forces. "In proportion as the policy of the country is adverse to extensive military establishments," so, he declared, "ought to be our care to render the principles of our military system as perfect as possible, and our endeavors to turn to the best account such force as we may at any time have on foot, and to provide an eligible standard for the augmentations to which particular emergencies may compel a resort."[91]

To this end Hamilton drew up a bill for a "medical establishment" and devised plans for the classification and organization of the militia, for military supplies, for the improvement of army discipline, for the maintenance and strengthening of the frontier posts, and for the fortification of New York. He favored a system of selective military service "for classing all persons from eighteen to forty-five inclusively, and for draughting out of them *in case of invasion*, by lot, the number necessary to complete the entire army of fifty thousand."[92] He believed the establishment of agencies for advanced military instruction to be essential and favored the creation of a national military academy.[93] In December, 1798, Hamilton urged upon McHenry, the Secretary of War, the necessity of good organization and management in the armed services, explaining that "an army is in many respects a machine; of which the displacement of any of the organs, if permitted to continue, injures its symmetry and energy, and leads to dis-

[91] Washington to McHenry, December 13, 1798, draft by Hamilton, *ibid.*, VII, 22.

[92] To Gunn, December 22, 1798, *ibid.*, p. 47.

[93] An account of the activities of Hamilton, Washington, Knox, and others in the establishment of the United States Military Academy may be found in Edward S. Holden, "Origins of the United States Military Academy, 1777–1802," *The Centennial of the United States Military Academy at West Point, New York, 1802–1902* (Washington: Government Printing Office, 1904), pp. 201–22.

order and weakness."[94] That he failed to convince was apparent when in August of the following year he wrote to McHenry deploring the want of organization in the services of supply and the immersion of the Secretary of War and the chiefs of the several divisions in a welter of detail to the neglect of the larger aspects of military planning.[95]

Hamilton's interest in a national military academy has been previously remarked. "The Plan for a Military Peace Establishment" observed that the technology required in the formation of officers of artillery and engineers called for institutions of scientific instruction. Although the report recommended the attachment of professors to the corps of engineers rather than the establishment of a military academy, it nevertheless indicated an academy as an object for future consideration. Hamilton's proposals concerning a military academy are interesting because they show the system by which he proposed to secure to America the benefits of military preparedness without the disadvantages of large standing armed forces. Although the method proposed has never been exploited to the fullest extent, it has in fact worked very nearly as he suggested:

Since it is agreed that we are not to keep on foot numerous forces instructed and disciplined, military science in its various branches ought to be cultivated with peculiar care, in proper nurseries, so that there may always exist a sufficient body of it ready to be imparted and diffused, and a *competent* number of persons qualified to act as instructors to the additional troops which events may successively require to be raised.

This will be to substitute the elements of an army to the thing itself, and it will greatly tend to enable the government to dispense with a large body of standing forces, from the facility which it will give of forming officers and soldiers promptly upon emergencies.

No sound mind can doubt the essentiality of military science in time of war, any more than the moral certainty that the most pacific policy on the part of a government will not preserve it from being engaged in war more or less frequently.

To avoid great evils, it must either have a respectable force prepared for service, or the means of preparing such a force with expedition. The latter, most agreeable to the genius of our government and nation, is the object of a military academy.[96]

Although a vast number of detailed reports and recommendations on military organization and procedure issued from Hamilton's pen during the years 1798–99, he did not fail to distinguish "the energy of the imagination dealing in general propositions from that of *execution* in *detail*."[97]

[94] *Works*, ed. Lodge, VII, 27.

[95] *Ibid.*, pp. 108–9.

[96] To McHenry, November 23, 1799, *ibid.*, pp. 180–81.

[97] To Rufus King, October 2, 1798, *ibid.*, X, 321.

In both respects he believed the administration of John Adams to be remiss, but the want of administrators with a generalizing grasp of policy was the more serious lack. "It is a pity, my dear sir, and a reproach," he declared to the Secretary of War, McHenry, "that our administration have no general plan. Certainly there ought to be one formed without delay."[98]

Although a disposition for comprehensive national planning certainly did not exist in the administration of John Adams, Hamilton's proposals nevertheless remain as a landmark in American administrative thought. Taken as a whole, these plans and recommendations developed during Hamilton's career as Inspector-General constitute his last serious attempt to institute a comprehensive unitary policy in the federal administration in contrast to the fragmentary system of policy formulation which was actually developing. It remained for his great rival Jefferson to make the final effort to effect a unitary administrative policy in the federal government. The failure of Jefferson's embargo system represented the end of unitary public policy in the early history of the Republic.

It is this conception of public administration as responsible for the formulation of a unifying national program that constitutes one of Hamilton's major contributions to political thought. The idea was indeed not born with Hamilton, but it was he who gave it original and effective expression in American political life. Obviously, the theory of a general public policy was better adapted to the monarchial and ministerial governments of Europe than to a federal republic wherein policy determination was divided among the several states and between the legislative and executive branches of the state and national governments. The American party system was hardly a satisfactory medium through which to effect unitary policy, for parties, in their effort to win the support of the diverse interests of society, customarily assembled their platforms to answer the special demands of separate groups, and no coherent program could therefore be expected. With the doubtful exception of the administrations of Jefferson and Jackson, the national administrations during the century following 1800 found the greatest force for unity in policy—the presidential executive power—limited or threatened by the presence of powerful political leaders in the presidential cabinet or in the Congress. The practice of placing the higher party leaders in the major administrative posts precluded unity in policy, for the jockeying of cabinet principals for the presidential succession bred a jealousy of reputation which resulted in fragmentary rather than unitary administration.

[98] June 27, 1799, *ibid.*, VII, 97.

The relative isolation of the executive from the legislative branch of the national government, the tradition of congressional government inherited from the confederation era, and the influence of party politics in the presidential cabinet all contrived to produce national policy which usually was a composite of divergent objectives. Hamilton fully realized that public policy must represent all major social interests, but he conceived the role of statesmanship to be the weaving of the conflicting elements into a rational program of ultimate benefit to all.

The failure of Hamilton's theories of national planning and unitary policy to win acceptance must in part therefore be ascribed to the obstacles presented by the constitutional structure and tradition of the Republic. But it can hardly be doubted that the individualism of the American people, their increasing adherence to laissez faire political economy, and the relative security and abundance which the nation enjoyed deprived Hamilton's system of the popular support necessary to its successful application in American politics. Nevertheless, Hamilton's administrative program set a precedent for coherence in public policy, an example of comprehensive public planning to which administrators might repair in future days for guidance. It was a major contribution to the thought on public administration in America.

CHAPTER VI

ADMINISTRATIVE POLICY AND THE PUBLIC SERVICE

THE preceding chapter having developed the planning and financial aspects of public policy as conceived by Alexander Hamilton, it remains to outline the general character of his thought on the administration of government personnel. In this area of public administration Hamilton left no systematic treatise comparable to his state papers on finance and manufactures. His Treasury circulars,[1] correspondence, and portions of his reports to the House of Representatives afford much of the evidence upon which a reconstruction of his theories must be based. It is possible that, as new sources of information about Hamilton's

[1] A collection of Hamilton's "Revenue Circulars," September 22, 1789, t9 March 29, 1793, is printed in The Works of Alexander Hamilton Comprising His Political and Official Writings . . . . , ed. J. C. Hamilton (7 vols.; New York: Charles S. Francis & Co., 1850–51), III, 537–74. Manuscript collections of circulars and correspondence with revenue collectors are "Treasury Circulars, 1789–96," Library of Congress, and "Collectors Small Ports, 1789–1802," National Archives.

Treasury career are uncovered, the picture of Hamilton as an administrator may be accented and enriched. But sufficient material now exists to indicate the main currents of Hamilton's personnel policies and to show that in general they followed the course of energetic, unifying, nationalizing action which characterized the other aspects of his program for the federal government.

APPOINTMENT

It is not easy to conceive a plan better calculated than this to promote a judicious choice of men for filling the offices of the Union; and it will not need proof that on this point must essentially depend the character of its administration.—"THE FEDERALIST," No. 76.[2]

It has been observed that Hamilton defended the constitutional method of appointment to federal office: nomination vested in the President with the power of confirmation lodged in the Senate. While admitting that the "sole and undivided responsibility of one man will naturally beget a livelier sense of duty and a more exact regard to reputation,"[3] he believed that the concurrence of the Senate in appointment "would be an excellent check upon a spirit of favoritism in the President, and would tend greatly to prevent the appointment of unfit characters from State prejudice, from family connection, from personal attachment, or from a view to popularity."[4] Thus the reflection of the federal personnel upon the character of the administration seemed to Hamilton more important than considerations of executive responsibility in the appointive process.

In determining the fitness of a candidate for public office, ability alone did not constitute an adequate measure, for character and political considerations were important in men upon whom the success of an administration so largely depended. Reliability and firmness were qualities especially to be desired where responsibility and discretion were involved. Writing to James Bayard on August 6, 1800, concerning the appointment of a president for Columbia College, he observed that "it is essential that he be a gentleman in his manners, as well as a sound and polite scholar; that his moral character be irreproachable; that he possess energy of body and mind, and be of a disposition to maintain discipline without *undue austerity;* and, in the last place, that his politics be of the right sort."[5]

Hamilton appears to have distinguished between the policy-determining and the merely executory posts of the civil service in the appointive

---

[2] Edward Mead Earle (ed.), *The Federalist* (Washington: National Home Library Foundation, 1937), p. 491.

[3] *Ibid.*, p. 492.

[4] *Ibid.*, p. 494.   [5] *Works*, ed. Lodge, X, 385.

function. In the subordinate positions political reliability was of less consequence than in the higher offices of government. In Hamilton's requests to the federal revenue collectors for the names of suitable appointees to minor Treasury posts, technical skill appears to be the determining factor in appointments. However, in requesting opinions on two candidates for district attorney of Rhode Island, Hamilton asked the collector at Providence "to state not only the qualifications of each, *but the collateral circumstances affecting the public service.*"[6] It is probable that Hamilton could assume that the collectors would not suggest persons whose loyalty to the administration was questionable, but the absence of partisan reference in the greater part of his correspondence may indicate that merit rather than patronage governed his choice of subordinates.

Although Hamilton distinguished between the requisites for civil and military appointment, the principles which he applied to the latter throw some light on the obscure areas of the former. He objected to an overly partisan policy in appointment and promotion in the armed services. Writing to McHenry on February 6, 1799, he declared his regret that "the objection against anti-federalism has been carried so far as to exclude several of the characters proposed by us."[7] Although he recognized the importance of appointing friends of the government to military stations, he argued that in certain instances particular merit justified relaxation of partisan considerations and warned against giving appointments too absolute a party feature.

Among those who opposed the ratification of the Constitution of 1787, many feared the creation of a vast federal bureaucracy whose influence would overshadow that of the state officialdoms. To quiet this fear, Hamilton observed that the state establishments of civil and military officers "infinitely surpassing any corresponding establishments in the General Government, will create such an extent and complication of attachments as will ever secure the predilection and support of the people."[8] Hence Hamilton's belief that the strength of an administrative system corre-

[6] To Jeremiah Olney, November 26, 1793, *ibid.*, p. 59. Also letter to General O. H. Williams, June 21, 1792, *ibid.*, p. 48.

[7] *Ibid.*, VII, 63. Washington's theory of appointment was in general nonpartisan; "suitable qualifications, personal merit, and former services" were his criteria for determining fitness for office, but also he opposed appointing anyone whose "political tenets are adverse to the measures which the general government are pursuing" (Worthington C. Ford [ed.], *Washington's Works* [14 vols.; New York: G. P. Putnam's Sons, 1889–93], XII, 107). See discussion in Gaillard Hunt, "Office Seeking during Washington's Administrations," *American Historical Review*, I (January, 1896), 270 ff.

[8] "Speech on the Senate of the United States, June 24, 1788," *Works*, ed. Lodge, II, 46.

sponds in some degree to the number of its functionaries appears to have influenced his recommendations on the appointment of federal officials. He was convinced that the federal government never could withstand state opposition until it created a numerous and independent corps of public servants. "Far the greatest number of offices and employments are in the gift of the States separately," he observed. "The weight of official influence will therefore be in favor of the State governments; and, with all these advantages, they cannot fail to carry the people along with them in every contest with the General Government."[9]

In the appointment of federal officials Hamilton recognized that the interests of the states could not be ignored, but he favored holding their influence to a minimum. Neither in the military nor in the civil services did Hamilton believe that a strict adherence to the practice of equalizing appointments on the basis of states could be observed without detriment to the services. The concentration of population in certain areas of the Union made apportionment by relative population a better formula for recruitment than the arbitrary division of an equal office to each state; but even the relative population of states should not, he believed, constitute a formula so rigid as to prevent the appointment of able men to office wherever they might be found.

It was to be expected that Hamilton would oppose a dependence upon state officers for the enforcement of federal measures. As early as 1783 he asserted the need for an independent federal civil service. He declared it expedient to introduce the influence of officers deriving their emoluments from, and, therefore, interested in supporting the power of, Congress; and in *The Continentalist*, No. VI, he explained that "the reason of allowing Congress to appoint its own officers of the customs, collectors of the taxes, and military officers of every rank, is to create in the interior of each State a mass of influence in favor of the Federal Government."[10] The expansion of the federal civil service which Hamilton's proposed system of comprehensive administration required might have greatly increased the influence of the central government, but the Washington administration as actually constituted provided no occasion for the elaborate regime which Hamilton envisaged. However, in the appointment of revenue collectors he attempted to heighten the prestige of the service by increasing the quality and compensation of personnel, thus partially overcoming the deficiency of numbers. It is, nevertheless, clear that he believed that the multiplication of federal offices would increase the strength and reputation of the na-

[9] "Speech on the Revenue System" (1787), *ibid.*, p. 208.
[10] *Ibid.*, I, 286.

tional administration, and to this end he favored the enlargement of the federal civil service.

Jefferson's charge that the Federalist administrations were responsible for an "undue multiplication of offices and officers," Hamilton described as "substantially a misrepresentation."[11] He declared that "it would be nothing less than a miracle if, in a small number of instances, it had not happened that particular offices and officers might have been dispensed with. For, in the early essays of a new government in making the various establishments relative to the affairs of a nation, some mistakes in this respect will arise, notwithstanding the greatest caution."[12]

In answer to Jefferson's declaration that the inspectors of internal revenue were unnecessary and served to obstruct the accountability of the institution, Hamilton explained that, when the excise on distilled spirits was established, great opposition was expected and experienced in certain states. In such states it was useful "to have the exertions of some men of weight and character . . . . to reconcile the discontented; to arrange the details of business, and to give energy to the measures for collection."[13] Observing that the active and vigilant superintendence of the inspectors was necessary until the excise had been established in full and uninterrupted operation, Hamilton questioned the soundness of Jefferson's assertion that their services were no longer necessary. "Nothing is more easy than to reduce the number of agents employed in any business, and yet for the business to go on with a reduced number," he observed, "but before the reduction is applauded, it ought to be ascertained that the business is as well done as it was before."[14]

Hamilton's views on the appointive process indicate his interest in the strength and reputation of the federal administration. Effective organization, adequate numbers, employees technically and politically qualified, and a minimization of state influence appear to have been the major considerations in his theory of appointment. His Treasury administration preceded the crystallization of party feeling in the United States, and Hamilton does not appear to have been excessively concerned with partisan politics in appointments. Indeed, his opportunities for appointment do not appear to have been unusually great, although the entire civil list of the federal government had to be filled during his Treasury career.[15]

[11] "Lucius Crassus," No. IX, January 18, 1802, *ibid.*, VIII, 296.   [12] *Ibid.*

[13] "Lucius Crassus," No. X, January 25, 1802, *ibid.*, pp. 301–2.

[14] *Ibid.*, pp. 302–3.

[15] According to Gaillard Hunt (*loc. cit.*), Washington made most of the appointments: 351 civil officers, not including judges of the Supreme Court, heads of departments, or miscellaneous

COMPENSATION AND PROMOTION

The nature of our popular institutions requires a numerous magistracy, for whom competent provision must be made, or we may be certain our affairs will always be committed to improper hands.—"THE CONTINENTALIST," No. VI.[16]

Hamilton's ideas concerning the rewards of the public service were entirely in keeping with his general conception of public administration. Able men were needed to fulfil the tasks that he expected administration to undertake, and accordingly the rewards of public life should be calculated to draw such men to the service of government. Hamilton was not oblivious to rewards other than pecuniary; the prestige of office, honors, citations, and promotions were all useful incentives to a public career. But adequate financial return was the indispensable compensation, although one which the American people seemed least willing to accord their public servants.

The collateral rewards in prestige and privilege which characterized the bureaucracies of the Old World were scanty, indeed, in republican America and promised to disappear once the "Jacobinical" Republicans came into power. As party fervor arose after 1793, the growing abuse of public officers in the partisan press and in Congress prompted a change of attitude on the part of considerable numbers of Americans toward public life. Federalist leaders of the old Colonial aristocracy held well-defined ideas about the dignity of office and the respect due high officers of state. They had little inclination to brave the slanderous abuse of a press which promised to set the all-time low-water mark for invective.

Thus, if good men were to hold public office, the one reward which they might count on was the earning of a living. But the disinclination of Americans to pay taxes, together with a Colonial legacy of suspicion toward holders of public office, resulted in the provision of meager compensation for most public services; and, wherever possible, private persons were employed to undertake part-time responsibilities, thus supplementing their private incomes with fees or some small salary compensation. Obviously, a responsible public service could never be erected on so weak a foundation.

---

small offices. Jefferson probably made more appointments than any of the other secretaries. Washington appears to have consulted Hamilton in the making of Treasury appointments. See Hamilton to Washington, December 2, 1790, and April 17, 1791, *Works*, ed. Lodge, IX, 474 ff. and 479 ff. See also *The Writings of George Washington, from the Original Manuscript Sources*, ed. John C. Fitzpatrick (37 vols.; Washington: Government Printing Office, 1931–40); Washington to Hamilton, September 27, 1790, *ibid.*, XXXI, 125; October 6, 1790, *ibid.*, p. 130; October 26, 1790, *ibid.*, p. 135; November 4, 1790, *ibid.*, p. 143.

[16] *Works*, ed. Lodge, I, 282.

Irresponsible, necessitous, and sometimes dishonest persons were attract-
ed to the lower civil positions, and the top executive offices were nearly impossible to fill properly. Washington's difficulties in replacing his Secretary
of State after the resignation of Jefferson are notorious, and Adams, it has
been alleged, retained Washington's cabinet throughout most of his own
administration because it had become virtually impossible to replace.

As early as 1782 Hamilton urged the adequate compensation of public
officials, admonishing that "experience will teach us that no government
costs so much as a bad one."[17] Writing to a correspondent in 1797, he deplored the unhappy state of public administration in the United States:

Public office in this country has few attractions. The pecuniary emolument is so
inconsiderable as to amount to a sacrifice to any man who can employ his time with
advantage in any liberal profession. The opportunity of doing good, from the jealousy
of power and the spirit of faction, is too small in any station to warrant a long continuation of private sacrifices. The enterprises of party had so far succeeded as materially to weaken the necessary influence and energy of the executive authority, to
take away the motives which a virtuous man might have for making sacrifices. The
prospect was even bad for gratifying in future the love of fame, if that passion was to
be the spring of action.[18]

Given these circumstances, the promises of public service were not
bright, but Hamilton worked to brighten them as much as possible. As
Secretary of the Treasury he pointed out to the Congress the wisdom of
making adequate provision for the collectors of the revenue. The security
of public funds depending upon the officers of the lowest grade, he declared it a policy "no less mistaken than common, to leave those officers
without such compensations as will admit of a proper selection of character, and prevent the temptation, from indigence, to abuse the trust."[19]
In recommending the employment of an officer for the procurement of
military supplies to be attached to the Treasury, he maintained that "the
compensation to such an officer ought . . . . to weigh nothing as an objection," for the services of an administrator prepared to give "close, constant and undivided attention" to this object and competent to make
"minute as well as extensive inquiries and investigations . . . . would produce savings to the United States with which the salary of the officer
could bear no comparison."[20]

In his administration within the Treasury Department Hamilton at-

[17] Ibid.

[18] To _____ Hamilton, May 2, 1797, ibid., X, 259.

[19] Report on Improvement of the Revenue System, January 31, 1795, ibid., III, 304.

[20] To Washington, December 2, 1794, ibid., X, 81.

tempted to correct inequalities in the compensation of the personnel, investigating the situations of those who believed themselves underpaid. Although he wished to correct any disparity between service and compensation, he held that the legislature must make provision in all cases needing adjustment and that, until such provision was lawfully made, the consequences of such disparities must be disregarded. He declared it "an important principle of public policy, that allowances to officers should not be extended by implication or inference as discretion on that head must from the nature of the thing, be liable to great abuses."[21] He persisted in his demands for adequate pay to federal employees, and after his retirement from the Treasury he embodied a strong plea for due compensation in the address he prepared for Washington to deliver to the Congress on December 7, 1796.

Without adequate rewards for public services he foresaw the affairs of the nation passing into incompetent or unfaithful hands. He held it repugnant to the principles of American government "to exclude men, from the public trusts, because their talents and virtues . . . . are unaccompanied by wealth."[22] The character and success of republican government depended, he believed, upon the capacity of the nation to command the services of its most able and virtuous citizens without regard to circumstances of class or fortune.

Hamilton had served in public office at great financial loss to himself. His urges to distinguish himself in public life, to command offices of state, and to make history were ever in conflict with the necessity of earning a living. Depending largely upon his legal practice for his livelihood, he was less favorably situated for public service than the landed gentry of Virginia or the inheritors of landed or mercantile wealth in the North. Writing to McHenry in 1798, he protested the lack of compensation for his services as Inspector-General in the new army: "It is utterly out of my power to apply my time to the public service without the compensations, scanty enough, which the law annexes to the office. If I were to receive them from the day of the appointment, I should be at least a thousand pounds the worse for my acceptance."[23]

Hamilton believed that provision for advancement within the administrative hierarchy was indispensable to effective performance and in itself constituted a type of reward for service. He did not believe, however, that opportunity for unlimited advancement was consonant with sound ad-

---

[21] "Treasury Circular," November 30, 1789.

[22] *Works*, ed. Lodge, VIII, 220–21.   [23] *Ibid.*, VII, 43.

ministrative principles, holding that the top executive offices must always be filled from the outside:

> Though a regular gradation of office is not admissible in a strict sense in regard to offices of a civil nature, and is wholly inapplicable to those of the first rank (such as the heads of the great executive departments), yet a certain regard to the relation which one situation bears to another is consonant with the natural ideas of justice, and is recommended by powerful considerations of policy. The expectation of promotion in civil as in military life is a great stimulus to virtuous exertion, while examples of unrewarded exertion, supported by talent and qualification, are proportionable discouragements. Where they do not produce resignations they leave men dissatisfied, and a dissatisfied man seldom does his duty well.
>
> In a government like ours, where pecuniary compensations are moderate, the principle of gradual advancement as a reward for good conduct is perhaps more necessary to be attended to than in others where offices are more lucrative. By due attention to it it will operate as a means to secure respectable men for offices of inferior emolument and consequence.[24]

Two observations can be made concerning Hamilton's ideas on compensation: first, he did not believe the duties of public office so simple that any person of ordinary ability could fulfil them. To secure the right man for the right place was the task of appointment, but that task could not be adequately undertaken unless due compensation could be promised for the services required of the appointee. Second, Hamilton conceived of a public service open to all able men of moderate means. This meant that compensation must be attached to public office sufficient to allow such men to serve without fear of insolvency. The importance of this latter viewpoint to a democratic administrative system is apparent, for without it the human resources for the top executive responsibilities would be limited to the few possessed of the wealth, leisure, and inclination to hold public office. Inadequacy of compensation meant plutocracy on the top and mediocrity at the bottom of the administrative structure.

TENURE

The standard of good behavior for the continuance in office . . . . is certainly one of the most valuable of the modern improvements in the practice of government.—"THE FEDERALIST," No. 78.[25]

It has been observed that duration of tenure was deemed by Hamilton to be requisite for good administration. But rotation in office was becoming a widely accepted article in American political creed, and Hamilton was strongly opposed to a general application of this principle to the public

---

[24] To Washington, April 17, 1791, *ibid.*, IX, 480–81.

[25] Earle, *op. cit.*, p. 503.

service. "I am convinced," he asserted, "that no government, founded on this feeble principle, can operate well."[26] In *The Federalist*, No. 72, Hamilton observed that an intimate connection existed between the duration of the executive magistrate in office and the stability of the system of administration. Every new president, declared Hamilton, would be induced to promote a change of men to fill the subordinate stations, and this circumstance could not fail to occasion a disgraceful and ruinous mutability in the administration of the government.

In *The Federalist*, No. 77, he sought further to protect the tenure of federal office-holders by urging that concurrence of the Senate should be required to effect their removal. "Those who can best estimate the value of a steady administration," he declared, "will be most disposed to prize a provision which connects the official existence of public men with the approbation or disapprobation of that body."[27] That this was Hamilton's final opinion on the matter seems doubtful, considering Madison's assertion that "Mr Hamilton had changed his view of the Constitution on that point."[28] Hamilton's conclusive opinion remains uncertain, but it is likely that he accepted the "decision of 1789" to the effect that the President may remove at pleasure executive officers appointed with the consent of the Senate, whose terms have not been fixed by Congress. Where, as in the case of the judiciary, the terms of office were fixed by the Constitution, neither Congress nor the President could exercise the power of removal, impeachment being the only political method of terminating tenure.

In considering Hamilton's idea of the postion of the judiciary in the structure of government, it was observed that Hamilton opposed Jefferson's attempt to remove Federalist judges by reducing the number of courts. His argument in the "Lucius Crassus" letters was that, since the office of judge was distinct from any particular court, the removal of judges could not be accomplished by an abolition of courts. Where the Constitution had created an office and fixed its tenure, he held Congress powerless to alter the constitutional conditions. Where Congress had created an office, but the Constitution had fixed its tenure, as in the case of the judges of the inferior federal courts, Congress could not defeat the tenure provisions by abolishing the office:

[26] "Speech on the Senate of the United States," June 25, 1788, *Works*, Lodge, ed. II, 57–58.

[27] Earle, *op. cit.*, p. 497.

[28] James Madison, *Letters and Other Writings of James Madison* . . . . (4 vols.; New York: R. Worthington, 1884), IV, 5. See also "Lucius Crassus," No. XVII, March 20, 1802, *Works*, ed. Lodge, VIII, 355 ff., wherein Hamilton seems to accept a freer interpretation of the removal power.

There are two modes known to the Constitution in which the tenure of office may be affected—one, the abolition of the office; the other, the removal of the officer. The first is a legislative act, and operates by removing the office from the person; the last is an executive act, and operates by removing the person from the office. Both equally cause the tenure, enjoyment, or *holding* of the office to cease.

. . . .

The constituent part of an office are its authorities, duties, and duration. These may be denominated the elements of which it is composed. Together they form its *essence* or *existence*. It is impossible to separate, even in idea, the duration from the existence. The office must cease to exist when it ceases to have duration. Hence, let it be observed that the word *tenure* is not used in the Constitution, and that in the debate it has been the substitute for duration. The words: "The judges shall hold their office during good behavior," are equivalent to these other words: "The offices of the judges shall endure or last so long as they behave well."

The conclusions from these principles are that existence is a *whole*, which includes tenure and duration as a part; that it is impossible to annul the existence of an office without destroying its tenure; and, consequently, that a prohibition to destroy the tenure is virtually and substantially a prohibition to abolish the office.[29]

As far as the judiciary was concerned, Hamilton concluded that the office of judge was distinguishable from the existence of a particular court; "that *Congress have a right to change or abolish inferior courts, but not to abolish the actual judges.*"[30] And Congress could not use the abolition of courts as a device for refusing compensation to the judges, for Hamilton contended that the emolument was annexed to the office, not to the court, and should be paid to a judge as long as he held his office. "Without doubt," Hamilton agreed, "the Constitution does contemplate service as the ground of compensation; but it likewise takes it for granted that the Legislature will be circumspect in the institution of offices; and especially that it will be careful to establish none of a permanent nature which will not be permanently useful."[31] The readiness of the officer to render service to the government was the consideration which justified his compensation, and as to the possibility "of an enormous abuse of power by creating a long list of sinecures and a numerous host of pensioners," Hamilton asserted that, should this happen, "it will constitute one of those extreme cases which, on the principle of necessity, may authorize extra-constitutional remedies."[32]

Regarding the tenure of civil officers other than judges the case was different where no constitutional provision barred an abolition of the office.

---

[29] "Lucius Crassus," No. XIII, February 27, 1802; No. XIV, March 2, 1802, *Works*, ed. Lodge, VIII, 323–24, 330–31.

[30] "Lucius Crassus," No. XVI, March 19, 1802, *ibid.*, p. 350.

[31] "Lucius Crassus," No. XVII, March 20, 1802, *ibid.*, p. 357.   [32] *Ibid.*, p. 358.

Hamilton contended that, because of the role of the chief executive in the enactment of laws, the abolition of a civil office and the consequent displacement of the officer could seldom happen against his pleasure. But the pleasure of the President "in all cases not particularly excepted" he held to be subject to the direction of the law. Whether the practical meaning of this contention supports or contradicts the "decision of 1789" is not clear and turns upon the implication of the phrase "not particularly excepted." A fair interpretation is that Hamilton believed that the President could not dismiss at pleasure and without legal justification officers whose tenure was fixed by congressional statute. Regarding the right of civil servants to retain offices without fixed tenure, he explained:

. . . . an officer during pleasure, having merely a revocable interest, the abolition of his office is no infringement of his right. In substance, he is a tenant *at the will of the government*, liable to be discontinued by the executive organ, in the form of a removal; by the legislative, in the form of an abolition of the office. These different considerations reconcile the legislative authority to abolish, with the prerogative of the Chief Magistrate to remove, and with the temporary right of individuals to hold.[33]

Hamilton's position that the tenure of executive officers might be terminated by the legislative as well as by the executive branch followed from his contention that executive "office is holden not of the President, but of the *Nation*."[34] He observed that "the Constitution has everywhere used the language, 'Officers of the United States,' as if to denote the relation between the officer and the sovereignty; as if to exclude the dangerous pretension that he is the mere creature of the Executive; accordingly, he is to take an oath to support the 'Constitution'; that is, an oath of fidelity to the government; but no oath of any kind to the *President*."[35] Hamilton pointed out that the situation of the British public officer was entirely different, as his allegiance was due the prince wherein the sovereignty of the nation was deemed to reside. But under the American Constitution the President was not sovereign; for sovereignty was vested in the government collectively—and "it is of the sovereignty, strictly and technically speaking, that a public officer holds his office."[36]

Hamilton clearly favored lengthy tenure of public office, consonant always with good performance and responsibility. He opposed the principle of rotation in office except where in quasi-public agencies, such as the United States Bank, private opportunities and public responsibility were too closely interwoven to make the permanent tenure of directorships by the same individuals acceptable to the public or desirable to the govern-

33 *Ibid.*, pp. 358–59.

34 *Ibid.*, p. 355.

35 *Ibid.*, pp. 355–56.

36 *Ibid.*, p. 356.

ment; but where responsibility to the public was clear and complete Hamilton considered long tenure as absolutely desirable. He opposed the doctrine of the spoils system and lent strength to the conception of the public service as a legitimate lifetime career.

Apparently, Hamilton gave insufficient attention to the termination of tenure in the Treasury Department, for during his administration Tench Coxe, commissioner of revenue, was giving secret aid to William Duane, editor of the bitterly anti-Hamiltonian *Aurora*, and informing Jefferson concerning the operation of Treasury affairs.[37] The dismissal of Coxe for "deliberate misconduct in office" was effected by Oliver Wolcott during the Adams administration. Coxe attributed his dismissal to Hamilton's hatred of Jefferson, but the dismissal was long overdue. Why Hamilton had himself neglected to remove Coxe was not explained. Seeing the Federalist star in descent and anxious to ingratiate himself with Jefferson in hope of securing a new civil appointment, Coxe evidently sought to take advantage of Jefferson's enmity toward Hamilton.[38] Under the Adams administration the cabinet officers enjoyed greater freedom in the selection of their personnel than the Washington cabinet had enjoyed. Nevertheless, Hamilton's failure to purge his own department of disloyalty remains difficult to explain, particularly in view of Washington's dislike of the opposition which Coxe supported.

CO-ORDINATION AND CONTROL

It is my earnest wish to cultivate an harmonious and cordial cooperation, and it is essential to this that correct opinions should be mutually entertained.—TREASURY CIRCULAR, JULY 20, 1792.[39]

Although Hamilton's great contribution to public administration derived from that capacity which he described as "the energy of the imagination dealing in general propositions," he was by no means deficient in that other aspect of the administrative art which involved *"execution in detail."* Early in his Treasury administration he requested the collectors of customs duties and the naval officers of the several ports to carefully note and from time to time communicate whatever might serve to discover the merits or defects of the revenue system and to point out the means of im-

[37] Gaillard Hunt, "Office Seeking during the Administration of John Adams," *American Historical Review*, II (January, 1897), 241 ff.

[38] *Ibid.* The political intrigues of Tench Coxe will perhaps remain obscure until the Coxe papers (some 60,000 pieces) are made accessible to study. When Harold Hutcheson wrote *Tench Coxe: A Study in American Economic Development* (Baltimore: Johns Hopkins University Press, 1938), the papers were still denied to scholars.

[39] "Treasury Circulars, 1789–96."

proving it. To this same end Hamilton requested information concerning complaints which though not infallible indications of defect might yet merit attention. His directions to the collectors of revenue were precise, systematic, and often accompanied by sample forms illustrating the manner in which reports to the Treasury were to be made. Regular quarterly returns were required of the collectors, and, although Hamilton appears to have experienced some difficulty in securing prompt conformity with this rule, he pressed the laggards with circulars requesting compliance.

Hamilton's use of standard forms to systematize the reporting function indicates his aptness for *"execution* in *detail."* He required separate reports on separate phases of revenue administration for the convenience of filing separately. He requested the submission to the Treasury of samples of all forms used in the offices of the collectors and not prescribed by the department, of any papers previously used by the state customs houses that might be available, and of any foreign samples which might be obtained. It was Hamilton's purpose, "with the Aid of these precedents, to digest a general and Uniform plan of Custom House Documents, which will conduce to Order, facilitate business and give Satisfaction."[40]

In his administration of Treasury expenditures Hamilton was not wanting in regard to economy. Concerning the supplies and repairs for the revenue cutters, he directed the collectors of the ports to whom the business was committed to observe "the strictest oeconomy in the disbursements which may be found consistent with the safety and comfort of the Officers and men; and the effectual execution of the public service."[41] He recommended that supplies be purchased on the lowest terms for cash, explaining that "the discounts on most goods purchased for ready money are considerable, and I wish the public to enjoy the benefit of that kind of dealing."[42] Writing to Benjamin Lincoln, collector of the Port of Boston, concerning the purchase of a coastal patrol boat, he observed that "the necessary regard to oeconomy and to the whole sum appropriated to this object, requires that you render the cost as moderate as possible."[43] The advantage of large-scale, centralized purchasing was appreciated by Hamilton, and he attempted to reduce the cost of sailcloth for the revenue cutters by purchasing for the several ports collectively.

In the enforcement of revenue measures Hamilton's administration evi-

[40] *Ibid.*, September 30, 1790.

[41] *Ibid.*, June 1, 1791.   [42] *Ibid.*

[43] To Benjamin Lincoln, October 1, 1790, "Collectors, Small Ports." See also letter to Benjamin Lincoln, November 22, 1790, *ibid.*

denced an energy in detailed execution which combined rigor with sound judgment. Several months after assuming his Treasury post, Hamilton directed the collectors to bring suit promptly on defaulted bonds taken as guaranty for the payment of customs duties. If the bonds were not paid as they fell due, the collectors were advised to put them in suit immediately and report the action to the Treasury. Hamilton admitted that this procedure might seem severe but explained that he considered the strict observance of federal legislation on the customs payments "as *essential* not only to the order of the finances, but even to the propriety of the indulgence, which the law allows—of procrastinated terms of payment of the duties."[44] This strictness he regarded "as eventually most convenient to Individuals as well as necessary to the public."[45] Although he urged that the convenience of the merchants be considered by the customs officers and a spirit of co-operation maintained in dealings with them, he nowhere indicated that favors might be shown or that laxity in regulation would be tolerated, and toward smugglers and the receivers of smuggled goods he urged vigorous prosecution. Although prompt to defend public measures against violation, Hamilton was equally prepared to rectify error on the part of the government toward private persons. Minor inequities were not wanting in attention, for on one occasion the collector at Annapolis was directed to refund a sum of $2.40 collected contrary to instructions and without authorization.[46]

In a new government unaccustomed to detailed administrative supervision the tasks of co-ordination and control were unusually difficult. Prompted by several instances of noncompliance with Treasury policy on the part of subordinates, Hamilton felt it necessary "to state the ideas which are entertained at the Treasury respecting the power of the head of the department 'to superintend the collection of the Revenue' and the obligations incident to it on the part of the officers immediately charged with that collection."[47] He sometimes found it necessary to countermand actions taken by his officers. When the collector at New Bern, North Carolina, proceeded to erect a stores building and scale house without proper authorization, Hamilton ordered construction stopped, declaring it improper to permit public money to be applied to objects "for the utility and costs of which I am in some degree responsible, without my being previously and sufficiently informed."[48]

[44] "Treasury Circular," December 18, 1789.   [45] *Ibid.*
[46] To John Davidson, June 18, 1791, "Collectors, Small Ports."
[47] "Treasury Circular," July 20, 1792.
[48] To John Daves, December 13, 1790, "Collectors, Small Ports."

Revenue officers were sometimes requested to perform duties which, although not required by law, were nevertheless of importance to the government and of public benefit. Treasury officers supplied some of the material used by Hamilton in his *Report on Manufactures*, and in 1789 customs collectors were requested to ascertain and report on "the mode of Navigating of the Several States; and of Foreign nations."[49] The use of diplomatic agents to supply information needed by the Treasury was proposed by Hamilton to Jefferson in 1791, but the developing antagonism between the two administrators appears to have frustrated this attempt at interdepartmental co-ordination.

Co-operation among departments was a natural concomitant of Hamilton's notion of unified administration, but his success in realizing a co-operative relationship was confined to the departments of Treasury and War, for, although he attempted initial co-operation with Jefferson's Department of State, the two antagonists found co-operative effort difficult. The procurement of supplies for the armed forces was the major instance of a co-ordinated undertaking between the War Department and the Treasury, and here Hamilton anticipated the contemporary practice of centralized purchasing by advocating a procurement officer to be provided in the Treasury Department. With the growth of the country the business of securing military supplies could not, be believed, "be conducted in detail by the head of the department, or by any existing officer of it, now charged with other duties, and without being less well executed than it ought to be, or interfering with other essential duties, or without a portion of both these inconveniences, to the material detriment of the public service."[50]

This interdepartmental co-operation did not survive Hamilton's departure from the cabinet, however, for when preparations for war were again under way in 1799, Hamilton, serving as Inspector-General in the Army, wrote to Washington on November 18, deploring the inefficiency of the departments and the lack of co-operation between them.[51] As for the War Department, Hamilton lectured McHenry on its organization and the responsibility for procurement of supplies, which had been returned to it. In effect Hamilton's criticism was that the Adams administration had failed to provide for a proper ordering of authority and responsibility. He admonished the incompetent McHenry that, "in my opinion, the want of a proper organization of agents in the various branches of the public service, and of a correct and systematic delineation of their relative duties,

[49] "Treasury Circular," October 15, 1789.

[50] To Washington, December 2, 1794, *Works*, ed. Lodge, X, 80.   [51] *Ibid.*, VII, 175.

has been a material cause of the imperfect results which have been experienced; that it continues to embarrass every operation, and that while it lasts it cannot fail to enfeeble and disorder every part of the service."[52]

Hamilton believed that administrative incompetence was frequently due to the failure of the administrator properly to delegate the detailed aspects of his duties. He warned McHenry on July 30, 1798, of the danger of failure to delegate:

I observe you plunged in a vast mass of details. I know from experience, that it is impossible for any man, whatever be his talents or diligence, to wade through such a mass, without neglecting the most material things, and attaching to his operations a feebleness and sloth of execution. It is essential to the success of the minister of a great department, that he subdivide the objects of his care, distribute them among competent assistants, and content himself with a general but vigilant superintendence. This course is particularly necessary when an unforeseen emergency has suddenly accumulated a number of new objects to be provided for and executed.[53]

It would therefore appear that Hamilton was familiar with the general requirements of good management as they are understood today. What personal success he enjoyed as a manager it is difficult to say. There is some reason to believe that his genius lay in the theory rather than in the practice of management, for it has already been observed that the art of control over others was the least of Hamilton's political talents. But a distinction obtains between political control and administrative proficiency. Hamilton appears to have been thoroughly competent in the administrative management of the Treasury Department, and such mistakes as may be charged to him seem the result of the multiplicity of his concerns rather than errors in administrative theory. He set a high standard of thinking concerning problems of administrative co-ordination, co-operation, and control, and his ideas had a validity that survived their failure to secure adoption. Critical thought on administration has always been rare, even among students of administration. Critical discussion on the level of Hamilton's reasoning represents a constant desideratum in public administration.

ADMINISTRATIVE RESPONSIBILITY

. . . . *every magistrate ought to be personally responsible for his behavior in office.*— "THE FEDERALIST," NO. 70.[54]

Although the general theories of Alexander Hamilton concerning responsibility as a principle of administration have been discussed in chap-

---

[52] September 16, 1799, *ibid.*, p. 126.

[53] *Ibid.*, VI, 484.   [54] Earle, *op. cit.*, p. 461.

ter iii, it remains to define more closely his conception of the particular responsibility of public administrators. Hamilton's interest in this respect was largely confined to the higher posts of the federal government, and his observations resulted largely from political controversies wherein issues of administrative responsibility were involved. Out of the contentions of the Washington and Adams administrations the problem of responsibility appeared in three distinguishable forms: the mutual responsibilities of the members of the administrative family; the responsibility of the administrators to the legislative branch; and the responsibility of the administrators to the public at large.

A corollary of Hamilton's belief that public policy should be unified and consistent was that fundamental differences of opinion should not operate within the administrative arm of government. Although he recognized that "difference of opinion between men engaged in any common pursuit, is a natural appendage of human nature," he held that such differences were permissible when exerted *"in the discharge of a duty*, with delicacy and temper, among liberal and sensible men,"[55] but intolerable when displayed "in a quarter where there is no responsibility, to the obstruction and embarrassment of one who is charged with immediate and direct responsibility."[56] Applied to the members of the executive administration of any government, he held that such opposition of views fostered factions in the community, distracted councils in the administration, and generally weakened government. A working unanimity among the members of an administrative family was therefore a requisite of responsible administration.

Hamilton's observations on the mutual responsibilities of administrators were largely the product of his controversy with Jefferson over the policies of the Washington administration. Writing in the *Gazette of the United States* under the pseudonym "Metellus," Hamilton asserted that, although a member of the executive department should not be held "to throw the weight of his character into the scale, to support a measure which in his conscience *he disapproved, and in his station had opposed*,"[57] it was a very different matter to volunteer opposition to a measure wherein no discharge of duty was involved:

The true line of propriety appears to me to be the following: A member of the administration, in one department, ought only to *aid* those measures of another which he approves—where he disapproves, if called upon to *act officially*, he ought to manifest his disapprobation, and avow his opposition, but out of an official line he ought not to

55 "Metellus," October 24, 1792, *Works*, ed. Lodge, VII, 285.

56 *Ibid.*, pp. 285–86.   57 *Ibid.*, p. 284.

interfere *as long as he thinks fit to continue a part of the administration.* When the measure in question has become a law of the land, especially with a direct sanction of the chief magistrate, it is peculiarly his duty to acquiesce. A contrary conduct is inconsistent with his relations as an officer of the government, and with a due respect as such for the decisions of the Legislature, and of the head of the executive department. The line here delineated, is drawn from obvious and very important considerations. The success of every government—its capacity to combine the exertion of public strength with the preservation of personal right and private security, qualities which define the perfection of a government, must always naturally depend on the energy of the executive department. This energy again must materially depend on the union and mutual deference which subsists between the members of that department and the conformity of their conduct with the views of the executive chief.[58]

Holding that, by opposing Treasury measures of which Washington approved, Jefferson violated his responsibility to the chief executive, Hamilton declared that, as the heads of the executive departments were auxiliaries to the President, their opposition to any measure of his, "except in the shape of frank, firm, and independent advice to himself, is evidently contrary to the relations which subsist between the parties."[59] That Hamilton was willing to co-operate with Jefferson in the interest of administrative unanimity appears from Jefferson's account of Washington's proposal that the two administrators "coalesce in the measures of the government."[60] But Hamilton's revelation in the public press of the dissensions of the cabinet had already done irreparable damage in violation of his own principles, and Jefferson's political future was served better by opposition to Hamilton than by a composition of mutual differences.

In the succeeding administration of John Adams the lack of confidence subsisting between the President and his executive officers elicited an observation by Hamilton on the responsibility of the chief executive to his cabinet:

As the President nominates his ministers, and may displace them when he pleases, it must be his own fault if he be not surrounded by men who, for ability and integrity, deserve his confidence. And if his ministers are of this character, the consulting of them will always be likely to be useful to himself and to the state. Let it even be supposed that he is a man of talents superior to the collected talents of all his ministers . . . . he may, nevertheless, often assist his judgment by a comparison and collision of ideas. The greatest genius, hurried away by the rapidity of its own conceptions, will occasionally overlook obstacles which ordinary and more phlegmatic men will discover, and which, when presented to his consideration, will be thought by himself decisive objections to his plans.

. . . .

[58] *Ibid.*, pp. 284–85. [59] *Ibid.*, p. 286.

[60] *The Anas*, February 7, 1793, *The Works of Thomas Jefferson*, ed. Paul Leicester Ford (12 vols.; Federal ed.; New York: G. P. Putnam's Sons, 1904), I, 251.

The stately system of not consulting ministers is likely to have a further disadvantage. It will tend to exclude from places of primary trust the men most fit to occupy them.

Few and feeble are the inducements to accept a place in our administration. Far from being lucrative, there is not one which will not involve pecuniary sacrifice to every *honest* man of preeminent talents. And has not experience shown, that he must be fortunate, indeed, if even the successful execution of his task can secure to him consideration and fame? Of a large harvest of obloquy he is sure.

If excluded from the counsels of the Executive Chief, his office must become truly insignificant. What able and virtuous man will long consent to be so miserable a pageant?

Every thing that tends to banish from the administration able men, tends to diminish the chances of able counsels. The probable operation of a system of this kind, must be to consign places of the highest trust to incapable honest men, whose inducement will be a livelihood, or to capable dishonest men, who will seek indirect indemnifications for the deficiency of direct and fair inducements.[61]

Hamilton therefore held the heads of the great executive departments as subordinate to the chief executive but entitled to his confidence and regard. It was their responsibility to promote the program of the administration so far as their duty and conscience indicated and to abstain from interference in matters lying beyond the jurisdiction of their offices. With this argument Jefferson might have agreed, but unfortunately the respective spheres of the executive departments was an uncertain matter. Jefferson's position that the Treasury was properly confined to the single object of revenue was not shared by Hamilton, who likewise dissented from Jefferson's notion that the Department of State embraced "nearly all the objects of administration."[62]

The responsibility of the heads of the executive departments to the Congress was an equally uncertain matter, although partially defined by the acts of Congress creating the departments. Strictly speaking, there were only two executive departments, State and War, which were clearly placed under presidential authority. The Treasury was not designated by Congress as an executive department, with the result that two quite opposing constructions of responsibility could be drawn. The provision that the Secretary of the Treasury was to "make report and give information to either branch of the Legislature, in person or in writing (as he may be required), respecting all matters referred to him by the Senate or House of

[61] "The Public Conduct and Character of John Adams, Esq. President of the United States," *Works*, ed. Lodge, VII, 338–39.

[62] Jefferson attributed this definition of departmental responsibilities to Washington, but Hamilton throughout his administrative association in Washington's administration was hardly governed by such limitation (see *The Anas*, February 29, 1792).

Representatives, or which shall pertain to his office," would seem to indicate his direct responsibility to the Congress. Whether this responsibility implied ministerial leadership or congressional control was doubtful. Hamilton assumed the former interpretation; Madison and the Republicans determined to enforce the latter.

Gallatin suggested that Hamilton wished to exercise presidential powers under cover of the ambiguous responsibility of the Treasury Department.[63] The constitutional position of the presidency was by no means clear in 1789, and with a lesser chief executive and a more politic secretary, the Treasury might have become analogous to the British Exchequer. Treasury leadership might have impaired executive unity but does not describe the inevitable, for Americans have evidenced a capacity for improvising workable arrangements out of unpromising situations. The development of a body of extra-constitutional conventions would have been necessary to insure Treasury leadership and executive unity, and the great powers of the President would have necessarily operated through the agency of the cabinet officers to a greater extent than under the presidential system.

Jefferson alleged that in practice Hamilton construed the responsibility of the Treasury to suit his convenience—that "he endeavored to place himself subject to the house when the Executive should propose what he did not like, and subject to the Executive when the house should propose anything disagreeable."[64] Both Hamilton and Jefferson were agreed that the heads of the other departments, as agents of the President, were not directly subject to the jurisdiction of the Congress, and Hamilton's opinion on this point seems to have moved from the ministerial to the presidential conception of responsibility, for, faced with a hostile faction in the House of Representatives, he did not care to rely on the indefinite statutory status of the Treasury Department to sustain his administrative leadership. Instead he assumed that the Treasury was actually an executive department and that the ultimate responsibility for departmental policy and action lay with the chief executive:

When it once appears that the President has constituted the head of a department his agent, for any general purpose, intrusted to him by law, all intermediate authorities from the President to the agent, being conformable with law, are to be presumed. The proper inquiry for the Legislature must be, whether the laws have been duly executed or not; if they have been duly executed, the question of sufficiency or deficiency

[63] *The Writings of Albert Gallatin,* ed. Henry Adams (3 vols.; Philadelphia: J. B. Lippincott & Co., 1879), I, 67.

[64] *The Anas,* April 2, 1792, *Works of Jefferson,* ed. Ford, I, 215.

of authority, from the President to his agent, must be, to the Legislature, immaterial and irrelavent. That question must, then, be a matter purely between the President and the agent, not examinable by the Legislature, without interfering with the province of the Chief Magistrate, to whom alone the responsibility is.[65]

Hamilton's career immensely strengthened the theory of executive responsibility in America, although the results of his work in this respect were not to be immediately apparent. Given the principle of absolute ministerial responsibility to the President and an elective presidency combined with a party system, it seems unlikely that heightened ministerial authority would have necessarily made for undemocratic or disunified administration. Had Hamilton's proposed presidency, elective for good behavior (life), been adopted, it is almost a certainty that a parliamentary system of administration would have evolved with the President's choice of departmental executives determined by the political majority in the Congress. For, although Hamilton distrusted direct popular government, he nevertheless believed that administrators should be held accountable to the representatives of the people for their conduct in office. Whether this accountability passed through the medium of the presidency or went directly to the legislative branch was merely a matter of mechanics; it was the factor of administrative responsibility that was significant.

Alexander Hamilton remains the nation's foremost advocate of "responsible" administration. "The Federal Government," he wrote, "should neither be independent nor too much dependent. It should neither be raised above responsibility or control, nor should it want the means of maintaining its own weight, authority, dignity, and credit."[66] He did not fear the power of government so long as it was "responsible" power. No great purpose, he believed, could be accomplished by a government inflexibly restrained by checks and divided into mutually exclusive branches. Energy, unity, power, and duration, the inescapable requisites of good government, were safely intrusted only to a government so constituted that its responsibility to the people was clear and undivided, and Hamilton feared that the Constitution of 1789, with its checks, balances, and divided responsibility, would never be able to provide the nation with a responsible government. It was this fear which lay behind his proclivity for the unified executive government that Jefferson described as monarchy. In a sense, Hamilton was for monarchy—but a monarchy remote from the ordinary connotation of the word. "Monarchy," he declared in the Constitutional Convention, was a term that marked neither the degree

[65] "To a Committee of Congress, April 1, 1794," *Works*, ed. Lodge, III, 186.

[66] *The Continentalist*, No. VI, *ibid.*, I, 283.

nor the duration of power. The prime minister of Great Britain or the President of the United States might answer to Hamilton's definition of a monarch. But it was the danger of an executive-legislative deadlock that rendered the American government potentially irresponsible, for a break in the reciprocal co-operation of the President and the Congress paralyzed authority and divided responsibility. Partially responsibile agents, Hamilton understood to be potentially, if not actually, irresponsible. This weakness of the national government remains, as indicted by Hamilton, a major administrative and constitutional problem. It was Hamilton's great contribution to thought on administration that he foresaw the problem in the Constitutional Convention; that he labored to solve it under the adopted Constitution; and that, in so doing, he defined for future generations the issue of "responsible" government and marked out conditions necessary to its attainment.

PART II

THE ADMINISTRATIVE THEORIES OF THOMAS JEFFERSON

THOMAS JEFFERSON: A BIOGRAPHICAL NOTE

Thomas Jefferson was born April 13, 1743, at "Shadwell," the farm of his father, Peter Jefferson, in Albemarle County, Virginia. From March, 1760, to April, 1762, he studied at William and Mary College in Williamsburg and upon completion of his academic training entered the law office of George Wythe. In 1767 he was admitted to the bar, and his political career began shortly thereafter, when in 1769 he was elected to the Virginia House of Burgesses. Re-elected in 1771, he began to associate himself with those opposing the colonial policy of the British ministry, and 1773 he became one of the first members of the Virginia Committee of Correspondence. When Virginia proposed, in 1774, to send delegates to a Continental Congress, Jefferson prepared a set of instructions which he hoped would be useful in guiding the conduct of the Virginian representatives. Although the instructions overreached the consensus of the assembly and were not adopted, their influence on the growing sentiment for Colonial autonomy was considerable. Printed under the title of *A Summary View of the Rights of British America*, Jefferson's pamphlet ran through several editions and resulted in the proscription of its author by the British Parliament.

Having placed himself among the leaders in the movement for American independence, Jefferson was elected to the second Continental Congress in 1775, and in June, 1776, was appointed one of a committee of five to draft a declaration of independence. The essential form and phraseology of the Declaration appear to have been determined by Jefferson, and its content was entirely in harmony with his political principles.

The break with Britain made, Jefferson returned to Virginia and, as a member of the House of Delegates, began the work of revising the legal system of the former colony. By 1779, when he was elected governor, Jefferson had succeeded in forcing the abolition of the legal institution of entail, had begun his fight for the abrogation of primogeniture and for the disestablishment of the Anglican church, and had taken initial steps in the establishment of a system of public education. As wartime governor of Virginia, Jefferson was beset with problems which would have perplexed one with greater aptitude and inclination for administrative duties than he displayed. In 1781 he retired from the governorship under a cloud of public disfavor, and vindication by the Virginia legislature in the autumn of that year failed to heal the wounds which public censure of his conduct had inflicted. In 1781 he had been elected to the Virginia legislature, but, following the death of his wife in 1782, he temporarily withdrew from all public life.

In 1783 Jefferson's career in national politics was resumed when he was elected a delegate to the Congress. In 1784 he was appointed Minister Plenipotentiary to the

Court of France, and until 1789 he remained abroad traveling in England and on the Continent, forming lasting friendships with the apostles of the "Age of Reason" and publishing his *Notes on Virginia*. He observed the opening phases of the French Revolution and informally counseled with the revolutionary leaders concerning the best method of establishing a liberal constitution for France.

Upon his return to America, Jefferson was asked by President Washington to assume the post of Secretary of State. After some hesitation he accepted the offer and in March, 1790, commenced his duties in the city of New York. The conservative reaction which had swept the Union while Jefferson lived abroad filled him with dismay, and he soon became equally alarmed at the efforts being made to transplant the industrial system of Great Britain to America, to establish banks, and to encourage urban development and the centralization of government, all of which he deemed unfavorable to his dream of a decentralized agrarian American republic. Accordingly, he soon clashed with Alexander Hamilton, who was attempting to construct an integrated, balanced American economy, requiring the stimulation of finance and manufacture and involving a degree of national governmental control over the economy which Jefferson associated with the centralized mercantile systems of the Old World monarchies. Jefferson and Hamilton quarreled, and, as Jefferson was unable to check Hamilton, and unwilling to co-operate with him, he retired from the administration in 1793 and resumed the life of a planter at Monticello.

Ostensibly in retirement, Jefferson was not inactive in politics. He maintained a vigorous correspondence with anti-Hamiltonian leaders throughout the Union and laid the foundation of the Democratic-Republican party. Between 1797 and 1801 he served as Vice-President in the administration of President John Adams, and in the election of 1800 he defeated Adams and the Federalists. In 1801 he was inaugurated President in his fifty-eighth year.

Jefferson served two administrations as chief executive, the first, 1801–5, largely successful and characterized by the purchase of Louisiana, and the second, 1805–9, characterized by the ill-fated embargo and the factiousness of John Randolph of Roanoke and filled with difficulty and discord. With his retirement from the presidency in 1809 Jefferson's active political career was ended.

In his twenty-eight remaining years he retained his interest in political affairs, but he devoted his efforts increasingly to science, agriculture, and education. In 1812 he renewed his friendship with John Adams, broken on the occasion of their political rivalry in 1800. Jefferson became the "sage of Monticello" and the object of pilgrimage for the great and humble of America and for distinguished travelers from abroad. He died on July 4, 1826, the fiftieth anniversary of the signing of the Declaration of Independence.

CHAPTER VII

THE PERSONALITY FACTOR IN JEFFERSON'S PHILOSOPHY OF ADMINISTRATION

QUALITIES OF INTELLECT

The last hope of human liberty in this world rests on us. We ought, for so dear a state to sacrifice every attachment and every enmity.—To WILLIAM DUANE.[1]

THERE is perhaps no figure in the history of the United States more difficult to interpret than Thomas Jefferson. This is true not only because of certain apparent inconsistencies in his policies and opinions but also because any treatment of Jefferson must strike some balance between the contrasting views of his numerous interpreters. The volume of Jeffersonian literature is indeed great, to which Jefferson himself contributed no small share.[2] Whether one could discover the real Jefferson by sifting this mass of writings is problematic and would require an undertaking of years. It is as true of Jefferson as of Hamilton that no really comprehensive, objective, and penetrating biographical study exists. Certainly, no thoroughgoing interpretation of the Jeffersonian personality can be undertaken here. But it is necessary to a proper understanding of his theory and practice of public administration that certain of Jefferson's personal characteristics be recognized.

The breadth of Jefferson's mind varied markedly with the context of its thought. His reputation for open-mindedness and regard for reason was entirely justified in the realms of natural science and education but was only partially justified where matters of politics and related social policy were concerned. As a recent biographer has suggested, "politics" affords

[1] March 28, 1811, *Works*, ed. Ford, XI, 193.

[2] Although no complete printed collection of Jefferson's writings is extant, the most comprehensive and accessible printed sources are:

The Writings of Thomas Jefferson, ed. H. A. Washington (9 vols.; Washington: Taylor & Maury, 1853–54).

The Works of Thomas Jefferson, ed. Paul Leicester Ford (12 vols.; Federal ed.; New York: G. P. Putnam's Sons, 1904–5). There is also an earlier edition of *The Works of Thomas Jefferson* edited by Ford and published by G. P. Putnam's Sons in 1892 in 10 volumes. This edition differs considerably from the Federal edition not only in pagination but in content.

Andrew A. Lipscomb (editor-in-chief) and Albert Ellery Bergh (managing editor), *The Writings of Thomas Jefferson, Containing His Autobiography, etc.* (20 vols.; Washington: Issued under the auspices of the Thomas Jefferson Memorial Association, 1903–5). Cited hereafter as "Memorial ed."

the notable exception to Jefferson's otherwise temperate and reasonable disposition.[3] His political thinking was governed by several articles of faith which withstood modification by reasoned argument or practical demonstration. In matters wherein his emotional bias was strong, as Henry Adams correctly observed, Jefferson saw what he wished to see and willed what he wished to believe.[4]

He was sincerely equalitarian, but he was coincidentally an individualist, loving men as persons, cherishing them collectively in the abstract, but distrusting them to the point of fear when massed together in cities. Jefferson's conception of the poeple was an idealization, yet he saw them not as masses but as individuals, independent farmers, tradesmen, and mechanics. His equalitarian philosophy was not that all should be alike but that all should as nearly as possible enjoy an equal opportunity to realize the rewards of ability and perseverance.

Jefferson inclined toward a provincial emotional bias, notwithstanding a cosmopolitan breadth of intellectual outlook. Although he had lived in Europe, he never overcame an ingrained suspicion of foreigners. He may have loved Europeans as individuals, but as nationalities he distrusted them. In America he had a strong proclivity toward his native Virginia and toward the South generally. He believed country people more virtuous than city dwellers and suspected the morals of those who did not derive their living from the land or from a skilled trade or learned profession.

Although Jefferson was capable of narrow prejudice and undue suspicion, he was nevertheless willing to change his mind when, by experience, he satisfied himself that policies once opposed were necessary to the public welfare. His speculative tendencies, his independence of tradition, and his versatility do not, however, imply a ready receptivity to new ideas. Where Jefferson doubted, he was distinctly conservative. He accepted the desirability of American manufactures only after years of observation and ultimately came to accept in some measure the internal improvements, the military preparations, and the aids to private enterprise which he condemned when they were urged by Hamilton. By some of his contemporaries he was considered a revolutionary thinker, but this belief was only in part correct.

Jefferson wished simplicity and harmony to characterize his living. Harmony meant friendship, the approbation of others, and the absence of dissension—personal or political. To achieve harmony, he was sometimes

[3] Saul K. Padover, *Jefferson* (New York: Harcourt, Brace & Co., 1942), p. 296.

[4] Henry Adams, *History of the United States during the Administration of Thomas Jefferson* (2 vols.; New York: Albert & Charles Boni, 1930), Book III, p. 58.

willing to sacrifice personal preferences to the objectives of his friends and followers, betraying what seemed to friends and enemies alike a craving for popularity.[5] But if Jefferson departed from principles to insure popularity, he exacted the price of loyalty to his political leadership and general objectives as the price of his conciliation. Secondary principles he would sacrifice on the altar of party and personal harmony, but fundamental principles never. Departures from one principle on behalf of another were exceptions which the exigencies of the public welfare might occasionally require but which did not shake his fundamental political convictions.

Jeffersonian simplicity did not preclude elegance in living, but it did imply a dislike for formality or complexity in ideas or social conventions. Jefferson's passion for simplicity and his generalizing turn of mind may explain why he sometimes accepted explanations far more simple than the facts would seem to indicate. He was impatient with complex social arrangement, and in particular he held complicated administration as a likely cover for the usurpation of power and privilege. But simplicity did not imply direct or forthright dealing in political or administrative affairs, for Jefferson not infrequently discovered that his desire for harmony and good will required most devious political arrangements.[6]

Jefferson was liberal in the literal sense of the word. He believed mankind entitled to the greatest degree of personal liberty reconcilable with the freedom and welfare of all individuals. And Jefferson had abundant faith in the capacity of the American people to order their affairs to their mutual well-being without the undue aid or interference of self-constituted or even publicly constituted authority. Selfishness and ignorance necessitated government to restrain the abuse or misdirection of personal freedom. But Jefferson's emotional bias was distinctly against the idea and implications of authority. His seemingly innate hostility to the arbitrary use of power deterred him from the use of force in human relationships, yet he held violence as a justifiable necessity when it was required to insure the triumph of freedom and equality over tyranny and privilege.[7]

Between his passion for freedom and for equality Jefferson faced the two horns of a dilemma. Freedom, as he understood it, might easily permit the growth of great inequalities in personal power which would destroy the

---

[5] *Ibid.*, p. 7.

[6] E.g., Jefferson's attempt to secure the Floridas without creating an international and domestic turmoil.

[7] Harry Elmer Barnes attributes Jefferson's dislike of authority to emotional conditioning resulting from his subjection during boyhood to the domination of a strong-willed father (see *The New History and the Social Sciences* [New York: Century Co., 1925], pp. 235–47).

conditions necessary for equality of opportunity. Conversely, to enforce an equality of status on all individuals would narrow the scope of personal liberty to the extent of rendering equality inequitable. To reconcile freedom and equality was a task which Jefferson left in large measure to his successors, but he did not believe that his work toward establishing freedom and equality in America fulfilled his responsibilities. Although he believed that the people would effect their own reconciliation in the course of time, he also believed that positive leadership toward this end was useful. One avenue of leadership, which lies beyond the province of this study, was public education. A second avenue of leadership was politics, and the function of politics was to develop and protect the political and social structure in which Jeffersonian freedom and equality could coexist in perfect harmony.

QUALITIES OF LEADERSHIP

*In a government like ours, it is the duty of the Chief Magistrate, in order to enable himself to do all the good which his station requires, to endeavor, by all honorable means, to unite in himself the confidence of the whole people.—*To J. GARLAND JEFFERSON.[8]

Jefferson's thought on administration was more closely defined by political ideology than was the corresponding thought of Hamilton. For, although Hamilton's theories of organization and administration were likewise governed by a general theory of politics, he cared as much about the substance but less about the form of government than did Jefferson. Hamilton advocated the unified executive power symbolized by the monarch, and he held it immaterial whether a chief executive be called "king," "president," or "prime minister." Jefferson contrastingly opposed the label and external trappings of royal monarchy, although in Louisiana he was willing to exercise the executive authority of a Spanish king in the interim between the acquisition of the colony and its organization into a republican territory. Nevertheless, the political creed of republicanism and Jefferson's temperamental inclination urged him toward party leadership rather than toward the politics of administration. Both Hamilton and Jefferson employed constitutional and partisan resources in their exercise of the executive power, but it was characteristic of Jefferson to rely where possible upon his power to marshal the support of his followers on behalf of his policies, whereas Hamilton preferred to rely on the prerogative of the executive, broadly interpreted, to support the position he wished to take.

Emotionally and intellectually Hamilton was admirably fitted for administrative leadership, and Jefferson was no less well qualified for leader-

---

[8] January 25, 1810, *Works*, ed. Ford, XI, 133.

ship in the field of political action. What forces induced Jefferson to concern himself with politics is difficult to determine, for, in spite of his adaptability to political leadership, he possessed no sharply marked traits which pointed to an inevitable public career. "I have no ambition to govern men," he wrote; "no passion which would lead me to delight to ride in a storm."[9] "I have never been so well pleased, as when I can shift power from my own, on the shoulders of others."[10] Yet if neither power nor command urged Jefferson toward politics, he was nevertheless not without ambition. If his own testimony is reliable, love of popularity was a compelling motive in his public life. The "approbation of my fellow citizens is the richest reward I can receive,"[11] he confessed; and he further averred that "the approving voice of our fellow citizens . . . . is the greatest of all earthly rewards."[12] Jefferson's letters and addresses are filled with allusions to the pleasures of popular good will, and one can readily agree with his remark to Madison that he valued present reputation above posthumous fame.

Hamilton believed as early as 1792 that Jefferson aimed with "ardent desire at the Presidential chair"[13] and that his elevation thereto was a major object of Republican party politics. Madison confirmed the latter thesis when he remarked to Monroe that "the Republicans, knowing that Jefferson alone can be started with hope of success, mean to push him. I fear much," he added, "that he will mar the project and insure the adverse election by a peremptory and public protest."[14]

It is apparent that Jefferson did not wish to be thought ambitious, and, although this reticence may have reflected a sincere modesty, he knew how to use self-effacement to good advantage. "Take things always by their smooth handle," he advised a young friend,[15] incidentally providing a perfect characterization of his political methods. Jefferson knew well the truism that in democratic politics one who aspires to lead must often be willing to follow.

[9] To Edward Rutledge, December 27, 1796, *ibid.*, VIII, 257.

[10] To Destutt Tracy, January 26, 1811, *ibid.*, XI, 186.

[11] To Richard M. Johnson, March 10, 1808, *Writings*, ed. Washington, V, 256.

[12] To New London Methodists, February 4, 1809, *ibid.*, VIII, 147.

[13] To Colonel Edward Carrington, May 26, 1792, *Works*, ed. Lodge, IX, 530.

[14] February 26, 1796, James Madison, *Letters and Other Writings of James Madison* . . . . (4 vols.; New York: R. Worthington, 1884), II, 83.

[15] To Thomas Jefferson Smith, February 24, 1825, *Writings*, ed. Washington, VII, 402. Cf. Henry S. Randall, *The Life of Thomas Jefferson* (3 vols; New York: Derby & Jackson, 1858), III, 524–25.

Although Jefferson appears to have been initially drawn into public life by keen interest in public affairs and by personal ambition, there is abundant evidence that the dissensions of politics and the drudgery of public office were truly distasteful to him. Although he was certainly not cured of political ambition as he professed to be in 1782, more than considerations of personal reputation compelled him to assume the role of national party leadership after 1790.

In order to determine the true source of Jefferson's power and the meaning of his career, he must be viewed in terms of historical context. For the leadership of Jefferson, like that of Hamilton, developed in response to the major social trends of his time. Jefferson's political career may be conveniently divided into three periods distinguished not so much by changes in his attitudes but by changes in his orientation. Prior to 1790 Jefferson's leadership was in the political sense revolutionary. He placed himself among those leaders aligned against the monarchical and aristocratic conventions of the Old World. He successfully led the movement to disestablish the state church in Virginia and abolish the legal appurtenances of aristocracy, primogeniture, and the law of entail. But the old order overthrown, a new social system appeared no less inimical to the agrarian democracy which Jefferson envisaged. The abolition of British mercantile controls opened the way for the rise of industrialism and capitalism in America. Alexander Hamilton became the apostle of the new economy and by 1791 seemed certain to succeed in replacing the imperial system of mercantile Britain with a domestic order of capitalist industrialism supported and controlled by a powerful centralized federal administration. Thus Jefferson's second political orientation was conservative and defensive. To preserve the liberties gained in the Revolution of 1776 and to insure the independence, perhaps, indeed, the dominance, of agrarian America in politics, Jefferson took issue with Hamilton. If Jefferson's triumph in the election of 1800 can be called a revolution, it must be called a conservative revolution; and Jefferson himself viewed it as a return to the pure republican principles of the Revolutionary era. The final period of Jefferson's leadership, the years after 1800, represented a continuation of his conservative point of view but a change in his political methods. Jefferson in power relaxed his opposition to the growing capitalist industrial system. He discovered that the common people in whose name he assumed the presidency were not of one mind about the economic future of the country.

Whether Jefferson distinguished between the forces of the past which he had helped to overthrow and the forces of the future which he resisted is problematic. Certainly, he sensed the growing power of trade and manufacturing, and, recognizing the futility of playing Canute to the rising tide of industrial economy, he preferred compromise to resistance.[16] Thus Jefferson in power maintained the essential elements of the Hamiltonian system which he had once opposed, modifying them only slightly to suit partisan exigencies.

Thus it happened that in the opening decades of the nineteenth century the American nation was committed to a theory of government and of public administration which was designed to reconcile agrarian political control with the rising economic power of the capitalist-industrial order. Hamilton would have provided America with a national system of public administration competent to deal with the vast economic and social problems of the new age. As he recognized the inevitable rise of industrialism in America, Hamilton was prepared to direct its development in the general interest. He believed that the new system held potentialities for great good and therefore was eager to encourage its development. Jefferson, hostile to industrialism, yet unable to discover effective means for resisting it, chose to leave it to its own resources. Unable to abolish the Hamiltonian system and equally unable to control it without recourse to the complex centralized administrative machinery which he had always feared, he adopted the expedient of laissez faire. Thus began the drifting-apart of government and the industrial economy which was to have profound consequences for the history of the American people.

For a century after Jefferson's triumph over the Federalists no American statesman successfully advanced the notion that the planning and direction of social evolution was a responsibility of public administration, and Jefferson's interest in the assisting hand of government in the distribution of public lands and the dissemination of public instruction was less often remembered than his warnings against centralized political and administrative power. Indeed, Jefferson's one great experiment with a centrally directed administrative program, the ill-fated embargo, seemed to testify to the wisdom of his laissez faire views. The Jeffersonian theory that most domestic public affairs could be properly controlled by the personal supervision of local majorities over local units of government was retained as a popular article of faith long after the conditions of Jefferson's day had ceased to exist. Thus Jefferson's influence on administrative ideas did not end with the pronouncement and practice of his theories but con-

[16] His compromise with Federalism is well brought out by Joseph Dorfman in "The Economic Philosophy of Thomas Jefferson," *Political Science Quarterly*, LV (March, 1940), 98–121.

tinued after his political career was ended, as a body of attitudes toward government which the American people rightly or wrongly understood as the teachings of Thomas Jefferson.[17]

Although the contrast between Jefferson's earlier role as reformer and his later conservative position affords ground for charges of inconsistency and love of popularity, the better explanation lies in what T. V. Smith has described as "Jefferson's doctrine of democratic means."[18] Continuing to hold to his earlier ideals, as ideals, he nevertheless recognized that as a political leader he must effect the public welfare by the means at his disposal. He did not believe the public good was to be attained by the suppression of those who did not share his ideals, and he recognized that the transaction of public business required that he work with men whose ideals he did not share. Thus in a sense Jefferson was the realistic politician whereas Hamilton remained a confirmed idealist, for only on such great occasions as the assumption of state debts and the election of Jefferson to the presidency could Hamilton subordinate his perfectionism to the mediocrity of political compromise. Perhaps an explanation of this contrast in political leadership, Hamilton's inflexibility and Jefferson's conciliation, lies in Jefferson's capacity to separate the ideal from the actual. Perhaps, as Smith has suggested, it is true "that for him means existed not primarily as agencies to realize ideals but as reproducers of themselves; that for him ideals existed not primarily as things to be realized through collective means but as ends of reflection to be enjoyed for their own sake."[19]

Jefferson's practical leadership must therefore be distinguished from his intellectual or moral leadership, although they sometimes constitute, as in his inaugural addresses, an interwoven pattern and cannot be separated. Jefferson's contribution to thought on public administration derives from both aspects of his leadership and from the traditions concerning his leadership, but it is fair to say that Jefferson's greater contribution derives

[17] Among the writers who have developed the idea of the Jefferson tradition as an influence in American history are: James Truslow Adams, *The Living Jefferson* (New York: Charles Scribner's Sons, 1936), and "Jefferson and Hamilton Today: The Dichotomy in American Thought," *Atlantic Monthly*, CXLI (April, 1928), 443–50; Gilbert Chinard, *Thomas Jefferson, the Apostle of Americanism* (Boston: Little, Brown & Co., 1929); C. M. Wiltse, *The Jeffersonian Tradition in American Democracy* (Chapel Hill: University of North Carolina Press, 1935); Carl Becker, "What Is Still Living in the Political Philosophy of Thomas Jefferson," *American Historical Review*, XLVIII (July, 1943), 691–706; and Francis G. Wilson, "On Jeffersonian Tradition," *Review of Politics*, V (July, 1943), 302–21. See also the articles in the *Virginia Quarterly Review*, Vol. XIX (spring, 1943), and *Ethics: An International Journal of Social, Political, and Legal Philosophy*, Vol. LIII (July, 1943).

[18] "Thomas Jefferson and the Perfectibility of Mankind," *Ethics*, LIII (July, 1943), 297.

[19] *Ibid.*, p. 302.

from the ideal. For, although ideal ends are distinguishable from means, it is the ends that ultimately determine the nature and direction of the means, and it is the Jeffersonian ideals which in large measure still persist in American political thought which have had a decisive influence in shaping the administrative theories and practices of American government.

CHAPTER VIII

THE POLITICAL BASIS OF JEFFERSON'S ADMINISTRATIVE IDEAS

I T IS not the purpose of this chapter to present a comprehensive review of Jefferson's political theory. Rather, the intent is to define those factors in his political thinking that governed his administrative ideas. This purpose assumes, as implied in the preceding chapter, that Jefferson's administrative ideas were largely determined by his more strictly political thinking, and, in the chapters to follow, evidence will be presented to show that this assumption is not unfounded. Obviously, not all of Jefferson's vast range of political ideas are germane to administrative theory, and, as the object of this chapter is only to formulate the basis of his administrative thought, any comprehensive account of Jeffersonian political doctrine is precluded.

THE PSYCHOLOGICAL BASIS OF JEFFERSONIAN POLITICAL THEORY

. . . . *whenever our affairs go obviously wrong the good sense of the people will interpose and set them to rights.*—To DAVID HUMPHREYS.[1]

The purpose for which all legitimate governments were instituted Jefferson declared to be the freedom and happiness of men. "The only orthodox object of the institution of government," he asserted, "is to secure the greatest degree of happiness possible to the general mass of those associated under it."[2] To effect the care of human life and happiness all governments were not equally fitted. "The republican is the only form of government which is not eternally at open or secret war with the rights of mankind,"[3] he declared. Nor were all the activities customarily undertaken by public authority suitable to promote the public good. Although he asserted

[1] March 18, 1789, *Works*, ed. Ford, V, 469.

[2] To Vander Kemp, March 22, 1812, *Writings*, ed. Washington, VI, 45.

[3] To William Hunter, mayor of Alexandria, March 11, 1790, *ibid.*, III, 128.

that "the legitimate powers of government extend to such acts only as are injurious to others,"[4] he believed that government might take preventive measures to forestall injurious acts; hence public support for education, the encouragement of small landowning, the reform of prisons, and improved transportation. But he averred that, even in republican societies, "the natural progress of things is for liberty to yield, and government to gain ground."[5] Therefore, in order that popular liberty, which he deemed a concomitant of republicanism, might be preserved, he would vest the ultimate political powers in the mass of the people. "Unless the mass retains sufficient control over those intrusted with the powers of their government, these will be perverted to their own oppression, and to the perpetuation of wealth and power in the individuals and their families selected for the trust."[6] No other depositories of power have ever yet been found, he asserted, "which did not end in converting to their own profit the earnings of those committed to their charge."[7]

Mankind thus inclined to selfishness, and government should afford no occasion for private interest to find expression at the cost of the public good. The way to keep government free from corruption was to keep it always responsible to the people in whose general interest it was created. To maintain this popular control of government was no simple matter for men divided on the question of where power ought to be vested. There was always a group, Jefferson observed, who would remove political power from the people and secure it in a select few who were deemed more able than the many to determine the best course for public affairs:

Men by their constitutions are naturally divided into two parties. 1. Those who fear and distrust the people, and wish to draw all powers from them into the hands of the higher classes. 2ndly those who identify themselves with the people, have confidence in them, cherish and consider them as the most honest and safe, altho' not the most wise depository of the public interests. In every country these two parties exist, and in every one where they are free to think, speak, and write, they will declare themselves. Call them therefore liberals and serviles, Jacobins and Ultras, whigs and tories, republicans and federalists, aristocrats and democrats or by whatever name you please, they are the same parties still and pursue the same object. The last appellation of aristocrats and democrats is the true one expressing the essence of all.[8]

[4] *Notes on Virginia* (1782), *ibid.*, VIII, 400; but cf. "Second Inaugural Address."

[5] To E. Carrington, May 27, 1788, *Works*, ed. Ford, V, 402. See also letter to David Humphreys, March 18, 1789, *ibid.*, pp. 470–71.

[6] To Vander Kemp, March 22, 1812, *Writings*, ed. Washington, VI, 45.

[7] To Samuel Kercheval, September 5, 1816, *Works*, ed. Ford, XII, 15.

[8] To Henry Lee, August 10, 1824, *ibid.*, p. 375.

Jefferson intimated that the basis for this tendency of men to divide on the question of the allocation of power was physiological, although complicated by factors of economic interest and moral understanding. "The weakly and nerveless, the rich and the corrupt seeing more safety . . . . in a strong executive," were the Tories of nature, whereas "the healthy, firm and virtuous feeling confidence in their physical and moral resources, and willing to part with only so much power as is necessary for their good government,"[9] were natural Whigs.

Whether the divisions aristocrat and democrat, Whig and Tory, were inevitable, probable, or merely fortuitous, Jefferson did not say. Writing to Henry Lee in 1824, he recalled his earlier contention that men were divided by nature into the two opposing political groups. Yet, writing in 1822 to William T. Barry, he had declared that the division into Whig and Tory was "worthy of being nourished, to keep out those of a more dangerous character."[10] The division of people into aristocrats and democrats was therefore only one of many possible groupings, for, although Jefferson believed that men were inclined by nature to divide upon this basis, one may deduce from his reference to other principles that he deemed other divisions possible.

The implication of his theory of party divisions is that he believed the driving forces of political society to be broadly psychological rather than narrowly economic, and his lifelong interest in popular education and in the advancement of science strengthens this view. This is not to deny that Jefferson recognized the importance of economic considerations in political efforts, for Charles A. Beard has demonstrated very clearly the significance of economic ideas in Jefferson's political career.[11] Certainly, Jefferson's wish that America be a land of small property owners, that the creation of a vast propertyless proletariat in the cities be avoided, that concentrations of wealth and power in the hands of the few, whether that few be private individuals or public officials, be resisted; all this reflects a keen awareness of the relation of wealth to politics.

The division of interests upon the basis of property distribution he deemed unhealthful in a republican society and accordingly labored for a reform of the property laws of Virginia which through the statutes of entail and primogeniture had tended to concentrate rather than to diffuse the distribution of wealth. "I am conscious that an equal division of prop-

---

[9] To Joel Barlow, May 3, 1802, *ibid.*, IX, 371.

[10] July 2, 1822, *Writings*, ed. Washington, VII, 255–56. See also letter to William Short, January 8, 1825, *Works*, ed. Ford, XII, 397.

[11] *The Economic Origins of Jeffersonian Democracy* (New York: Macmillan Co., 1915).

erty is impracticable,"[12] he declared. But in the enormous inequalities which he observed in France of the old regime he saw need for political action to relieve the misery of the multitude by a subdivision of property.

The danger of great inequality in wealth was that those who possessed the bulk of property would abuse their power and destroy the public liberty in their attempt to safeguard their fortunate position from attack by those who had less. Accordingly, Jefferson believed that great wealth tended to breed aristocracy and oligarchy.[13] He opposed monopolistic power in hands not subject to direct popular control,[14] but the danger of concentrated economic powers to the democratic processes of government rather than the resulting fact of economic inequality occasioned his fear. That economic inequality might reach a point where it resulted in a concentration of wealth capable of opposing the public good, Jefferson recognized. Thus he considered the undue concentration of wealth rather than the unequal distribution of property to be the dangerous factor in society.

That popular economic interests would obtrude into the area of public policy, Jefferson fully recognized. Writing to Congressman Hugh Nelson in 1820, he observed the clamor of contending manufacturing, commercial, and agricultural groups to secure political favors at the expense of the welfare of the others. This, declared Jefferson, proves that without political favoritism the conflicting interests of society will check one another. "The egotism of the whole," as he expressed the thought, happily balances the "cannibal appetites" of these groups to eat one another. "I do not know," he added, "whether it is any part of the petitions of the farmers that our citizens shall be restrained to eat nothing but bread, because that can be made here. But this is the common spirit of all their petitions."[15]

Thus the forces which united and divided society were both political and economic, but Jefferson seemed to believe that the political differences were fundamental, whereas the economic differences were of secondary importance. Although Jefferson recognized the importance of economic factors in political policy, he likewise considered the administrative structure, the form of constitution, the geographical extent of government,

[12] To James Madison, October 28, 1795 [1785], *Works*, ed. Ford, VIII, 195–96.

[13] Charles M. Wiltse suggests in *The Jeffersonian Tradition in American Democracy* (Chapel Hill: University of North Carolina Press, 1935), pp. 88–89, that Jefferson was influenced by Madison's economic interpretation of government.

[14] To Francis Hopkinson, March 13, 1789, *Works*, ed. Ford, V, 457; to James Madison, December 20, 1787, *ibid.*, p. 371.

[15] February 7, 1820, *ibid.*, XII, 157.

and the social inheritance of the governed as major factors in politics. His contention that the differences between the Whigs and Tories, the natural parties into which men tend to segregate, are to be found in mental attitudes based in part upon physiological qualities would seem to indicate a belief that basic political alignments were not necessarily determined by the production and distribution of wealth. Indeed, Jefferson's faith in the power of ideas sets him apart from other leaders in the founding of the nation. Although the revolutionary and federal leaders were profoundly aware of the relation of popular psychology to politics, their thought was directed toward the formation of attitudes through administrative and legislative machinery rather than in the stimulation and cultivation of popular thinking. This unique position of Jefferson may be illustrated most effectively by contrasting the relatively low value which he placed on a permanent constitution, on administrative machinery, on precedent, on titles, and on the formation of political habits with the emphasis given all these devices by Hamilton, John Adams, and Washington.

Hamilton and Adams were no less concerned for the welfare of the people than Jefferson, but they mistrusted the capacity of people generally to think correctly about affairs of state. The Federalist statesmen preferred to do the people's thinking for them. Jefferson, although recognizing the limitations of most people for constructive thought, nevertheless believed that people, to remain free, must learn to do their own thinking. This belief became a cardinal principle with him and is absolutely fundamental to his administrative theory, for it led directly to two conclusions about political organization: (1) that government must be decentralized to the extent that each citizen may personally participate in the administration of public affairs and (2) that government must serve to school the people in political wisdom and must train a self-reliant citizenry "to know ambition under all its shapes" and to be "prompt to exert their natural powers to defeat its purposes."[16] This latter conclusion implied that not only public education but political responsibility, which Jefferson considered one of the best teachers, should be accessible to as many as were capable of fulfilling its demands. Not only did this suggest the theory of administrative decentralization, but it further implied frequent rotation of office, the avoidance of an "administrative class," and, above all, the formal education of people generally for the responsibilities of citizenship.

The tendency which Jefferson saw in power to corrupt and the inclination of men to make self-interested use of such advantages as they could

[16] "A Bill for the More General Diffusion of Knowledge" (1779), *ibid.*, II, 415.

gain provide assumptions which governed Jefferson's theories of politics and administration. To minimize the arbitrary powers of the state and to maximize the political insight of the people were the two methods by which good government was to be effected. Thus the objectives of the Jeffersonian state were predisposed toward what might best be called a "liberal conservatism." To guard republican government from the degeneration to which he believed all governments subject was a constant object; to use the public power to insure the freedom of the people to work out their own destiny was another. The Jeffersonian state, therefore, would be a bulwark against the undesirable inclinations of men toward power and avarice and would serve to encourage the human qualities of honesty, independence, and open-mindedness which Jefferson believed conducive to the happiness of the multitude. Accordingly, a description of the political system by which these objectives were to be accomplished is in order.

THE JEFFERSONIAN CONCEPTION OF THE STATE

What constitutes a State?
Not high-raised battlements, or labor'd mound,
Thick wall, or moated gate;
Not cities proud, with spires and turrets crown'd;
No: men, high minded men;
Men, who their duties know;
But know their rights; and knowing, dare maintain.
These constitute a State.

—FROM AN ODE "IN IMITATION OF ALCAEUS," BY
SIR WILLIAM JONES.[17]

With the thought of the poet Jefferson agreed and quoted approvingly in a letter to that redoubtable republican, John Taylor of Caroline. Although the duties and rights of men and their preservation seemed more the province of the political theorist than of the poet, in the formulation of his political principles Jefferson relied more upon experience and intuition than upon the speculations of philosophers. "History, in general, only informs us what bad government is,"[18] he declared to John Norvell. But he considered history as a valuable educative device to avail the people of "the experience of other times and other nations; it will qualify them as judges of the actions and designs of men; it will enable them to know ambition under every disguise it may assume; and knowing it, to defeat

---

[17] To John Taylor, May 28, 1816, *ibid.*, XI, 531.

[18] June 14, 1807, *ibid.*, X, 416.

its views."[19] Jefferson held the political theories of Europe generally in-applicable to American experience, and he believed of the publicists as he declared of the great work of Montesquieu that their writings, although containing a great number of political truths, embodied an equal number of heresies so that readers must be constantly on guard in appraising them. Indeed, he held the state of political literature in general to be far from satisfactory, maintaining that a good elementary work on the organization of society into civil government did not exist.[20]

That Jefferson could not find a good elementary treatise on the organization of civil government in accordance with natural principles was hardly surprising in view of the fact that the publicists were given to the construction of administrative systems and political machinery, whereas Jefferson looked to the reduction of government as a force superimposed upon the ordinary activities of men. The political theories of anarchy and pluralism would perhaps have been more to his liking,[21] but their place in the political literature available to Jefferson was small indeed. That he should have declared that on the practice of government "there is no better book than *The Federalist*"[22] is curious not only because the greater part of the treatise was written by Alexander Hamilton (a fact which Jefferson may not have fully appreciated) but also because of its emphasis on centralized government and the limitation of direct popular control in the formulation of public policy.

Jefferson's theory of the state appears, therefore, to have been little influenced by the writings of the systematic political theorists. As Merriam observes, "Jefferson's theory followed a line of thought already marked out during the English revolution by Milton, Sidney, and Locke."[23] This body of thought, adopted by Colonial writers and developed by Jefferson in the direction of minimized government and popular control, represents the major influence of political writing upon his political ideas. But the treatises of the English revolutionary spokesmen provided no comprehensive theory of the state, and, although Jefferson's political interest lay in pragmatic reform rather than in philosophical

[19] *Notes on Virginia*, Query XIV, *ibid.*, IV, 64.

[20] To John Norvell, June 14, 1807, *ibid.*, X, 416.

[21] Jefferson was not favorably disposed to anarchy as he understood the term: "Our falling into anarchy would decide forever the destinies of mankind, and seal the political heresy that man is incapable of self-government" (to John Hollins, May 5, 1811, *Works* [Memorial ed.], XIII, 58).

[22] To T. M. Randolph, May 30, 1790, *Works*, ed. Ford, VI, 63.

[23] Charles E. Merriam, *A History of American Political Theories* (New York: Macmillan Co., 1903), p. 169.

speculation, he developed a framework of political theory sufficient to clarify the position of his republican commonwealth in a world of governments.

The nearest systematic approximation of Jefferson's political views was contained in the political writings of his friend, John Taylor of Caroline, whose *Inquiry into the Principles and Policy of the Government of the United States* Jefferson received in the spring of 1816.[24] To this treatise Jefferson acknowledged himself indebted for many valuable ideas and for the correction of some errors of early opinion. "Colonel Taylor and myself," he declared, "have rarely, if ever, differed in any political principle of importance."[25] Writing to Taylor, Jefferson expressed accord with the principles set forth in the *Inquiry* and added certain observations of his own on the nature of government.

Republican government precisely defined, wrote Jefferson, "means a government by its citizens in mass, acting directly and personally, according to rules established by the majority; and that every other government is more or less republican, in proportion as it has in its composition more or less of this ingredient of the direct action of its citizens."[26] Such a government, he confessed, "is evidently restrained to very narrow limits of space and population."[27]

This pure republicanism Jefferson viewed as impractical for the government of a state or nation. But, holding that "the further the departure from direct and constant control by the citizens, the less has the government of the ingredient of republicanism,"[28] he maintained that representative government should be so instituted as to render the representatives of the people subject to popular will.

That American government fell short of the degree of republicanism necessary to protect the rights and interests of the people, Jefferson in later life admitted. This he ascribed not to want of republican dispositions in those who had formed the American constitutions but "to a submission of true principle to European authorities, to speculators on government, whose fears of the people have been inspired by the populace of their own great cities, and were unjustly entertained against the independent, the happy, and therefore orderly citizens of the United States."[29]

[24] For an analysis of this work see Beard, *op. cit.*, chap. xii; Benjamin F. Wright, Jr., "The Philosopher of Jeffersonian Democracy," *American Political Science Review*, XXII (November, 1928), 870–92; and E. T. Mudge, *The Social Philosophy of John Taylor of Caroline* (New York: Columbia University Press, 1939).

[25] To Thomas Ritchie, December 25, 1820, *Works*, ed. Ford, XII, 176.

[26] To John Taylor, May 28, 1816, *ibid.*, XI, 529. [27] *Ibid.* [28] *Ibid.*, p. 530. [29] *Ibid.*, p. 532.

Jefferson was apprehensive that the golden moment for reforming the heresies from republicanism was past. "The functionaries of public power rarely strengthen in their dispositions to abridge it,"[30] he observed. Yet, although he despaired of achieving a truly republican commonwealth, he would provide against the deterioration of existing institutions into less republican forms.[31] This conviction of Jefferson's in the evening of his career that republicanism was not entirely safe, that the centralizing forces of trade and finance were still at work to corrupt the representatives of the people into betraying republican principles, and that the judiciary of the United States, a "subtle corps of sappers and miners,"[32] was constantly working underground to undermine the foundations of the confederated union increased his insistence upon limited and decentralized administration. He congratulated John Taylor on having uncovered the attempt of John Adams to open "the mantle of republicanism to every government of laws, whether consistent or not with natural right."[33] But, as Henry Adams was later to observe, he failed to distinguish between centralization as an administrative principle and centralization as an appurtenance of monarchy.[34] To Jefferson, republicanism, democracy, and decentralized government remained forever concomitant.

If decentralized limited governments were the only safe administrators of republican principles, how and to what extent was government to be organized to effect legitimate public purposes? Jefferson believed that a federal organization of the state was the way to combine public strength with individual freedom. He described a graduation of authorities, the elementary republics of the wards, the county republics, the state republics, and the Republic of the Union forming a comprehensive political system. Good government, he declared, was effected not by the consolidation or concentration of powers but by their distribution, each division of the country to do for itself what concerns itself directly. "It is by this partition of cares," he declared, "descending in gradation from general to particular, that the mass of human affairs may be best managed for the good and prosperity of all," and, he added, "were we directed from Washington when to sow, and when to reap, we should soon want bread."[35]

---

[30] *Ibid.*

[31] *Ibid.*, pp. 532–33.

[32] To Thomas Ritchie, *ibid.*, XII, 177.   [33] To John Taylor, *ibid.*, XI, 529.

[34] *History of the United States during the Administration of Thomas Jefferson* (2 vols.; New York: Albert & Charles Boni, 1930), Book I, pp. 209–10.

[35] *Autobiography, Works*, ed. Ford, I, 123.

But Jefferson was concerned not only with the structure of government but with the moral principles which he felt must guide its administration. Writing to George Logan in 1816, he exclaimed: "It is strongly absurd to suppose that a million of human beings collected together are not under the same moral laws which bind each of them separately."[36] In the *Notes on Virginia* he had maintained that "civil government being the sole object of forming societies, its administration must be conducted by common consent."[37] But if consent of the governed was necessary to justify the administration of government, what proportion of the governed constituted popular consent? Obviously, unanimous consent was not to be secured.[38] In his "First Inaugural Address" Jefferson attempted an answer, declaring that "absolute acquiescence in the decisions of the majority,—the vital principle of republics, from which is no appeal but to force, the vital principle and immediate parent of despotism,"[39] was an essential principle of the American government, and, consequently, one which ought to shape its administration. But Jefferson was not prepared to admit that the rule of the majority, though legitimate, was always to be considered just; for, he promised, "though the will of the majority is in all cases to prevail, that will, to be rightful, must be reasonable," and added that "the minority possess their equal rights which equal laws must protect, and to violate would be oppression."[40]

He did not believe that majorities could rightfully require of others that from which they exempted themselves. Certainly, majorities were not entitled to abuse the right of majority rule by ruling unjustly. The abuse of the principle did not, however, imply its invalidation. Jefferson saw with concern the discrimination which the Republican citizens of Connecticut suffered from an unjust majority; however, the remedy lay not in the abrogation of majority rule but in the correction of its perversion. Jefferson's attitude toward democracy, as John Dewey rightly observed, embodied a "moral idealism" that is inseparable from his political doctrines. Political interest he held to be inseparable in the long run from moral right; rule by the majority could never justify tyranny by the ma-

[36] November 12, 1816, *ibid.*, XII, 43.

[37] *Writings*, ed. Washington, VIII, 331.

[38] Jefferson recognized exceptions to the rule that government must be based upon popular consent. For contrasting opinions in this respect see letters to DeWitt Clinton, December 2, 1803 (*Works*, ed. Ford, X, 55), and to Albert Gallatin, November 24, 1818 (*The Writings of Albert Gallatin*, ed. Henry Adams [3 vols.; Philadelphia: J. B. Lippincott & Co., 1879], II, 88–89).

[39] "First Inaugural Address," March 4, 1801, *Works*, ed. Ford, IX, 198.

[40] *Ibid.*, p. 195.

jority, but without a common standard of moral conduct the power of the majority would become merely the rule of the strong over the weak.

Not only morality but understanding and experience were requisites for democratic self-rule. Holding that the qualifications for self-government in society are the result of habit and long training, he observed to Joseph Priestly that "some preparation seems necessary to qualify the body of a nation for self-government."[41] Again, writing to Lafayette, he expressed his belief that self-government unaccompanied by experience and a common morality could not endure.[42]

Free government was not to be maintained solely upon the basis of consent, for Jefferson observed that, although good men would be governed by the principle of civic duty, bad men would obey only the principle of fear. On the proper use of coercive force Jefferson's position was not entirely consistent. In 1795 he denounced the use of military force for civil purposes in enforcing the federal internal revenue measures in western Pennsylvania during the Whiskey Rebellion. He declared that "the servile copyist of Mr. Pitt . . . . must have his alarms, his insurrections and plots against the Constitution."[43] If he had believed an insurrection to in fact exist he would perhaps have sanctioned the use of military force. But he described the disorders as merely an occasional riot and a few special cases of resistance to the law, asserting that Hamilton's expedition was designed only to strengthen the government and increase the public debt. In 1808 the shoe was on the other foot, and Jefferson wrote to his Secretary of War, Henry Dearborn: "We have such complaints of the breach of embargo by fraud and force on our northern water line, that I must pray your cooperation with the Secretary of the Treasury by rendezvousing as many new recruits as you can in that quarter."[44] He declared to Albert Gallatin in Hamiltonian style that it was "important to crush every example of forcible opposition to the law."[45] But with Jeffersonian caution he subsequently added, "I am clearly of the opinion this law ought to be enforced at any expense, *which may not exceed our appropriation.*"[46]

Upon the role of public opinion in the administration of government,

[41] November 29, 1802, *ibid.*, p. 404.

[42] February 14, 1815, *Writings*, ed. Washington, VI, 421.

[43] To James Monroe, May 26, 1795, *Works*, ed. Ford, VIII, 177.

[44] July 18, 1808, *Writings*, ed. Washington, V, 323.

[45] April 19, 1808, *ibid.*, p 271.

[46] August 11, 1808, *Works*, ed. Ford, XI, 41.

Jefferson laid great stress. "No government," he declared to Washington in 1792, "ought to be without censors; and where the press is free, no one ever will."[47] He went on to explain that "if virtuous, it need not fear the fair operation of attack and defense. Nature has given to man no other means of sifting out the truth, either in religion, law, or politics."[48] To counsel patience to Washington, chafing under the attacks of Republican editors, was one matter—to bear the attacks and misrepresentations of critics one's self was quite another. In 1806 President Jefferson complained to William Duane of the unreasonableness of the critics:

Our situation is difficult; and whatever we do is liable to the criticisms of those who wish to represent it awry. If we recommend measures in a public message, it may be said that members are not sent here to obey the mandates of the President, or to register the edicts of a sovereign. If we express opinions in conversation, we have then our Charles Jenkinsons, and back-door counsellors. If we say nothing, "we have no opinions, no plans, no cabinet."[49]

Yet he held it his consolation and encouragement to serve a just public which he felt would be indulgent to any error committed honestly. He believed it beneath the dignity of the government to notice either its sycophants or its censors, and he refused to prosecute his calumniators at law, trusting his character, as he expressed it, "to my own conduct, and the good sense and candor of my fellow citizens."[50]

What, then, was the essential character of the Jeffersonian state? Briefly, it was a decentralized federation, democratically governed, insuring the greatest amount of liberty consonant with justice. Its governors were only the agents of the people and absolutely responsible to them, and, although they were vested with the dignity of office, that dignity derived not from titles, power, or patronage but from the representation of the public will. The responsibility of the governors required of them submission to public censorship. The responsibility of the people required obedience to the public will expressed in law. Education and the personal participation of each citizen in the administration of public affairs were the ways by which republicanism was to be maintained. History and the political science of Europe taught America what to avoid in government, and in the evolution of a political system Jefferson would have America look to her own experience rather than risk misguidance by the errors and heresies of the Old World.

[47] September 9, 1792, *Writings*, ed. Washington, III, 467.

[48] *Ibid.*

[49] March 22, 1806, *Works*, ed. Ford, X, 242.

[50] To W. C. Nicholas, June 13, 1809, *ibid.*, XI, 109.

THE CONSTITUTIONAL BASIS OF PUBLIC ADMINISTRATION

. . . . a wise and frugal government, which shall restrain men from injuring one another, shall leave them otherwise free to regulate their own pursuits of industry and improvement, and shall not take from the mouth of labor the bread it has earned.

This is the sum of good government. . . . .—"First Inaugural Address."[51]

Although Jefferson never constructed a constitutional doctrine to support his ideal political order, the elements of such a structure were nevertheless to be found throughout his writings. In certain of his major public papers circumstances required a statement of constitutional theory, and Jefferson's response, though calculated to reflect the views of Americans generally, clearly represented his own opinions. On three critical occasions in his political career—on the eve of the American Revolution, on the occasion of the Declaration of Independence, and on his inauguration as President—Jefferson felt required to expound his theory of the constitutional basis of government and to do so as the spokesman of the American people. The first occasion arose in the late summer of 1774, when Virginia was preparing to send delegates to the First Continental Congress.

Although Jefferson later confessed that the leap he proposed was too long for the mass of citizens, yet he attempted to formulate an American interpretation of the constitution of the British colonies. To guide the action of the Virginia delegates to the Congress, Jefferson prepared *A Summary View of the Rights of British America*, which argued the thesis that the constitution of the Americans was based upon natural law and that the natural rights of Americans had been historically derived from Britain of Saxon times and had never been permanently abridged by king or Parliament. It was a compromise view, reflecting the shift of Colonial argument from the defense of British constitutional rights as enjoyed by Americans to the natural-rights argument of the Declaration of Independence. But the natural rights of the individual citizen in the political order provided the foundation upon which Jefferson's historical and legal arguments were based.

The natural-law basis of Jefferson's constitutional theory underlay all of his discussion on the causes and objectives of the American Revolution and achieved most notable expression in the Declaration of Independence. In the Declaration, Jefferson's natural-law theories remained those of the *Summary View* but with emphasis shifted to meet the needs of political independence.[52] This was the second major occasion for an exposition of his theory of the basis of constitutional government, and the circum-

---

[51] March 4, 1801, *ibid.*, IX, 197.

[52] *A Summary View of the Rights of British America, ibid.*, II, 64–65.

stances permitted the freest expression of his belief that legitimate governments were bottomed on natural law. The historical derivation of constitutional liberties was put aside and reliance placed in the view that

all Men are created equal and independent; that from that equal Creation they derive Rights inherent and unalienable; among which are the Preservation of Life, and Liberty, and the Pursuit of happiness; that to secure these Ends, Governments are instituted among Men, deriving their just Powers from the Consent of the governed; that whenever, any form of Government, shall become destructive of those ends, it is the Right of the People to alter, or to abolish it, and to institute new Government, laying its Foundation on such Principles, and organizing its Powers in such Form, as to them shall Seem most likely to effect their Safety and Happiness.[53]

Even a cursory examination of the *Summary* and the Declaration will reveal that their author viewed the constitutional basis of government from an individualist, natural-law point of view. It is the sovereign people upon whose consent government depends. It is not the will of the nation— a general will distinct from the objectives of individuals. The sovereignty of the people is no abstraction. "All men," reads the first draft of the Declaration, "are created equal and independent." Men as independent individuals unite to form governments which are instituted for purposes common to men as individuals. Government is therefore a creature of utility. It possesses no metaphysical spirit of its own. Men institute governments to do certain things for them collectively which they are unable to accomplish individually. What the government may undertake depends upon what men believe necessary to their safety and happiness. "Those of firm health and spirits," observed Jefferson, "are unwilling to cede more of their liberty than is necessary to preserve order, those of feeble constitutions will wish to see one strong arm able to protect them from the many. These are the whigs and tories of nature. These mutual jealousies produce mutual security: and while the laws shall be obeyed all will be safe."[54]

For his own part Jefferson preferred the independence of those of "firm health and spirits," yet he believed that men must relinquish liberties that would impair the liberties of others and ultimately their own. Thus in his "First Inaugural Address," Jefferson found a third occasion to express his constitutional theory and finally to define it by specific illustration. His administration was to be based upon the principles of the Decla-

[53] *Ibid.*, pp. 200–201. Text of the copy in John Adams' handwriting, evidently the original draft of the Declaration and differing somewhat from the draft reported by the congressional committee, the engrossed copy, and the revised copy included by Jefferson in his *Autobiography*.

[54] Note in Jefferson manuscripts possibly intended for use in the "First Inaugural Address" (*ibid.*, IX, 193).

ration of Independence, and, upon undertaking the office of President, he deemed it proper to state in more precise terms the manner in which those principles ought to be expressed. "It is proper you should understand what I deem the essential principles of our Government and consequently those which ought to shape its Administration," he declared. "I will compress them within the narrowest compass they will bear, stating the general principle, but not all its limitations."[55]

Equal and exact justice to all men, of whatever state or persuasions, religious or political; peace, commerce, and honest friendship with all nations, entangling alliances with none; the support of the State governments in all their rights, as the most competent administrations for our domestic concerns, and the surest bulwarks against antirepublican tendencies; the preservation of the General Government in its whole constitutional vigor, as the sheet anchor of our peace at home and safety abroad; a jealous care of the right of election by the people—a mild and safe corrective of abuses which are lopped by the sword of revolution where peaceable remedies are unprovided; absolute acquiescence in the decisions of the majority, the vital principle of republics, from which is no appeal but to force, the vital principle and immediate parent of despotism; a well-disciplined militia, our best reliance in peace and for the first moments of war, till regulars may relieve them; the supremacy of the civil over the military authority; economy in the public expense, that labor may be lightly burthened; the honest payment of our debts and sacred preservation of the public faith; encouragement of agriculture, and of commerce as its handmaid; the diffusion of information and arraignment of all abuses at the bar of the public reason; freedom of religion; freedom of the press, and freedom of person under the protection of the habeas corpus, and trial by juries impartially selected. . . . .[56]

This marshaling of principles might well be termed the "Constitution Democracy," although, like written constitutions generally, it called for interpretation through practice to make its meaning clear. This practical interpretation and commentary Jefferson was himself to provide, and it may be found in the public documents and in the private correspondence of the balance of his career. Of particular importance to an understanding of Jefferson's conception of constitutional government was his notion of the relation between basic natural law and the written constitutions and statutes created by political action.

In his official opinion as Secretary of State upon the question whether the President should veto the bill declaring that the seat of government should be transferred to the Potomac in the year 1790, Jefferson took occasion to explain the way in which natural law became statutory law and the method by which natural rights might be abridged by government:

[55] "First Inaugural Address," March 4, 1801, James D. Richardson (comp.), *A Compilation of the Messages and Papers of the Presidents, 1769–1897* (10 vols.; Washington: Government Printing Office, 1896–1900), I, 323–24.

[56] *Ibid.*

Every man, and every body of men on earth, possesses the right of self-government. They receive it with their being from the hand of nature. Individuals exercise it by their single will; collections of men by that of their majority; for the law of the *majority* is the natural law of every society of men. When a certain description of men are to transact together a particular business, the times and places of their meeting and separating, depend on their own will; they make a part of the natural right of self-government. This, like all other natural rights, may be abridged or modified in its exercise by their own consent, or by the law of those who depute them, if they meet in the right of others; but as far as it is not abridged or modified, they retain it as a natural right, and may exercise them in what form they please, either exclusively by themselves, or in association with others, or by others altogether, as they shall agree.[57]

To the historical accuracy of Jefferson's natural-law theories objections might easily be raised, and, as one of his more penetrating biographers has suggested, his legal notions constituted a "sort of sublimation and legal justification of the pioneer spirit."[58] But the importance of these theories to the history of American law and administration should not be underestimated. Although gradually falling into disrepute among the multitude of lawmakers, administrators, and judges, the Jeffersonian conception of law was embodied in the basic political document of the Republic, the Declaration of Independence, and by virtue of the first ten amendments was incorporated into the Constitution of the United States, which in other respects represented a diminution of the natural-law enthusiasm of 1776.[59]

The natural-rights argument has been pre-eminently an opposition argument and, as such, has served better those who disliked the course of political action than those who were charged with the administration of public affairs. Nevertheless, the argument of Jefferson remained in the patriotic tradition of the nation and could always be drawn upon with good effect in cases where encroachment upon the traditional freedom of the American people was alleged. Thus the body of natural law, natural-rights traditions, although it has afforded a salutary check upon the ambitions of public officials and has been, indeed, an invisible bulwark against the undue centralization of public power, has sometimes been a factor in retarding the extension of public administration to areas where the public welfare seemed to require its services.

[57] "Opinion on Residence Bill," July 15, 1790, *Works*, ed. Ford, VI, 98.

[58] Gilbert Chinard, *Thomas Jefferson, Apostle of Americanism* (Boston: Little Brown & Co., 1929), p. 50.

[59] For a discussion of Jefferson's legal theories see L. K. Caldwell, "The Jurisprudence of Thomas Jefferson," *Indiana Law Journal*, XVIII (April, 1943), 193–213.

The close relationship which Jefferson saw in law to politics strengthened his belief that law must apply political opinion and that, where it fails to reflect the considered judgment of the community, it should no longer be held valid. In this conception of law as an instrument of political action lies the explanation of many of Jefferson's better-known constitutional principles: his opposition to judge-made law, his belief that the laws of one generation could not rightfully bind another, and his insistence on the equal right of the three departments of government to construe the meaning of the law in areas of their respective jurisdiction. He declared that laws and institutions must go hand in hand with the progress of the human mind. Nothing, he believed, was unchangeable "but the inherent and inalienable rights of man."[60]

Within this framework of psychological, political, constitutional, and philosophical ideas, Jefferson developed his theories of public administration. But he did not find it easy to reconcile his notions of a minimized, decentralized state hedged by constitutional limitations derived from natural law with the exigencies of administrative situations. Jefferson in retirement had declared that "every power is dangerous which is not bound up by general rules."[61] Jefferson in power found that authority is not easily confined by mere rules; that his desire to serve the public interest and honestly to adhere to professed principles compelled him on occasions to be inconsistent and even to confess that he had been forced into the paradox of violating some of his principles in order to maintain others. Jefferson's letter of August 12, 1803, to John C. Breckinridge concerning the purchase of Louisiana reveals a curious attempt to combine republican principles with Hamiltonian conduct. "The Executive," he confessed, "have done an act beyond the Constitution."[62] He compared himself to a guardian investing the money of his ward. He could not bind the nation, he admitted, but he was sure that the people would not disavow him.

Although in practice Jefferson brought about a notable expansion of public power through his educational, land, embargo, and foreign policies, yet his political theories considered apart from his actual conduct provided no broad road to expanded administrative authority. Limitations—structural, financial, and philosophical—demanded that every public measure be jealously examined before enactment and that its administration be vested in the unit of government nearest the individuals to be served. Thus the federal Union would be intrusted only with those

---

[60] To John Cartwright, June 5, 1824, *Writings*, ed. Washington, VII, 359.

[61] To Philip Mazzei, November ?, 1785, *Works*, ed. Ford, IV, 480.

[62] *Ibid.*, X, 7.

powers which could not properly be placed elsewhere, and in Jefferson's opinion this was primarily the power to govern foreign relations.

The constitutional doctrines of Jefferson, based on natural-law jurisprudence, tended in practice to restrict rather than to expand the sphere of political activity. The theme of his arguments in the *Summary View*, the Declaration of Independence, and the "First Inaugural Address" was limited government, although his constitutional theories led him to sympathize with revolutions designed to bring the legal order into line with contemporary needs. His continuing major objective in the administrative posts in which he served was to bring public policy into harmony with his political principles, for he held these to be the principles of the majority of his fellow-countrymen. To guide his administration of public affairs upon truly republican lines, Jefferson developed, perhaps unwittingly, certain principles of administration which, though seldom expressed as formal rules for administrative procedure, nevertheless afford a bridge between his political theories and the practical policies and decisions which marked his administrative career.

CHAPTER IX

JEFFERSONIAN PRINCIPLES OF ADMINISTRATION

IN THE development of the general principles which governed his thought on administration Jefferson did not lose sight of the political objectives toward which he believed administration should be directed. It is therefore hardly surprising that Jefferson's interest in government by local majorities, in freedom for the adaptation of institutions to human needs, in the prevention of public extravagance and corruption, and in harmonious unity among men of republican principles should be reflected in his administrative methods. More important, Jefferson's interpretation of administrative responsibility was a formula which made possible both accountability and leadership in the administration of a democratic commonwealth wherein the separation of powers was applied to render policy-making only in part an executive function. Hamilton's administrative principles were formulated to effect the unitary, policy-making administrative system which he hoped America would adopt. Jefferson's principles described the rules by which administrators ought to be guided in the pluralistic system of government to which America adhered. Both sets of principles represent a contribution to administrative theory, although Jefferson does not appear to have developed his ideas with the same acuteness with which Hamilton described the functions of energy, unity, duration, and adequate power in *The Federalist*, Nos. 70–74. That Jefferson was guided by a different set of principles need not suggest that he would have disagreed with Hamilton's rules. Rather it indicates a differing emphasis in Jefferson's administrative thought which one might expect in view of the contrasting political philosophies of the two leaders.

HARMONY

I have thought it among the most fortunate circumstances of my late administration that, during its eight years' continuance, it was conducted with a cordiality and harmony among all the members, which never were ruffled on any, the greatest or smallest occasion.—To WILLIAM DUANE.[1]

Although harmonious co-operation has ever been an objective of administration, not often has it been raised to a principle governing administrative policy. Harmony more often has been a means by which the ends of administration were to be effected rather than an end in itself. With Jefferson, however, harmony was both end and means; it was a principle by which some of his most significant administrative decisions were guided.

Writing to Governor McKean of Pennsylvania near the beginning of his first administration, Jefferson declared that he considered the most perfect harmony and interchange of accommodations and good offices with the state governments as among the first objects of his administration.[2] Within his administrative family Jefferson placed harmony as a major concern. "Indeed, the affectionate harmony of our Cabinet," he later wrote, "is among the sweetest of my recollections."[3] He looked back with peculiar satisfaction, he declared to his former Secretary of the Navy, "on the harmony and cordial good will which, to ourselves and to our brethren of the cabinet, so much sweetened our toils."[4]

The harmony which Jefferson cherished was, however, more apparent than real. Beneath the outward cordiality of the Jefferson cabinet raged a bitter conflict between Albert Gallatin, the Secretary of the Treasury, and Navy Secretary Robert Smith and his friends in the Congress. The actual state of affairs in Jefferson's harmonious cabinet may be gathered from the following remark of Gallatin's concerning Smith's administration of the Navy Department: "On this subject, the expense of the navy greater than

[1] August 12, 1810, *Writings*, ed. Washington, V, 533.

[2] February 2, 1801, *Works*, ed. Ford, IX, 175.

[3] To Caesar Rodney, March 16, 1815, *Writings*, ed. Washington, VI, 448.

[4] To Robert Smith, June 10, 1809, *ibid.*, V, 451.

the object seemed to require, and a merely nominal accountability, I have, for the sake of preserving perfect harmony in your councils, however grating to my feelings, been almost uniformly silent; and I beg that you will ascribe what I now say to a sense of duty and to the grateful attachment I feel for you."[5] During his two terms as President, Jefferson's personal authority held the discordant elements in abeyance, but upon his retirement the conflict became public and culminated in the attempted resignation of Gallatin and in the dismissal of Robert Smith from the Madison cabinet in 1811. To disharmony within and without his official family Jefferson lent a deaf ear. Writing to Dr. George Logan, he held that "the duty of an upright administration is to pursue its course steadily, to know nothing of these family dissensions."[6]

Recognizing the necessity for sacrificing personal opinion in the interest of harmony, Jefferson was prepared to set an example to his party. The stormy career of Alexander Hamilton was evidence to testify to the inharmonious results of energetic policy. Jefferson proposed to refrain as far as possible from errors of commission. "The path we have to pursue is so quiet that we have nothing scarcely to propose to our Legislature," he wrote to his friend Thomas Cooper; "a noiseless course, not meddling with the affairs of others, unattractive of notice, is a mark that society is going on in happiness."[7] But though his temperamental aversion to controversy and his recognition of the need for legislative-executive harmony in effective government might indicate a policy of political quietism, Jefferson's urge to leadership impelled his pursuit of policies which could scarcely be followed along "a noiseless course." Louisiana, war with Tripoli, patronage controversies, and, finally, the embargo represented a trend of policy which could hardly be described as "unattractive of notice."

Jefferson's difficulties in preserving a harmonious administration derived from those same faults in the constitutional relations between the executive and legislative branches which had baffled Washington and contributed to the frustration of Hamilton. But it was Jefferson, through the development and control of a political party, who first discovered the way in which the constitutional separation of powers could be made to serve the ends of responsible government. And so the principle of harmony became not only a maxim of administrative procedure but also a measure of party discipline. To the recalcitrant Republican editor, William Duane, Jefferson recalled that the harmonious unity of the party had been the constant

---

[5] May 30, 1805, *The Writings of Albert Gallatin*, ed. Henry Adams (3 vols.; Philadelphia: J. B. Lippincott & Co., 1879), I, 234.

[6] May 11, 1805, *Works*, ed. Ford, X, 142–43.   [7] November 29, 1802, *ibid.*, IX, 403.

theme of his exhortations and recommended that, "while our functionaries are wise, and honest, and vigilant, let us move compactly under their guidance, and we have nothing to fear."[8]

The utilization of party discipline to effect harmony in policy-making implied the exercise of the presidential patronage power with a view to party regularity as well as to administrative efficiency. Indeed, the utilization of the party system to promote administrative purposes rendered considerations of party harmony and administrative effectiveness nearly inseparable. It is therefore difficult to appraise Jefferson's use of the patronage power to preserve party unity solely in terms of its consequences for the administrative personnel of the federal government. Carl Russell Fish may have overemphasized the genesis of the spoils system under Jefferson's administration, but Jefferson's efforts to conciliate all branches of his party without particular regard to the moral integrity of factional leaders led to a decline in the care with which public offices were filled, and hence to a lowered respect for the civil service which prepared the way for avowed spoils politics in the decades ahead.[9] Although Jefferson professed to know no differences between party factions in the distribution of public trusts, it was this aloofness which permitted him to overlook the abuse of public office by the unscrupulous masters of machine politics in New York and Philadelphia, where his party had become strong. Under such circumstances impartiality toward all partisan groups meant in practice the support of those ill-deserving of the confidence of the people.

Through this effort to maintain administrative effectiveness Jefferson introduced the factor of legislative leadership through party control into the American presidency. The administrations of Washington and Adams had revealed an unwillingness on the part of the Congresses to accept an interpretation of the constitutional separation of powers which would vest the responsibility for policy-making in the executive branch. The attempts of the congressional leaders to direct the formulation of administrative policy over the opposition of President John Adams clearly demonstrated that any President who failed to exercise commanding legislative influence was in danger of being rendered powerless to fulfil the actual duties of office.

Given a constitutional system which seemed to place Congress and the President in potential opposition, Jefferson's insistence upon political harmony at the possible expense of administrative efficiency does not seem unreasonable. The degree to which executive patronage was required to

[8] March 28, 1811, *ibid.*, XI, 194.

[9] Carl Russell Fish, *The Civil Service and the Patronage* (Cambridge: Harvard University Press, 1921).

effect this harmony remained a problem for future administrations, but it was in Jefferson's presidency that the problem of the relation of politics to the public service assumed the form in which it was to be most manifest during the century ahead.

SIMPLICITY

The accounts of the United States ought to be, and may be made as simple as those of a common farmer, and capable of being understood by common farmers.—To JAMES MADISON.[10]

Simplicity in the administration of public affairs was a first principle with Jefferson. Believing that public functionaries readily seized upon the opportunities of public office for aggrandizement of power, prestige, and fortune, he proposed to reduce to the minimum the occasions for public corruption. He did not encourage any but the ablest men to seek public appointment; he favored low wages and short terms and the abolition of offices wherever possible. "Our public economy also is such as to offer drudgery and subsistence only to those entrusted with its administration," he explained; "a wise and necessary precaution against the degeneracy of the public servants."[11] Civic duty rather than rewards of money or power should be the incentives for a public career. In part, Jefferson's insistence that public administration be reduced to the simplest possible form reflected a belief that the administration of public affairs was in fact a simple matter. There are no mysteries in public administration, he declared. "Difficulties indeed arise; but common sense and honest intentions will generally steer through them, and, where they cannot be surmounted, I have ever seen the well-intentioned part of our fellow citizens sufficiently disposed not to look for impossibilities."[12] To James Sullivan he declared that "the ordinary affairs of a nation offer little difficulty to a person of any experience."[13]

Accordingly, Jefferson did not believe that a large and complicated public administrative system was necessary or desirable. "I am for a government rigorously frugal and simple,"[14] he declared. Extravagance and complexity were charges he leveled at the Federalists, and upon his accession to the presidential office he held it the duty of his administration "to reform the prodigalities of our predecessors . . . . and to bring the government to a simple and economical course."[15] To a French correspondent he

[10] March 6, 1796, *Writings*, ed. Washington, IV, 131.
[11] To M. DeMeusnier, April 29, 1795, *Works*, ed. Ford, VIII, 174.
[12] To Dr. J. B. Stuart, May 10, 1817, *Writings*, ed. Washington, VII, 64.
[13] March 3, 1808, *ibid.*, V, 252.
[14] To Elbridge Gerry, January 26, 1799, *Works*, ed. Ford, IX, 18.
[15] To James Monroe, January 13, 1803, *Writings*, ed. Washington, IV, 455.

wrote of his administration that "we are endeavoring too to reduce the government to the practice of a rigorous economy, to avoid burthening the people, and arming the magistrate with a patronage of money, which might be used to corrupt and undermine the principles of our government."[16] He declared himself against the multiplication of salaries merely to make partisans and held that "the multiplication of public offices, increase of expense beyond income, growth and entailment of a public debt, are indications soliciting the employment of the pruning-knife."[17]

Jefferson's letters and public addresses are filled with the insistence on a plain and frugal government, and the influence of his emphasis in this respect upon the history of administrative thought cannot be doubted; but, in spite of his insistence on a reduced civil service, the personnel of government tended to increase. In his old age Jefferson continued to oppose expanded government. "I think, myself," he declared, "that we have more machinery of government than is necessary, too many parasites living on the labor of the industrious," and, he added, "I believe it might be much simplified to the relief of those who maintain it."[18]

Yet Jefferson did not believe that simplicity in government required that the public be denied benefits which only government could confer. Thus he advocated the public support of schools, universities, and libraries in the several states, and in his second presidential term, when in the face of a Treasury surplus he might have proposed a reduction in federal taxation, he proposed instead to distribute federal funds among the states to be expended on useful public works. Nevertheless, the tenor of Jefferson's pronouncements on simplicity in government was calculated to discourage unproductive public spending so that, as he declared in his first annual message to Congress, "it may never be seen here that, after leaving to labor the smallest portion of its earnings on which it can subsist, government shall itself consume the residue of what it was instituted to guard."[19]

ADAPTABILITY

This I hope will be the age of experiments in government.—To John Adams.[20]

The degree of permanence which one attributes to administrative institutions and practices is likely to qualify one's attitude toward administration. Jefferson did not believe that permanent political or administrative

[16] To M. Pictet, February 5, 1803, *ibid.*, p. 463.

[17] To Spencer Roane, March 9, 1821, *Works*, ed. Ford, XII, 201.

[18] To William Ludlow, September 6, 1824, *Writings*, ed. Washington, VII, 378.

[19] December 8, 1801, *Works*, ed. Ford, IX, 335–36.

[20] February 28, 1796, *ibid.*, VIII, 219.

arrangements could be or ought to be possible. Each generation had, in his opinion, the right to form its political arrangements to its own liking. Thus precedent and tradition were discounted, and fixed statutory, economic, or constitutional arrangements deemed contrary to the natural rights of men. These natural rights alone were permanent—political methods and institutions were merely temporary arrangements which men should be free to alter with time and experience.

"In so complicated a science as political economy," wrote Jefferson to Benjamin Austin, "no one axiom can be laid down as wise and expedient for all times and circumstances."[21] Jefferson believed that there must be a progressive change in political institutions to meet the needs of successive generations: "Laws and institutions must go hand in hand with the progress of the human mind. As that becomes more developed, more enlightened, as new discoveries are made, new truths disclosed, and manners and opinions change with the change of circumstances, institutions must advance also, and keep pace with the times."[22] Each generation, Jefferson averred, "has the usufruct of the earth during the period of its continuance. When it ceases to exist, the usufruct passes on to the succeeding generation, free and unencumbered, and so on, successively, from one generation to another forever." We may, he added, "consider each generation as a distinct nation, with a right, by the will of its majority, to bind themselves, but none to bind the succeeding generation, more than the inhabitants of another country."[23]

Jefferson's insistence upon the adaptation of institutions to circumstances indicated a pragmatic approach to problems of administrative organization. Within the confines of the states Jefferson believed that circumstances dictated a decentralized control of domestic affairs, with limitations in the main construed against the extension of public administration. In the territories beyond the states the absence of effective local political units and the character and distribution of the population indicated far-reaching federal controls which Jefferson proposed as readily there as he would have opposed the same measures within the geographical limits of the states.[24] So far, therefore, as Jefferson's philosophy of adaptation bears upon the administration of government, it is apparent that his influence was essentially liberating.

[21] January 9, 1816, *ibid.*, XI, 505.   [22] To Samuel Kercheval, July 12, 1816, *ibid.*, XII, 12.

[23] To John Wayles Eppes, June 24, 1813, *ibid.*, XI, 298.

[24] See, e.g., Jefferson's drafts of constitutional amendments to govern the Louisiana territory (*ibid.*, X, 3–12) and his report on the proposed government of the territory northwest of the Ohio River (*ibid.*, IV, 251–55).

DECENTRALIZATION

. . . . it is not by the consolidation or concentration of powers, but by their distribution, that good government is effected.—"AUTOBIOGRAPHY."[25]

Of the foregoing principles which governed Jefferson's administrative thought, none could truthfully be said to have fundamentally altered the course of administrative development in American government. Harmony, simplicity, adaptability—all strongly marked Jefferson's thinking on administrative problems, but they represented personal predilections for administrative arrangements rather than a coherent and systematic theory of administration. In effect the principle of decentralization differed sharply from the others. It, indeed, reflected a personal preference for local control of political affairs and evidenced a highly subjective distrust of professionalized administration and complex administrative machinery, but it was a principle capable of being expressed in objective terms, susceptible of concrete application in constitutions and statutes and in the platforms of political parties.

"In government, as well as every other business of life, it is by division and subdivision of duties alone," he asserted, "that all matters, great and small, can be managed to perfection."[26] By a decentralization of duties he held that every citizen personally might partake in the administration of public affairs, thus insuring the maximum degree of republicanism in government. Accordingly, he held it an axiom that good administration would provide for the greatest degree of decentralization possible to the successful execution of public policy. To those who asserted that decentralization of authority would weaken the federal Union, Jefferson declared "that government to be the strongest of which every man feels himself a part."[27] To Jefferson only a decentralized government could be free, and "a free government," he declared, "is of all others the most energetic."[28]

Jefferson never ceased to identify centralized government with arbitrary and oppressive rule. Writing to his friend and mentor, John Taylor, he declared: "While our State governments are the very *best in the world*, without exception or comparison our general government has, in the rapid course of nine or ten years, become more arbitrary, and has swallowed more of the public liberty than even that of England."[29] In the Kentucky Resolutions Jefferson expressed the constitutional basis for decentralized

---

[25] *Ibid.*, I, 122.   [26] To Samuel Kercheval, July 12, 1816, *ibid.*, XII, 9.

[27] To Governor H. D. Tiffin, February 2, 1807, *Writings*, ed. Washington, V, 38.

[28] To John Dickinson, March 6, 1801, *Works*, ed. Ford, IX, 202.

[29] November 26, 1798, *ibid.*, VIII, 481.

government which he held the true public law of the Union. He held the central government bound by the special delegations and reservations solemnly agreed to in the federal compact. Although the circumstances of the Resolutions and popular constitutional theory required the justification of state resistance to federal authority on grounds of states' rights, the fundamental principle which Jefferson defended was not states' rights so much as decentralized government.

Jefferson never overcame his hostility to centralization. "Consolidation is but toryism in disguise,"[30] he declared, and maintained that it had destroyed the liberty and rights of man in every government which had ever existed. He hoped "never to see all offices transferred to Washington, where, further withdrawn from the eyes of the people, they may more secretly be bought and sold as at market."[31] Yet, toward the close of his career, he saw the federal government "now taking so steady a course as to show by what road it will pass to destruction, to wit, by consolidation first, and then corruption, its necessary consequence."[32]

How far this centralizing trend might go without destroying the constitutional structure of the Union, Jefferson did not know. Though he believed the trend should be resisted, the dissolution of the Union he deemed only the last resource. Separation he held should come only when the "sole alternatives left, are the dissolution of our Union . . . . , or submission to a government without limitation of powers."[33] That the fatal consequences of centralization could be avoided he had little hope. Yet he did not entirely despair that the decentralized republic for which he had labored might be restored. In the last months of his life he wrote: "Although I have little hope that the torrent of consolidation can be withstood, I should not be for giving up the ship without efforts to save her. She lived well through the first squall, and may weather the present one."[34]

RESPONSIBILITY

In questions of power . . . . let no more be heard of confidence in man, but bind him down from mischief by the chains of the Constitution.—KENTUCKY RESOLUTIONS (1798).[35]

Although Jefferson described responsibility as "a tremendous engine in a free government,"[36] he did not believe that any single interpretation of

[30] To Nathaniel Macon, February 21, 1826, *ibid.*, XII, 460.

[31] To William Johnson, June 12, 1823, *ibid.*, pp. 258–59.

[32] To Nathaniel Macon, October 20, 1821, *ibid.*, pp. 208.

[33] To William Branch Giles, December 26, 1825, *ibid.*, p. 426.

[34] To C. W. Gooch, January 9, 1826, *Writings*, ed. Washington, VII, 430.

[35] *Works*, ed. Ford, VIII, 475.   [36] To Archibald Stuart, December 23, 1791, *ibid.*, VI, 351.

responsible conduct was applicable to all administrative situations. Jeffersonian responsibility was essentially an effort to insure the accountability of public servants to the public and yet to provide for the exercise of the judgment and initiative of statesmen on behalf of the public welfare. Therefore, in his definition of responsibility, Jefferson qualified the strict accountability of public officers for a literal conformity to the law with a most important exception governing the conduct of high officers of state in times of crises.

Denying that responsibility required that public officers be permitted a flexible exercise of powers under ordinary circumstances, Jefferson asked: "Is confidence or discretion, or is *strict limit*, the principle of our Constitution?"[37] He believed that limitation was the only correct principle of responsible power; a written constitution and supplementary statutes should prescribe certain explicit duties of public officers and provide certain means for accomplishing what the law required. Responsibility, as understood by Jefferson, implied administration closely checked by legal requirements and exactions, whereas Hamilton's theory of responsibility had the opposite result of vesting top administrators with a wide latitude of discretion in ordinary as well as extraordinary circumstances. Jefferson most clearly, though indirectly, defined his notion of responsibility in the Kentucky Resolutions of 1798, declaring that "free government is founded in jealousy, and not in confidence."[38]

Yet Jefferson did not discount the necessity for public confidence in administrators. In the Kentucky Resolutions he had described confidence as the "parent of despotism," and in his inaugural address in 1801 he guarded his request for confidence, saying, "I ask so much confidence only as may give firmness and effect to the legal administration of your affairs."[39] However, as his administration proceeded, his requests for confidence reflected less the austere patriot of 1798 and more the public servant eager for approval. In 1807 he wrote to Dr. Horatio Turpin that the energy of the government, "depending mainly on the confidence of the people in the chief magistrate, makes it his duty to spare nothing which can strengthen him with that confidence."[40] Thus did Jefferson confess it his duty to pursue what less than a decade before he had denounced as the "parent of despotism." "In a government like ours it is necessary to embrace in its administration as great a mass of public confidence as possible,"[41] wrote the states-

[37] To Jedediah Morse, March 6, 1822, *ibid.*, XII, 224.

[38] *Ibid.*, VIII, 474.   [39] March 4, 1801, *ibid.*, IX, 199.

[40] June 10, 1807, *Writings*, ed. Washington, V, 90.

[41] April 15, 1806, *The Anas, Works*, ed. Ford, I, 391–92.

man who had once declared: "Let no more be heard of confidence in man."[42] It is evident from an examination of his writings after 1801 that, although confidence might not substitute for responsibility, it was nevertheless essential to the success of public administration. In his last years Jefferson wrote to President Monroe, "It is not wisdom alone but public confidence in that wisdom which can support an administration."[43]

If administration must possess public confidence, and confidence obtained only from a disinterested execution of the law in conformity with the law, the successful Jeffersonian administrator was not likely to pioneer administrative frontiers. But, to Jefferson, confidence in the highest officers of the state required of them a conception of responsibility which exceeded the narrow limits of discretion by which lesser officials should be confined:

> A strict observance of the written laws is doubtless *one* of the high duties of a good citizen, but it is not *the highest*. The laws of necessity, of self-preservation, of saving our country when in danger, are of higher obligation. To lose our country by a scrupulous adherence to written law, would be to lose the law itself, with life, liberty, property and all those who are enjoying them with us; thus absurdly sacrificing the end to the means.

.   .   .   .

> From these examples and principles you may see what I think on the question proposed. They do not go to the case of persons charged with petty duties, where consequences are trifling, and time allowed for a legal course, nor to authorize them to take such cases out of the written law. In these, the example of overleaping the law is of greater evil than a strict adherence to its imperfect provisions. It is incumbent on those only who accept of great charges, to risk themselves on great occasions, when the safety of the nation, or some of its very high interests are at stake. An officer is bound to obey orders; yet he would be a bad one who should do it in cases for which they were not intended, and which involved the most important consequences. The line of discrimination between cases may be difficult; but the good officer is bound to draw it at his own peril, and throw himself on the justice of his country and the rectitude of his motives.[44]

Thus Jefferson held that the duty of the chief executive to enforce the provisions of the Constitution took precedence over observance of the statutory requirements of the legislature and might justify violation of those requirements if incompatible with the executive's larger duty.[45] Where the purpose of legislative action was impeded by contradictory or inadequate measures for execution, the chief executive—or governor—was justified in times of crises in deviating from legislative prescription to effect the intent

---

[42] Kentucky Resolutions (1798), *ibid.*, VIII, 475.

[43] July 18, 1824, *ibid.* (1892 ed.), X, 316.

[44] To John B. Colvin, September 20, 1810, *ibid.* (1904–5 ed.), XI, 146, 149.

[45] To Judge Spencer Roane, September 6, 1819, *ibid.*, XII, 137–39.

of the lawmakers by other legitimate means.[46] Yet this latitude of executive discretion represented the exception rather than the rule, for the weight of Jefferson's opinion was against the discretionary use of power. He recognized the need for a degree of executive freedom in the choice of administrative methods, and he stood for the independence of the executive branch from legislative or judicial interference, yet he also held it "inconsistent with the principles of civil liberty, and contrary to the natural rights of the other members of the society, that any body of men therein should have authority to enlarge their own powers, prerogatives, or emoluments without restraint."[47]

Strict limitation of powers became, therefore, the ordinary rule by which administrative responsibility was exacted, and confidence in the republican character of the government required that public officers on all but extraordinary occasions be held to the rules as stated by the people's representatives in the legislature and by the Constitution of the commonwealth. But Jefferson wisely left open the door for leadership in times of common peril, for popular confidence could hardly be retained by a political system designed only for fair weather. Thus Jefferson acted within the logic of his principles when he exceeded his statutory powers in the purchase of Louisiana, when he chose to defend Americans against the depredations of the Tripoli pirates without a congressional declaration of war, and when he ordered the seizure and transportation of the Burr conspirators in New Orleans in disregard of the written law of the territory.[48] And it is this principle of responsibility, now generally accepted by the American people, which has throughout the history of the Republic united security from arbitrary and irresponsible administration in times of peace with executive responsibility for energetic and effective leadership in times of danger.

Although one cannot gauge the extent to which Jefferson's administrative principles, other than decentralization and responsibility, affected the course of American administrative thought, there is no doubt that they presaged the actual developments of the American political system. As long as the American people disliked taxes and could refuse to vote them, simplicity in government was unavoidable. The rise of the political party system made harmony in the administration of public affairs something more

[46] To W. H. Cabell, August 11, 1807, *Writings*, ed. Washington, V, 158–59.

[47] "A Bill for Giving the Members of the Assembly an Adequate Allowance," December 12, 1778, *Works*, ed. Ford, II, 347–48.

[48] Illustrative of Jefferson's notion of responsibility was his suggestion to John Adams in July, 1785, that the two ministers exceed their instructions from Congress in order to secure more favorable terms in projected treaties with the European powers (see letter to John Adams, July 28 and 31, *Works* [Memorial ed.], V, 42, 46–49).

than the preference of an amiable Virginian gentleman. The rise of sectionalism, particularly after 1820, insured resistance to the centralizing trend of Jefferson's "monarchial-federalists" for years to come. If Jefferson's "age of experiments in government" fell short of its potentialities, the necessity and desirability of institutional change remained a theme, though not the main theme, in American administrative thought. The half-century between the retirement of President Jefferson and the inauguration of President Lincoln was marked by the administration of the Union mainly in conformity with Jeffersonian principles. And this half-century left an impression upon American practices and ideas too deep to be easily effaced by the partial return of Hamiltonian theories to public favor after 1861. The summation of Jeffersonian administrative principles was limited government; and, although under the exigencies of political crises the American people have been willing to allow the chief executive almost unlimited authority to protect the public interest, as Jefferson himself recommended, they have never rejected his basic assumptions concerning the limitations of public power. The student and practitioner of public administration in America accordingly can ignore Jeffersonian principles only at the peril of seriously misunderstanding a traditional disposition of public opinion toward the personnel and practice of the public service.

CHAPTER X

PUBLIC ADMINISTRATION AND THE DISTRIBUTION
OF AUTHORITY

IN THE foregoing chapter emphasis has been given to Jefferson's preference for decentralized government. Yet, because Jefferson opposed the centralization of public authority in the national government, one should not infer that he was less thoroughgoing a nationalist than Alexander Hamilton. Jefferson's nationalism contrasted with Hamilton's in its emphasis on the preservation of the political freedom of Americans rather than on the necessity for a unitary administrative structure and policy. Hamilton wished to make America strong by uniting the national strength under the directive power of the national government. Jefferson would insure the strength and permanence of the federal Union by developing the freedom and responsibility of the states and localities to work together for the realization of mutually beneficial ends. But this decentralized co-operative commonwealth needed a strong and unified leadership in matters of common concern, and therefore in the areas which he thought proper to its jurisdiction Jefferson would grant the national government powers as extensive as he believed the national interests required.

Although Jefferson stood for government of restricted scope, he favored limits broad enough to include the public needs, and he insisted that the limits be amendable to enlarge or confine the area of public policy in accordance with the will of the majority. He agreed with Hamilton that "undefined powers are discretionary powers, limited only by the object for which they were given,"[1] but he believed that, unless those objects be clearly defined and sanctioned by the electorate, discretion would degenerate into license. Jefferson was no enemy to power, public or private, but he was an implacable opponent of the abuse of power and was keenly aware of the tendency in men to use power for ends incompatible with the general good.

Jefferson believed that the control of power was best effected by its proper distribution. Certain powers, notably the conduct of foreign relations, he would centralize in the executive branch of the national government. Other powers, particularly those involving public works, he would decentralize as to actual construction but centralize as regards over-all planning and direction. The ordinary police powers of day-to-day concern he would completely decentralize into local communities. Accordingly, Jefferson's preference for decentralized government was not inconsistent with a considerable exercise of centralized authority, for it was neither the concentration nor diffusion but the proper *distribution* of power that Jefferson believed characterized good government.

THE UNION, THE TERRITORIES, AND THE STATES

The best general key for the solution of questions of power between our governments, is the fact that "every foreign and federal power is given to the federal government, and to the States every power purely domestic." . . . . The federal is, in truth, our foreign government, which department alone is taken from the sovereignty of the separate States.—To ROBERT J. GARNETT.[2]

Jefferson's love of simple distinctions was well served by his notion that American government comprised two clear divisions: a national government for foreign affairs and the state governments to administer domestic concerns. In his address to the Rhode Island Assembly in 1801 he declared that "to the united nation belong our external and mutual relations; to each State, severally, the care of our persons, our property, our reputation,

[1] To James Duane, September 3, 1780, *Works*, ed. Lodge, I, 215.

[2] February 14, 1824, *Works*, ed. Ford, XII, 342.

and religious freedom." This wise distribution Jefferson held would prove that "while smaller governments are better adapted to the ordinary objects of society, larger confederations more effectually secure independence and the preservation of republican government."[3]

Jefferson's description of the Union as a confederation was neither mere rhetoric nor accident. In a letter to Judge Spencer Roane written in 1821 he rejected the notion that either the federal government or the states enjoyed a balance of superior power in the Union, and described the states as being independent as different nations in matters of domestic concern.[4] Yet the fact that Jefferson viewed the states as in certain respects distinct nations adds meaning to his description of the federal government as instituted chiefly for foreign affairs. Writing to Edward Livingston in 1824, he declared that "the radical idea" of the Constitution which he adopted as a key in cases of doubtful construction was that the whole field of government was divided into two departments, "domestic and foreign (the states in their mutual relations being of the latter)."[5] Thus the entire field of interstate relations—variously described by Jefferson as "mutual" or "federal" concerns—was distinguished in his mind from purely "domestic" or intrastate matters. Interstate relations were therefore a modified species of foreign affairs. "I recollect no case," declared Jefferson, "where a question simply between citizens of the same State, has been transferred to the foreign department, except that of inhibiting tenders but of metallic money, and *ex post facto* legislation."[6] The great advantage in this delineation of state and federal powers lay in its flexibility, a consideration in keeping with Jefferson's administrative principles. For as the area of interstate concern expanded with the growth of commerce, industry, and agriculture, the activities of the general government could properly expand to meet the common needs in those matters wherein it had been granted jurisdiction.

Jefferson was fully aware of the desirability of nation-wide uniformity in the treatment of many matters not subject to federal jurisdiction. Congratulating James Sullivan upon his election as Republican governor of Massachusetts, he expressed his satisfaction in "the harmony it has introduced between the legislative and executive branches, between the people and both of them, and between all and the General government."[7] This harmony, Jefferson declared, made for "that union of action and effort in all its parts, without which no nation can be happy or safe."[8] But it was

[3] May 26, 1801, *Writings*, ed. Washington, IV, 398.

[4] June 27, 1821, *Works*, ed. Ford, XII, 203.

[5] April 4, 1824, *ibid.*, p. 349.

[6] *Ibid.*

[7] June 19, 1807, *ibid.*, X, 420.

[8] *Ibid.*

by means of political solidarity and intergovernmental harmony rather than through administrative centralization that this desirable unity was to be realized. Jefferson agreed with Governor Sullivan's proposal for closer working relations between the President and the state executives and took occasion to express his own notion of how national unity and decentralized government might be harmoniously effected.

> Your opinion of the propriety and advantage of a more intimate correspondence between the executives of the several States, and that of the Union, as a central point, is precisely that which I have ever entertained; and on coming into office I felt the advantages which would result from that harmony. I had it even in contemplation, after the annual recommendation to Congress of those measures called for by the times, which the Constitution had placed under their power to make communications in like manner to the executives of the States, as to any parts of them to which the legislatures might be alone competent. For many are the exercises of power reserved to the States, wherein an uniformity of proceeding would be advantageous to all. Such are quarantines, health laws, regulations of the press, banking institutions, training militia, &c., &c.[9]

Although Jefferson was deterred by political considerations from his proposed annual message to the executives of the states, he never doubted his constitutional authority to make such recommendations, for he declared that "as to the portions of power within each state assigned to the general government, the President is as much the Executive of the State, as their particular governor is in relation to State powers."[10] Where the independent or reserved rights of the states were concerned, Jefferson held that state and federal executives "if they are to act together, must be exactly coordinate," for in those cases he deemed each "the supreme head of an independent government."[11] However, in cases involving federal powers, Jefferson believed that "the general executive is certainly pre-ordinate" and that a state governor must be subject to receive orders from the federal department heads "as any other subordinate officer would."[12]

Jefferson hoped that the states and the central government would in time establish a beautiful equilibrium "unexampled but in the planetary system itself,"[13] but he feared that the balance of power was likely to be upset by one or the other of the major divisions. Under the old Confederation the states had disturbed the federal equilibrium, and Jefferson be-

[9] *Ibid.*, pp. 420–21.

[10] To Mr. Goodnow, June 13, 1822, *Works*, ed. Washington, VII, 251–52.

[11] To James Monroe, May 29, 1801, *Works*, ed. Ford, IX, 261.

[12] *Ibid.*   [13] To Peregrine Fitzhugh, February 23, 1798, *ibid.*, VIII, 377.

lieved that some provision for enforcing federal authority should be provided. By 1798, however, he believed that a contrary situation had developed and that too little respect was accorded the states by the Federalist administration of the national government.

The theory of two co-ordinate powers, foreign and domestic, neither having control over the other but in its own department, Jefferson explained frequently and at length, for he believed that some Americans and most foreigners misunderstood the American system, assuming that the states were in every instance subordinate to the Union.[14] This co-ordinate division of power he held to be one of the two sheet anchors of the Union—and it is apparent that he could not but oppose the centralizing tendencies of Hamilton which would have cut away the one anchor entirely. The other anchor was the republican form of government, and Jefferson believed that in the destruction of the constitutional division of powers Hamilton in fact aimed at the subversion of republicanism. This Jeffersonian interpretation of the structure of the Union and of Hamiltonian politics partly explains, as Henry Adams has observed, why Jefferson thought his assumption of power in 1801 to be "as real a revolution in the principles of our government as that of 1776 was in its form."[15]

Between the government of the states and the government of federal territories Jefferson drew a sharp distinction. The lands northwest of the Ohio River, and in the old southwest and trans-Mississippi areas, Jefferson viewed as held in trust for their future inhabitants by the federal government. He would not accord the territorial inhabitants the latitude of local control which he deemed rightful to the citizens of states. The federal government, he believed, should take positive measures to insure the future welfare of the states-to-be. Accordingly, he favored congressional prohibition of slavery in the northwest territories and held it proper that Congress require the setting-aside of public lands to support a portion of the cost of future public education.[16]

In recommending provision for the government of the territory of Louisiana, Jefferson opposed the doctrinaire republicanism of the majority in Congress, who, as he wrote to DeWitt Clinton, "cannot bring them-

[14] E.g., letters cited to Spencer Roane, June 27, 1821; Edward Livingston, April 4, 1824; William Johnson, June 12, 1823; also to James Madison, December 20, 1787; to E. Carrington, August 4, 1787; to Elbridge Gerry, January 26, 1799; to Samuel H. Smith, August 2, 1823; to John Cartwright, June 5, 1824.

[15] Henry Adams, *History of the United States during the Administration of Thomas Jefferson* (2 vols.; New York: Albert & Charles Boni, 1930), Book I, p. 216.

[16] "Report of Government for the Western Territory," March 22, 1784, *Works*, ed. Ford, IV, 275; to James Monroe, August 28, 1785, *ibid.*, p. 454.

selves to suspend its principles for a single moment."[17] He described the inhabitants of Louisiana "as yet as incapable of self-government as children"[18] and believed that a period of preparation for the responsibilities of self-government was necessary.

The constitutional amendment which Jefferson prepared for use, if necessary, to legalize the annexation of Louisiana reveals the great authority which he would permit to the federal government in the administration of the territory. He would have the government authorized "to work salt springs, or mines of coal, metals and other minerals within the possession of the United States, or in any others with the consent of the possessors; to regulate trade and intercourse between the Indian inhabitants and all other persons; to explore and ascertain the geography of the province, its productions and other interesting circumstances; to open roads and navigation therein where necessary for beneficial communication; and to establish agencies and factories therein for the cultivation of commerce, peace and good understanding with the Indians residing there."[19]

Thus Jefferson's theory of distribution of powers appears motivated not essentially by the philosophy of political laissez faire but primarily by considerations of constitutional law and decentralization. In the absence of an effective local government, as in the territories, he would permit an extensive exercise of power by the central government and would sanction the enactment of congressional measures which might qualify the right of subsequent state legislatures fully to determine their own constitutional law. Thus Jefferson appears as a practical theorist rather than a doctrinaire visionary. He sought certain results from government— chiefly the freedom and welfare of individuals—and, although he held strongly defined notions about how these ends were best obtained, he was willing to put aside his preferences where a satisfactory result seemed more readily obtainable under other methods.

By ultimate extension of statehood to the territories, Jefferson saw the steady growth of the federal Republic. "Who can limit the extent to which the federative principle may operate effectively," he exclaimed.[20] "The larger our association, the less will it be shaken by local passions."[21] Nor did the Missouri struggle of 1821, though it filled him with fear for the future, alter his convictions that expansion would strengthen the bond of

[17] December 2, 1803, ibid., X, 55.

[18] Ibid.

[19] "Drafts of an Amendment to the Constitution," July, 1803, ibid., pp. 9–11.

[20] "Second Inaugural Address," March 4, 1805, ibid., p. 131.   [21] Ibid.

union. In 1821 he expressed his belief to Henry Dearborn that "the Western extension of our Confederacy will ensure its duration, by overruling local factions, which might shake a smaller association."[22]

In his theory of the internal organization of the states themselves, Jefferson's decentralizing principle was most emphatically expressed. In a detailed letter to Samuel Kercheval written July 12, 1816, Jefferson set forth the plan of organization which he believed most certain to establish and to maintain republican government. Because of the insight into his thought on administration which these recommendations provide, they are worthy of citation at length:

> The organization of our county administrations may be thought more difficult. But follow principle, and the knot unties itself. Divide the counties into wards of such size as that every citizen can attend, when called on, and act in person. Ascribe to them the government of their wards in all things relating to themselves exclusively. A justice, chosen by themselves, in each, a constable a military company, a patrol, a school, the care of their own poor, their own portion of the public roads, the choice of one or more jurors to serve in some court, and the delivery, within their own wards, of their own votes for all elective officers of higher sphere, will relieve the county administration of nearly all its business, will have it better done, and by making every citizen an acting member of the government, and in the offices nearest and most interesting to him, will attach him by his strongest feelings to the independence of his country, and its republican constitution. . . . . We should thus marshal our government into, 1, the general federal republic, for all concerns foreign and federal; 2, that of the State, for what relates to our own citizens exclusively; 3, the county republics, for the duties and concerns of the county; and, 4, the ward republics, for the small, and yet numerous and interesting concerns of the neighborhood; and in government, as well as in every other business of life, it is by division and subdivision of duties alone, that all matters, great and small, can be managed to perfection. And the whole is cemented by giving to every citizen, personally, a part in the administration of the public affairs.[23]

This plan of government by wards was in fact the New England township system, which Jefferson described to Kercheval as "the wisest invention ever devised by the wit of man for the perfect exercise of self-government."[24] He declared that, in the case of the embargo, "I felt the foundations of the Government shaken under my feet by the New England townships,"[25] and he attributed the overthrow of his embargo policy to the articulate opposition of the misguided but thoroughly representative town

[22] August 17, 1821, *ibid.*, XII, 206.

[23] *Ibid.*, pp. 8–9. See also letter to John Tyler, May 26, 1810, *ibid.*, XI, 143, for a similar exposition on decentralized administration.

[24] July 12, 1816, *ibid.*, XII, 9.

[25] To J. C. Cabell, February 2, 1816, *Writings*, ed. Washington, VI, 5–44.

meetings. Call a county meeting in Virginia, he lamented, "and the drunken loungers at and about the court houses would have collected, the distances being too great for the good people and the industrious generally to attend." The character of those who really met, he added, "would have been the measure of weight they would have had in the scale of public opinion."[26] "As Cato, then, concluded every speech with the words 'Carthago delenda est,' " he admonished, "so do I every opinion, with the injunction, 'divide the counties into wards.' "[27]

By the general adoption of the ward system Jefferson hoped to accomplish two major objectives relating to administration: first, to vest the management of the greatest number of common concerns in a governmental unit subject directly to the oversight and control of the people and, second, to avoid the creation of a bureaucracy of professional holders of public office by giving each citizen, to the greatest practical extent, a personal share in the business of public administration. The decentralization of political and administrative authority was directed not only at the federal Union but at the states themselves and at their subsidiaries—the counties. The difficulties inherent in the plan—the certain inequality of the wards in wealth and population and the problem of securing uniformity among the wards where state-wide uniformity might be desirable—would have been more impressive to a later generation than to that of Jefferson. The township system, and the elementary republics of the wards, never came into existence in the sense of the basic level of government which Jefferson wished to see. The practical significance of his thought on county organization was not therefore in the actual realization of his ideas but rather in the emphasis they gave to his faith in decentralized administration and his dislike of a professionalized public service removed from the direct scrutiny of a jealous public.

In his thought concerning the central administration of state government Jefferson showed a realization of the importance of good organization to administration. In a period of legislative reaction against the prerogative of the colonial executive he anticipated the future movement for a strong governor and a reformed legislature.[28] In his *Notes on Virginia* he declared against the confounding of executive functions with the legislative, and to Archibald Stuart he observed that the only antidote to the increasing centralization of power in the federal government was a more effective organization of the states:

[26] *Ibid.*, p. 544.   [27] *Ibid.*

[28] Cf. Leslie Lipson, *The American Governor from Figurehead to Leader* (Chicago: University of Chicago Press, 1939), chap. ii.

It is important to strengthen the state governments: and as this cannot be done by any change in the federal constitution, ... it must be done by the states themselves, erecting such barriers at the constitutional line as cannot be surmounted either by themselves or by the general government. The only barrier in their power is a wise government. A weak one will lose ground in every contest. To obtain a wise and an able government, I consider the following changes as important. Render the legislature a desirable station by lessening the number of representatives (say to 100) and lengthening somewhat their term, and proportion them equally among the electors: . . . . Render the Executive a more desirable post to men of abilities by making it more independent of the legislature. To wit, let him be chosen by other electors, for a longer time, and ineligible for ever after.[29]

Jefferson therefore did not believe that decentralized governments were of necessity weak. Rather he held that only efficient and effective state government could stem the trend toward centralization. His recommendations have been substantially those to which the better-governed states of later times have resorted. And as long as centralization and decentralization continue to be perennial issues in government, the relevance of Jefferson's thought on federalism to public administration seems assured.

THE LEGISLATURE AND THE EXECUTIVE

The leading principle of our Constitution is the independence of the Legislative, executive and judiciary of one another.—TO GEORGE HAY.[30]

The theory upon which Jefferson would distribute the powers of the central governments of the Union and of the states was that of the separation of powers. The principle of the federal Constitution he held to be the separation of legislative, executive, and judiciary functions, except in cases specified. "If this principle be not expressed in direct terms," he declared to Madison, "yet it is clearly the spirit of the constitution, and it ought to be so commented and acted on by every friend of free government."[31] In a letter to Judge Spencer Roane written in 1819, Jefferson declared that "each department is truly independent of the others, and has an equal right to decide for itself what is the meaning of the Constitution in the cases submitted to its action; and especially, where it is to act ultimately and without appeal."[32]

Although Jefferson's feud with Chief Justice John Marshall and the federal judiciary provides at least a partial explanation for his pronounced views on constitutional construction, the mutual independence of the

[29] December 23, 1791, *Works*, ed. Ford, VI, 351.

[30] June 20, 1807, *ibid.*, X, 404.

[31] January 22, 1797, *ibid.*, VIII, 272.   [32] September 6, 1819, *ibid.*, XII, 137.

three major divisions was not, however, advocated merely as a political expedient.[33] As early as 1782 Jefferson had defended the separation of powers in his *Notes on Virginia*, and in 1790 he declared that the executive and judiciary, possessing the rights of self-government from nature, cannot be controlled in the exercise of them but by law, passed in the form of the Constitution.[34] Writing from Paris to his friends in America, Jefferson urged the separation of the executive business of the United States from the Congress.[35] During his membership in the Congress of the Confederation, Jefferson had pressed upon individual members the desirability of an executive committee "to act during the sessions of Congress, as the Committee of the states was to act during their vacations."[36] An independent executive was necessary to free government, an independent legislature no less so. Jefferson declared to President Washington that "if the equilibrium of the three great bodies, Legislative, Executive and judiciary, could be preserved, if the Legislature could be kept independent, I should never fear the result of such a government but that I could not but be uneasy when I saw that the Executive had swallowed up the legislative branch."[37] And although he was prepared to resist the encroachment he believed the judiciary to be making upon the political branches of the government, he declared that he was against writing letters to judiciary officers. "I thought them independent of the Executive," he said, "not subject to its coercion and therefore not obliged to attend to its admonitions."[38] The passing of years saw no change in his conviction, for he wrote in 1820 that if the three major divisions maintained their independence, the government might last long, "but not so if either can assume the authorities of the other."[39]

[33] Jefferson's view was partially calculated to resist the encroachments of the Supreme Court upon the executive power. His letters to George Hay, United States District Attorney for Virginia, explaining his refusal to obey the summons of John Marshall to testify at the trial of Aaron Burr in Richmond in the summer of 1807 are important documents in the history of American public administration, constituting a notable defense by an American chief executive of his constitutional independence of judicial control (see letters in *ibid.*, X, 394–409).

[34] "Opinion on Residence Bill," July 15, 1790, *ibid.*, VI, 102. This report reveals the natural-law basis of Jefferson's theory of the separation of powers. Natural rights to self-government, rather than functional division of authority, was the basis of his theory of organization. See also "Opinion on Territorial Authority," December 14, 1790, *ibid.*, pp. 166–67; "Opinion on the Powers of the Senate," April 24, 1790, *ibid.*, pp. 49–52.

[35] E.g., to James Madison, June 20, 1787, *ibid.*, V, 284; to Edward Carrington, August 4, 1787, *ibid.*, p. 319.

[36] To James Madison, June 20, 1787, *ibid.*, V, 284.

[37] *The Anas*, 1792, *ibid.*, I, 236.   [38] September 4, 1793, *ibid.*, p. 323.

[39] To W. C. Jarvis, September 28, 1820, *ibid.*, XII, 164.

Jefferson's opinion of the necessity of a distinct executive agency does not appear to have initially implied a unitary executive. Prior to the framing of the Constitution, he appears to have leaned toward a plural executive consisting of an executive committee—the personnel of such committee evidently to be derived from the members of the Congress. Hamilton had similarly advocated a composite executive for want of a better arrangement but favored the appointment of certain executive ministers by Congress, to be selected from the men best fitted for their respective posts regardless of congressional membership. What Hamilton proposed was an independent ministry rather than an executive committee of the legislature.

The experiment of the French Directory, Jefferson watched with great interest. "The republican world," he declared, "has been long looking with anxiety on the two experiments going on, of a *single* elective Executive here, & a *plurality* there. Opinions have been considerably divided on the event in both countries."[40] He deemed the greater opinion there to favor plurality, whereas in America the single executive was generally, but not unanimously, favored. At first, Jefferson confessed uncertainty as to which form was best, but by 1796 he had become convinced of the superiority of the unitary executive, for in a letter to John Adams he exclaimed:

I fear the oligarchical executive of the French will not do. We have always seen a small council get into cabals & quarrels, the more bitter and relentless the fewer they are. We saw this in our committee of the states; & that they were from their bad passions, incapable of doing the business of their country. I think that for the prompt, clear & consistent action so necessary in an executive, unity of person is necessary as with us.[41]

By 1820 Jefferson's opposition to plural executives had become confirmed, for, writing to James Madison, he declared unequivocally that all executive directories become "mere sinks of corruption and faction."[42] "For if experience has ever taught a truth," he wrote to a European correspondent, "it is that a plurality in the supreme executive will forever split into discordant factions, distract the nation, annihilate its energies, and force the nation to rally under a single head, generally an usurper."[43] Thus it was Jefferson's final opinion that unity of the executive power was essential to good government.

[40] To Harry Innes, January 23, 1800, *ibid.*, IX, 101–2.
[41] February 28, 1796, *ibid.*, VIII, 218.
[42] November 29, 1820, *ibid.*, XII, 175.
[43] M. Coray, October 31, 1823, *Writings*, ed. Washington, VII, 321.

It should not be deduced from Jefferson's theories of decentralization, the separation of powers, and the constitutional independence of the three branches of the national government that he favored a rigidly restrictive interpretation of the executive power. No less a witness than Alexander Hamilton declared untrue the allegation that Jefferson opposed the extensive exercise of executive authority:

> But it is not true, as is alleged, that he is an enemy to the power of the Executive, or that he is for confounding all the powers in the House of Representatives. It is a fact which I have frequently mentioned, that, while we were in the administration together, he was generally for a large construction of the Executive authority and not backward to act upon it in cases which coincided with his views. Let it be added that in his theoretic ideas he has considered as improper the participations of the Senate in the Executive authority.[44]

As Secretary of State, Jefferson had energetically resisted the attempts of the Senate to extend its authority over the field of foreign relations. "The transaction of business with foreign nations is Executive altogether," he declared in his "Opinion on the Powers of the Senate."[45] Exceptions to this rule he held to be construed strictly against the claims of the Senate. "The senate," he asserted in sweeping language, "is not supposed by the constitution to be acquainted with the concerns of the executive department."[46]

Equally he had opposed the pretensions of the House of Representatives to command the persons, papers, and records of the executive branch of the government in matters pertaining to their investigations. That the House might properly institute inquiries and call for papers, both Jefferson and Hamilton agreed; but they held that, although the President ought to comply with any reasonable request, his discretion should determine what papers, or testimony, should be submitted and what withheld in the public interest.[47] They were also agreed in denying the unqualified right of Congress to executive sources of information. To Jefferson opposition to legislative encroachment was no new thing, for in 1789 he had declared to Madison: "The executive in our governments is not the sole, it is scarcely the principal object of my jealousy. The tyranny of the legislatures is the most formidable dread at present, and will be for long years."[48]

[44] To James A. Bayard, January 16, 1801, *Works*, ed. Lodge, X, 413.

[45] April 24, 1790, *Works*, ed. Ford, VI, 50.

[46] *Ibid.*, p. 51.

[47] *The Anas*, April, 1792, *ibid.*, I, 214-15.

[48] To James Madison, March 15, 1789, *ibid.*, V, 463.

As President, Jefferson attempted to reconcile his notions of legislative and executive independence with the free exercise of his presidential authorities. In the interest of simplicity and legislative independence he proposed to address all his communications to Congress by message, "to which no answer will be expected." The personal appearance of the chief executive in the legislature had been held by Republicans as advantageous to executive influence. Alexander Hamilton's desire to appear personally before the House of Representatives, like a British minister before Parliament, had been frustrated,[49] but the President's personal appearance to deliver his annual message retained the character of an address from the throne. This relic of monarchy Jefferson proposed to abolish along with the customary reply given by Old World parliaments to their sovereigns. Jefferson's personal distaste for public speaking may have contributed to his decision, but it is interesting to observe that the practice of presidents to deliver their messages in person to the Congress was not restored until American presidents a century later began to assert the constitutional right of the chief executive to leadership in the legislative branch and to claim for themselves a representative character equal to, if not greater than, that possessed by the Congress itself.

The significant change which Jefferson instituted in the relations between the presidency and the legislative branch was in the substitution of party leadership as an adjunct of the executive power for the formality and constitutional prerogatives upon which the Federalists had relied to maintain the independence of the executive from legislative interference. Thus Jefferson in the early years of his presidency could emphasize the constitutional independence of the legislature from executive influence with full knowledge that party regularity would carry his measures through Congress without overt influence from the executive. He could afford to be generous with the formal prerequisites of power so long as he held the ultimate power of political control. Before his election to the presidency, he had decried administration influence in the Congress, and he continued to avoid any public manifestation of his personal influence with congressmen long after he had learned of the embarrassment which his "independent legislature" could heap upon his "independent adminis-

---

[49] In 1792 Jefferson wrote to Thomas Pinckney that the Republicans were complaining that "the influence and patronage of the Executive is to become so great as to govern the Legislature. They endeavored a few days ago to take away one means of influence by condemning references to the heads of department. They failed by a majority of five votes. They were more successful in their endeavor to prevent the introduction of a new means of influence, that of admitting the heads of department to deliberate occasionally in the House in explanation of their measures" (*ibid.*, VII, 191).

tration." But the mischievous opposition of John Randolph soon taught him to rely upon his influence with members of the Congress for the successful promotion of what he confessed were "administration measures." Writing to Barnabas Bidwell, the administration leader in the House, Jefferson expressed the view that legislators should be something less than independent where the President's measures were concerned:

> I do not mean that any gentleman, relinquishing his own judgment, should implicitly support all the measures of the administration; but that, where he does not disapprove of them, he should not suffer them to go off in sleep, but bring them to the attention of the House, and give them a fair chance. Where he disapproves, he will of course leave them to be brought forward by those who concur in the sentiment.[50]

The inevitable criticism which Jefferson's use of congressional adherents aroused injured his sense of good intentions and honest republicanism. He denied that he was attempting surreptitiously to promote his measures through others, and, insisting upon the independence of the congressmen, he complained that "when a gentleman, through zeal for the public service, undertakes to do the public business, we know that we shall hear of the cant of backstairs councillors." But, declared Jefferson in a revealing sentence, "we never heard this while the declaimer[51] was himself a backstairs man, as he calls it, but in the confidence and views of the administration, as may more properly and respectfully be said."[52]

In summary, the most significant aspect of Jefferson's thought on the relations between the legislature and the executive powers appears to be his preference for political leadership over constitutional authority in the conduct of public administration. Although Jefferson "was generally for a large construction of the executive authority and not backward to act upon it in cases which coincided with his views," he nevertheless preferred to use his influence as a party leader to further his objectives rather than to employ powers which might threaten the intergovernmental harmony which he cherished. His choice may have been dictated by temperament rather than by reason, but the results were nonetheless significant. The political character of the American presidency was initially shaped by Thomas Jefferson and has not been substantially altered by his successors. Although Washington and Adams contributed to the character of the presidency as an executive institution, neither represented the type of party leadership which was to become an inseparable part of the presidency during and after Jefferson's time.

[50] July 5, 1806, *Works* (Memorial ed.), XI, 115–16; *Writings*, ed. Washington, V, 15–16.

[51] John Randolph.

[52] To Mr. Bidwell, July 5, 1806, *Writings*, ed. Washington, V, 16.

THE JUDICIARY AND PUBLIC ADMINISTRATION

The legislative and executive branches may sometimes err, but elections and dependence will bring them to rights. The judiciary branch is the instrument which, working like gravity, without intermission, is to press us at last into one consolidated mass.—To ARCHIBALD THWEAT.[53]

It is not the intention to review here the opinions of Thomas Jefferson on the role of the judiciary, a task which has been undertaken, more than once, by specialists in the investigation of judicial history. Rather the purpose is to complete the discussion of the distribution of public authority as advocated by Jefferson, placing the courts in the relation which he felt they properly held to the executive and legislative branches of the government and to the federal structure of the Union.

Jefferson's theory of constitutional separation of powers provided no place for an exclusive interpretation of constitutional law by either the executive, the legislature, or the courts; and, upon the premise that each major department was independent of the others, Jefferson held that none could control the others within their lawful sphere. Because he believed that the Constitution had "wisely made all the departments co-equal and co-sovereign within themselves,"[54] he held that the legislature, the executive, and the judiciary alike were competent to decide questions of constitutional interpretation in cases properly before them. It is a very dangerous doctrine, he declared, "to consider the judges as the ultimate arbiters of all constitutional questions."[55] In his opinion the Supreme Court of the United States did not constitute the ultimate authority for the interpretation of constitutional law. "The Constitution has erected no such single tribunal," he declared, "knowing that to whatever hands confided, with the corruptions of time and party, its members would become despots."[56]

The independence of the judiciary Jefferson believed had been carried too far by the framers of the constitutions, state and federal. "At the establishment of our constitutions," he explained, "the judiciary bodies were supposed to be the most helpless and harmless members of the government. Experience, however, soon showed in what way they were to become the most dangerous; that the insufficiency of the means provided for their removal gave them a freehold and irresponsibility in office."[57]

[53] January 19, 1821, *Works*, ed. Ford, XII, 196.

[54] To William C. Jarvis, September 28, 1820, *ibid.*, p. 162.

[55] *Ibid.*   [56] *Ibid.*

[57] To M. Coray, October 31, 1823, *Writings*, ed. Washington, VII, 322.

The judiciary of the United States is the subtle corps of sappers and miners constantly working underground to undermine the foundations of our confederated fabric. They are construing our constitution from a coordination of a general and special government to a general and supreme one alone. . . . . Having found from experience, that impeachment is an impracticable thing, a mere scare-crow, they consider themselves secure for life; they skulk from responsibility to public opinion, the only remaining hold on them, under a practice first introduced into England by Lord Mansfield. An opinion is huddled up in conclave, perhaps by a majority of one, delivered as if unanimous, and with the silent acquiescence of lazy or timid associates, by a crafty chief judge, who sophisticates the law to his mind, by the turn of his own reasoning. A judiciary law was once reported by the Attorney General to Congress, requiring each judge to deliver his opinion *seriatim* and openly, and then to give it in writing to the clerk to be entered in the record. A judiciary independent of a king, or executive alone, is a good thing; but independence of the will of the nation is a solecism, at least in a republican government.[58]

The circumstances of this gradual usurpation by the federal judge called loudly, Jefferson opined, for the exercise of the checks which the distribution of power among the three branches of government was intended to provide. Accordingly, he suggested a variety of devices by which the judges were to be rendered responsible for their conduct. His favorite method was to limit their tenure to an interval of several years and subject their continuation to the approval of both houses of Congress.[59]

Judges, like other public servants, were susceptible to the common weaknesses of ordinary men, but as agents of public justice they possessed more than ordinary resources for the aggrandizement of personal power and the indulgence of political prejudice. "In truth," Jefferson declared, "man is not made to be trusted for life, if secured against all liability to account."[60] Accordingly, Jefferson would render all public officers in all branches of the government responsible to the people directly or to their representatives. In part his attack upon the judiciary was motivated by this purpose. He would remove the temptations to the usurpation of power, which he believed life-tenure of office exaggerated; and, by solemn protest recorded in the houses of Congress, he would bring any departure from the proper judicial sphere before the bar of public opinion.

In 1816 the long-litigated case of *Martin* v. *Hunter's Lessee*[61] came before the Supreme Court, and the opinion of the Court, delivered by Joseph Story, confirmed all the mistrust with which Jefferson saw his ap-

[58] To Thomas Ritchie, December 25, 1820, *Works*, ed. Ford, XII, 177–78.

[59] To James Pleasants, December 26, 1821, *ibid.*, pp. 214–15.

[60] To M. Coray, October 31, 1823, *Writings*, ed. Washington, VII, 322.

[61] 1 Wheat. 304, L. Ed. 97 (1816).

pointment to the Cushing vacancy.[62] The Virginia Court of Appeals had declared Section 25 of the Judiciary Act of 1789 to be contrary to the Constitution, and, in a strongly "consolidationist" opinion, Story had overruled the decision of the state court. In Virginia, Story's remarks touched off a veritable powder keg of controversy, led by Jefferson's old friend, John Taylor of Caroline, and by Judge Spencer Roane of the Virginia Court of Appeals, to whom Jefferson looked as a "bulwark" of republican liberties. Jefferson's sympathies were entirely with the Virginians, and he read the discourses of Judge Roane "with great approbation," declaring that he subscribed "to every tittle of them."[63]

Marshall's opinion in the case of *Cohens* v. *State of Virginia*[64] added fuel to the controversy, and Jefferson declared that Roane, under the signature of Algernon Sidney, had pulverized every word of Marshall's obiter dissertation.[65] The Cohens decision Jefferson viewed as striking at the foundations of the Constitution in general and the Eleventh Amendment in particular. To the contention of the Chief Justice that the Constitution required "an ultimate arbiter somewhere," Jefferson agreed, but he was not prepared to admit that the courts were the proper repository of that function. "The ultimate arbiter is the people of the Union, assembled by their deputies in convention, at the call of Congress, or of two thirds of the States. Let them decide to which they mean to give an authority claimed by two of their organs."[66] The federal judiciary, usurping the function of constitutional amendment, was at war both in theory and in practice with the Jeffersonian conception of responsibility and principle of decentralization.

Jefferson's hostility to the federal judiciary was in part, therefore, a result of a controversy over constitutional principles involving administrative independence and political organization. His unwillingness to submit to judicial interference in the conduct of the presidential office maintained and strengthened the position of the executive branch of the government. Had Jefferson obeyed the summons of Marshall to testify at the trial of Aaron Burr in Richmond, the prestige of the executive office would have suffered a blow fraught with unpredictable consequences. Jefferson's personal conduct, added to his advanced notions of executive

[62] Roy J. Honeywell, "President Jefferson and His Successor," *American Historical Review*, XLVI (October, 1940), 64–75. The article contains useful observations on Jefferson's theory of patronage; see also Jefferson to James Madison, May 25, 1810, *Works*, ed. Ford, XI, 140.

[63] To Judge Spencer Roane, September 6, 1819, *Works*, ed. Ford, XII, 135 ff.

[64] 6 Wheat. 264; 5 L. Ed. 257 (1821).

[65] To William Johnson, June 12, 1823, *Works*, ed. Ford, XII, 252 ff.   [66] *Ibid.*, p. 259.

independence in constitutional interpretation, strengthened the hands of his presidential successors in latter-day struggles with the courts. As the growth of administrative adjudication created problems as to the ultimate decision of questions of constitutional law and fact, the Jeffersonian view of the distribution of executive and judicial powers afforded useful historical precedent for the advocates of administrative finality.

The relation of federal to state courts is a matter primarily judicial rather than administrative, but Jefferson's wish to see disputes over the constitutional distribution of power decided by constitutional amendment rather than by a supreme judicial body evidences again his distrust of centralized government by professional public servants and his desire to widen the basis of actual participation in governmental affairs. The alleged inconvenience of the amendment procedure could never justify the judicial usurpation of that function in Jefferson's mind, for he knew that, in matters of public administration and lawmaking alike, the inconvenience of self-government was the price of liberty. For those who preferred prompt efficiency and convenience to personal freedom Jefferson recommended the despotisms of the Old World, whose judges and functionaries relieved the people of all inconveniences in the conduct of public affairs, except the supreme inconvenience of enforced obedience to the arbitrary decisions of the bureaucracy. Thus, in determining the merits of every issue involving the distribution of authority, Jefferson was guided by the maxim which he laid down in his *Autobiography:* "But it is not by the consolidation or concentration of powers, but by their distribution, that good government is effected."[67]

CHAPTER XI

PUBLIC ADMINISTRATION AND PUBLIC POLICY

IN DETERMINING what constituted the proper business of public administration, Jefferson never lost sight of his fundamental principles, although he was willing to modify their application in the interest of a clear public benefit. To Jefferson, policy-making was a dangerous power in direct proportion as it was removed from the hands of the electorate. It is, therefore, not surprising that Jefferson narrowed the sphere of policy determination in the federal as contrasted with the state

[67] *Ibid.,* I, 122.

and local governments, for these he believed closer to the people than the central administration.

It should not be inferred that Jefferson subscribed to a narrow conception of public power because he favored the imposition of well-defined limits on the extent of public authority. Distinction between the scope and degree of public power is fundamental to an understanding of Jefferson's political philosophy. He believed the scope of national government as defined by Alexander Hamilton to be so broad as to actually lack definition. He agreed that the powers of government ought to extend to all great public purposes but believed that the electorate through their representatives should define exactly what they held those purposes to be. In practice Jefferson sometimes approximated Hamilton's idea of public power of indefinite scope, for in the purchase of Louisiana he acted, despite constitutional scruples, to define by his own discretion the extent of his authority. But, in so doing, Jefferson acted in accordance with his principle that, where an authority was exclusively and clearly lodged, full powers should be exercised to effect the public purpose underlying that authority. The Constitution had not allowed for the acquisition of foreign territory nor had Congress agreed to so extensive a purchase as Jefferson effected. But the direction of foreign policy and of national defense was lodged exclusively in the national executive, and if Jefferson had failed through a restricted interpretation of his authority to secure the Mississippi and Missouri valleys for the protection and expansion of the American people, he would have violated his own theory of administrative responsibility. He believed it incumbent upon those who accepted great charges to assume if necessary great risks on behalf of the public good. He preferred to govern in accordance with strictly enumerated authority, but he insisted on power adequate to realize his duties and to this end would exceed the provisions of the statutes in fulfilment of the larger sense of his responsibility.

In determining the sphere of public action, Jefferson believed that as the conduct of public affairs was removed from the immediate surveillance of the electorate there should be a corresponding diminution in its scope. The central government would be endowed with every power necessary to effect its ends, and neither states nor localities could challenge its authority in its exclusive sphere. But the area of this centralized authority would be limited as precisely as public exigencies would admit.

With regard to the extent of state and local authority Jefferson felt less concern, for he believed the close supervision of the electorate would insure the responsible exercise of power. The sphere of public action as defined by Jefferson was accordingly conditioned by his theories of decentralization and responsibility. Centralization and toryism were concomitant in his philosophy, and to the very end of his life he adhered to his governing principle of "cherishing and fortifying the rights and authorities of the people in opposition to those who fear them, who wish to take all power from them, and to transfer all to Washington."[1]

DOMESTIC POLICY AND PUBLIC WELFARE

If we can prevent the government from wasting the labors of the people, under the pretense of taking care of them, they must become happy.—To THOMAS COOPER.[2]

In a consideration of the proper sphere of government as understood by Jefferson, his assumptions regarding the natural division of men should be recalled. He believed that "the weakly and nerveless, the rich and the corrupt seeing more safety and accessibility in a strong executive," were the Tories of nature; "the healthy, firm and virtuous, feeling confidence in their physical and moral resources, and willing to part with only so much power as is necessary for their good government, and therefore to retain the rest in the hands of the many,"[3] were natural Whigs. The former favored the protection of government, whereas the latter preferred to depend upon their own resources to insure their welfare. In these distinctions Jefferson reflected the strongly marked individualism of the American farm and frontier. "It is not the policy of the government . . . . to give aid to works of any kind," he replied to an inquiry about America. The American states, he explained, "let things take their natural course without help or impediment, which is generally the best policy."[4] But if he opposed the wasting of the people's labor by the government under the "pretense of taking care of them," his hostility toward paternalism reflected no lack of concern for the welfare of the people. He shared Hamilton's desire to see a strong and prosperous nation, but he did not believe that strength and abundance must be purchased at the cost of self-government and individual freedom, which he believed would result from the centralized authority of the Hamiltonian state. Instead he held that general welfare would be the sure result of a wise and frugal government which would preserve the public order, give no man an artificial advantage over his fellows, and hold all accountable to the laws. Yet he was prepared

---

[1] To Nathaniel Macon, February 21, 1826, *Works*, ed. Ford, XII, 459–60.

[2] November 29, 1802, *ibid.*, IX, 403.

[3] To Joel Barlow, May 3, 1802, *ibid.*, p. 371.

[4] To Thomas Digges, June 19, 1788, *ibid.*, V, 410.

to proceed beyond these basic objectives to promote a positive program of public welfare where he believed the majority approved and the fundamental law permitted.

Private enterprise, Jefferson believed, managed much better than government all concerns to which it was equal.[5] Illustrative of this belief was his attitude toward the establishment of government-owned and government-operated mines, which had been a favored scheme of the Federalists. Jefferson, opposing this policy, prepared to lease the government mines to private operators.[6] In answer to an offer to convey an iron mine to the public, he reviewed his experience with public business enterprise:

> Having always observed that public works are much less advantageously managed than the same are by private hands, I have thought it better for the public to go to market for whatever it wants which is to be found there; for there competition brings it down to the minimum of value. I have no doubt we can buy brass cannon at market cheaper than we could make iron ones. I think it material too, not to abstract the high executive officers from those functions which nobody else is charged to carry on, and to employ them in superintending works which are going on abundantly in private hands. Our predecessors went on different principles; they bought iron mines, and sought for copper ones. We own a mine at Harper's Ferry of the finest iron ever put into a cannon, which we are afraid to attempt to work. We have rented it heretofore, but it is now without a tenant.[7]

In the same month that Jefferson refused the conveyance of an iron mine, he rejected a proposal that the government assume a sharehold in the New Orleans Canal Company. Replying to Governor Claiborne, Jefferson declared this measure "too much out of our policy of not embarking the public in enterprises better managed by individuals, and which might occupy as much of our time as those political duties for which the public functionaries are particularly instituted."[8]

Reinforcing Jefferson's conviction that productive enterprise was not the proper sphere of government was his belief that the federal government in particular lacked constitutional authority to embark upon entrepreneurial projects. In his "Opinion on the Constitutionality of a National

---

[5] "Sixth Annual Message," December 2, 1806, *ibid.*, X, 318.

[6] To Albert Gallatin, November 8, 1807, *Writings*, ed. Washington, V, 210. However, Jefferson was quite willing to have the government work mines where public necessity dictated; e.g., he urged the full exploitation of the Virginia lead mines during the Revolution (to the Governor of Virginia, July 16, 1776, *Works*, ed. Ford, II, 226–27).

[7] To William B. Bibb, July 28, 1808, *Writings*, ed. Washington, V, 326. Cf. *Works*, ed. Ford, X, 9.

[8] July 17, 1808, *Writings*, ed. Washington, V, 319.

Bank," Jefferson held to a strict interpretation of the power of the federal government

to lay taxes to provide for the general welfare of the United States, that is to say, "to lay taxes for *the purpose* of providing for the general welfare." For the laying of taxes is the *power*, and the general welfare the *purpose* for which the power is to be exercised. They are not to lay taxes *adlibitum for any purpose they please;* but only *to pay the debts or provide for the welfare of the Union.* In like manner, they are not *to do anything they please* to provide for the general welfare, but only to *lay taxes* for that purpose. To consider the latter phrase, not as describing the purpose of the first but as giving a distinct and independent power to do any act they please, which might be for the good of the Union, would render all the preceding and subsequent enumerations of power completely useless.

It would reduce the whole instrument to a single phrase, that of instituting a Congress with power to do whatever would be for the good of the United States; and, as they would be the sole judges of the good or evil, it would be also a power to do whatever evil they please.

It is an established rule of construction where a phrase will bear either of two meanings, to give it that which will allow some meaning to the other parts of the instrument, and not that which would render all the others useless. Certainly no such universal power was meant to be given them. It was intended to lace them up straitly within the enumerated powers, and those without which, as means, these powers could not be carried into effect.[9]

Hamilton's *Report on Manufactures* (December, 1791) accentuated Jefferson's alarm over the rapid expansion of federal authority under the guiding hand of the Treasury. He declared to Washington that Hamilton's report went far beyond any proposition yet advanced, "and to which the eyes of many were turned as the decision which was to let us know whether we live under a limited or an unlimited government."[10] The *Report* expressly assumed, asserted Jefferson, that "the general government has a right to exercise all powers which may be for the *general welfare*, that is to say, all the legitimate powers of government: since no government has a legitimate right to do what is not for the welfare of the governed." There was, indeed, he added, "a sham-limitation of the universality of this power *to cases where money is to be employed.*" But, he asked, "about what is it that money cannot be employed?"[11]

As evidence that the framers of the Constitution intended no such sweeping interpretation of power as Hamilton expounded, Jefferson declared that the Constitutional Convention, having rejected specific proposals to grant the general government powers of incorporation and

[9] February 15, 1791, *Works*, ed. Ford, VI, 199.

[10] *The Anas*, February, 1792, *ibid.*, I, 197.

[11] To Washington, September 9, 1792, *ibid.*, VII, 139.

powers to open canals and to erect banks, the specific enumeration of powers as stated in the written Constitution itself must be taken as describing the extent of federal authority.[12] Nor should those powers, specifically delegated, be stretched by construction to cover all undertakings conceivably related to them. "The power to regulate commerce," said Jefferson, "does not give a power to build piers, wharves, open ports, clear the beds of rivers, dig canals, build warehouses . . . . set up manufactories, cultivate the earth, to all of which the power would go if it went to the first."[13] Although Jefferson agreed to the building of piers in the Delaware River under the power to maintain a navy and declared of the building of lighthouses under the commerce power that "the utility of the thing has sanctioned the infraction,"[14] he warned that to build a second infraction upon the first, and on the second a third, would soon result in unlimited government.[15]

Writing from Philadelphia in 1800 to Robert R. Livingston, Jefferson described the "filiation of necessities" by which the Federalist majority in Congress used the necessary and proper clause to override constitutional limitation:

We are here engaged in improving our constitution by construction, so as to make it what the majority thinks it should have been. The Senate received yesterday a bill from the Representatives incorporating a company for Roosevelt's copper mines in Jersey. This is under the *sweeping clause* of the Constitution, and supported by the following pedigree of necessities. Congress are authorized to defend the country: ships are necessary for that defense: copper is necessary for ships: mines are necessary to produce copper: companies are necessary to work mines: and" this is the house that Jack built."[16]

Writing again to Livingston in the following year, Jefferson declared himself against a proposal that Congress incorporate an agricultural society. "I am against that," he wrote, "because I think Congress cannot find in all the enumerated powers any one which authorizes the act, much less the giving the public money to that use."[17] Although Jefferson favored the uniting of the several state agricultural societies into a central body, he believed that they would thrive best if left to themselves without the interference of government.

Rejection of the sweeping interpretation of the general welfare and nec-

---

[12] *The Anas*, 1792, *ibid.*, I, 197; "Opinion on the Constitutionality of a National Bank," 1791, *ibid.*, VI, 199.

[13] To Albert Gallatin, October 13, 1802, *ibid.*, IX, 399.

[14] *Ibid.*

[15] *Ibid.*

[16] April 30, 1800, *ibid.*, p. 134.

[17] February 16, 1801, *ibid.*, p. 181.

essary and proper clauses, Jefferson held a tenet of orthodox republicanism. Should the Federalist interpretation prevail, "all limits to the Federal
Government are done away," he declared. This opinion he formed "on
the first rise of the question" occasioned by the administrative policies of
Alexander Hamilton, and he affirmed that a quarter-century of reflection
on the issues, "whether in or out of power," had strengthened his belief
in the necessity for a strict limitation upon the powers of government.[18]
Although he was willing to see the powers of the federal government enlarged by amendment to permit the payment of premiums and internal
improvements, he held that any countenance to the constructive expansion of federal powers, by any regular organ of the government, would be
"more ominous than anything which has yet occurred."[19]

Jefferson's attitudes on the issues of public works, public finance and
taxation, the protection of manufacturing, public education, and public
lands illustrate and clarify his theory of the sphere of public administration.[20] He would place the responsibility for the public welfare as regards
each of these interests upon those levels of government best able to meet
the public needs. It has been observed that he opposed public manufacturing and mining where private resources were adequate to public necessities. Initially he opposed the federal undertaking of public works and internal improvements, holding that this was the proper responsibility of
the states and their subdivisions. He declaimed against Hamilton's comprehensive schemes for administering the Union into a consolidated nation, only to discover that his followers were willing to embark upon the
substance of Hamilton's proposals once they themselves came into power.
Even before the Republican victory of 1800, Jefferson rebuked his lieutenants for promoting federal projects. Writing to Madison in 1796, he
asked:

Have you considered all the consequences of your proposition respecting post roads?
I view it as a source of boundless patronage to the executive, jobbing to members of
Congress and their friends, and a bottomless abyss of public money. You will begin
by only appropriating the surplus of the post office revenues; but the other revenues
will soon be called into their aid, and it will be a scene of eternal scramble among the
members, who can get the most money wasted in their State; and they will always get
most who are meanest. We have thought hitherto, that the roads of a State could
not be so well administered even by the State legislature, as by the magistracy of the

[18] To Judge Spencer Roane, October 12, 1815, *ibid.*, XI, 490.

[19] *Ibid.*

[20] Jefferson's positive role as a formulator of public policy is developed by Charles E. Merriam and Frank P. Bourgin in "Jefferson as a Planner of National Resources," *Ethics*, LIII
(July, 1943), 284-92.

county, on the spot. What will it be when a member of N.H. is to mark out a road for Georgia? Does the power to *establish* post roads, ... mean that you shall *make* the roads, or only *select* from those already made, those on which there shall be a post? If the term be equivocal, (and I really do not think it so), which is the safer construction? That which permits a majority of Congress to go to cutting down mountains and bridging rivers, or the other, which if too restricted, may refer it to the states for amendment, securing still due measure and proportion among us, and providing some means of information to the members of Congress tantamount to that ocular inspection, which even in our county determinations, the magistrate finds cannot be supplied by any other evidence? The fortification of harbors were liable to great objection. But national circumstances furnished some color. In this case there is none. The roads of America are the best in the world except those of France and England. But does the state of our population, the extent of our internal commerce, the want of sea and river navigation, call for such expense on roads here, or are our means adequate to it?[21]

Writing to Madison on the same subject four years later, Jefferson declared that "the mines of Peru would not supply the monies which would be wasted on this object, nor the patience of any people stand the abuses which would be incontrolably committed under it."[22] To Caesar Rodney he described the Roads Bill as a "bottomless abyss for money . . . .—the richest provision for jobs to favorites that has ever yet been proposed."[23]

With the growth of the West and the reduction of the national debt during Jefferson's presidency came a growing popular demand for internal improvements at public expense. Albert Gallatin brought an enthusiasm and aptitude for large-scale administrative planning into Jefferson's cabinet, and during his second presidential term Jefferson veered from his earlier unfriendly view to a strong, though guarded, advocacy of federal support for internal improvements. In his "Second Inaugural Address" he recommended that, with the redemption of the national debt, "the revenue thereby liberated may, by a just repartition among the states, and a corresponding amendment to the constitution, be applied, *in time of peace*, to rivers, canals, roads, arts, manufactures, education and other great objects within each state."[24]

In his annual message of 1806 Jefferson again urged the amendment of the Constitution to permit the federal support of public education and public works, and in his *Report of April 6, 1808*, Gallatin proposed an extensive program for the development of a national transportation system. Hamilton had urged the utility of such a plan in his *Report on Manufac-*

[21] March 6, 1796, *Works*, ed. Ford, VIII, 226–27; cf. letter to Governor Claiborne, April 27, 1806, *ibid.*, X, 255, wherein Jefferson had evidently changed his mind concerning the power of Congress to construct post roads.

[22] December 19, 1800, *ibid.*, IX, 159.

[23] December 21, 1800, *ibid.*, IX, 160.   [24] March 4, 1805, *ibid.*, X, 130.

tures and again in letters written in 1799 and in 1801. Unfortunately, war necessities and sectional opposition prevented the realization of the comprehensive program, but its presentation indicates Jefferson's approval and illustrates the degree to which he was prepared to modify earlier views when convinced that the public welfare required that which he had formerly opposed.

Although Jefferson himself does not appear to have prepared an amendment to the Constitution adding expenditures for internal improvements to the enumeration of federal powers, the absence of such action can hardly be construed as acceptance of Hamilton's implied-power doctrine. In 1824 he explained to Edward Livingston that he favored an amendment to the federal Constitution granting specifically the power to finance internal improvements from Treasury surplus, but he would modify this authority by the proviso that "the federal proportion of each State should be expended within the State."[25] He declared that "with this single security against partiality and corrupt bargaining, I suppose there is not a State, perhaps not a man in the Union, who would not consent to add this to the powers of the general government."[26] In the absence of such an amendment, he was prepared to resist all efforts to extend federal authority by interpretation, and in December, 1825, he proposed a "solemn Declaration and Protest of the Commonwealth of Virginia on the principles of the Constitution of the United States of America and on the violations of them."[27] Submitted to Madison and Monroe, it was not approved by them and was never acted upon. Yet this restatement of constitutional principles coming at the close of his long life and public career underlines all his previous contentions regarding the limitations on governmental authority and his distrust of the discretionary use of consolidated power.

Jefferson appears to have originally held no theoretical objection to the undertaking of public works by the states. Indeed, the first of the public undertakings of which he considered himself the instrument was an act of the Virginia assembly providing for the clearing of obstructions in the Rivanna River. In 1784, in a letter to Madison, he urged that Virginia lay a tax for the purpose of opening a canal between the Ohio and Potomac rivers, fearing that Pennsylvania "will be beforehand with us and get possession of the commerce."[28] In 1789 he suggested to Washington that Maryland and Virginia jointly undertake such a canal, holding that this

[25] April 4, 1824, *ibid.*, XII, 351.

[26] *Ibid.;* cf. also letter to R. J. Garnett, February 14, 1824, *ibid.*, p. 342.

[27] *Ibid.*, pp. 418–21.

[28] February 20, 1784, *ibid.*, IV, 246.

and similar navigation projects should be done at public rather than at private expense.[29] In later life, however, Jefferson's enthusiasm for works projects of this type noticeably waned, perhaps because of his compelling interest in securing adequate support for a state university. His precepts in public finance had been taken too much to heart by his fellow-citizens, and only with greatest difficulty was he able to secure the most modest appropriations for the great institution of learning which he hoped to leave his state.

In his theories regarding the public credit and taxation Jefferson conformed to those same principles and assumptions which governed his thought on internal improvements. He would limit the scope of federal authority by maintaining the independence of the states in public finance. He did not concur in Hamilton's contention that the federal government should enjoy clear and undisputed priority over the sources of taxation. In his "First Inaugural Address" he declared "economy in the public expense, that labor may be lightly burthened," an essential principle which would shape his administration. The credit of the government he wished to maintain at a high level but to use only as an absolute necessity. Writing to his son-in-law, John W. Eppes, in 1813, he described his theory of public finance:

It is a wise rule, and should be fundamental in a government disposed to cherish its credit, and at the same tme to restrain the use of it within the limits of its faculties, "never to borrow a dollar without laying a tax in the same instant for paying the interest annually, and the principal within a given term; and to consider that tax as pledged to the creditors on the public faith." On such a pledge as this, sacredly observed, a government may always command, on a *reasonable interest*, all the lendable money of their citizens, while the necessity of an equivalent tax is a salutary warning to them and their constituents against oppressions, bankruptcy, and its inevitable consequence, revolution. But the term of redemption must be moderate, and at any rate within the limits of their rightful powers. But what limits, it will be asked, does this prescribe to their powers? What is to hinder them from creating a perpetual debt? The laws of nature, I answer. The earth belongs to the living, not to the dead. The will and the power of man expire with his life, by nature's law.[30]

Referring to Hamilton's management of the national debt, Jefferson warned Monroe: "We are ruined, Sir, if we do not overrule the principles that the more we owe, the more prosperous we shall be; that if ours should be once paid off, we should incur another by any means however extrava-

[29] May 10, 1789, *ibid.*, V, 474.

[30] June 24, 1813, *Writings*, ed. Washington, VI, 136. Cf. Alexander Hamilton, *First Report on the Public Credit*, January 9, 1790, *Works*, ed. Lodge, II, 283: "The creation of debt should always be accompanied with the means of extinguishment."

gant."[31] Writing to John Taylor in 1798, Jefferson expressed the wish that by constitutional amendment the federal government might be deprived of its powers to borrow money. "I would be willing to depend on that alone for the reduction of the administration of our government to the genuine principles of its constitution," he exclaimed.[32] Thirty years of experience and reflection on public affairs did not alter Jefferson's hostility to public debt where redemption was unprovided, for, writing to Nathaniel Macon in 1821, he declared the nation undone if it did not cease borrowing money and commence to pay off the debt. Indicating the extent to which he would go to achieve freedom from debt, he added: "If this cannot be done without dismissing the army, and putting the ships out of commission, haul them up high and dry, and reduce the army to the lowest point at which it was ever established. There does not exist an engine so corruptive of the government and so demoralizing of the nation as a public debt."[33]

At the root of Jefferson's fear of public debt lay his dislike of taxation and his desire to see taxes held to the lowest possible level consonant with the public welfare. Writing to Samuel Kercheval in 1816, he described the fatal connection between debt and taxes:

> We must make our election between *economy and liberty*, or *profusion and servitude*. If we run into such debts, as that we must be taxed in our meat and in our drink, in our necessaries and our comforts, in our labors and our amusements, for our callings and our creeds, as the people of England are, our people, like them, must come to labor sixteen hours in the twenty-four, give the earnings of fifteen of these to the government for their debts and daily expenses; and the sixteenth being insufficient to afford us bread, we must live, as they now do, on oatmeal and potatoes; have no time to think, no means of calling the mismanagers to account; but be glad to obtain subsistence by hiring ourselves to rivet their chains on the necks of our fellow sufferers.[34]

Jefferson believed that taxes may be based upon capital, income, or consumption and that a government may select either of these bases for the establishment of its system of taxation.[35] But when once the particular source of revenue had been selected, he believed that the taxation of special articles from either of the other bases constituted double taxation. This he held theoretically unjust but perhaps justifiable under special conditions. The governing principle of taxation, he believed, was to draw from each member of society his proportion of the public contributions.

[31] April 17, 1791, *Works* (1892 ed.), ed. Ford, V, 320.

[32] November 26, 1798, *ibid.* (1904–5 ed.), VIII, 481.

[33] August 19, 1821, *ibid.*, XII, 207.

[34] July 12, 1816, *ibid.*, p. 10.

[35] To Joseph Milligan, April 6, 1819, *Writings*, ed. Washington, VI, 573.

The utility of taxation as a device for effecting social policy was readily understood by Jefferson.[36] Although he believed an equal division of property to be impracticable, he nevertheless feared the consequences of such enormous inequalities in wealth as characterized France under the *ancien régime*. Accordingly, he favored a scheme of progressive taxation "to exempt all from taxation below a certain point, and to tax the higher portions of property in geometrical progression as they rise."[37] The extent to which Jefferson would carry this progressive tax is not clear, but one may safely conclude that its objective was the removal of gross inequities in wealth rather than the creation of an equalitarian society. In the edition of Destutt de Tracy's *Economie politique* which he translated and edited, he observed that to take from one, because it is thought that his own industry and that of his father has acquired too much, in order to spare to others who, or whose fathers, have not exercised equal industry and skill, is to violate arbitrarily the first principle of association, "the *guarantee* to everyone of a free exercise of his industry, and the fruits acquired by it."[38]

It therefore appears that Jefferson wished to use the taxing power to supplement such basic reforms in property ownership as the abolition of entail and primogeniture which he effected in Virginia. The objective of these measures was clearly the broadening of the base of property ownership. Jefferson believed that property was a civil rather than a natural right and hence subject to social regulation. He nevertheless deemed the desire for ownership a characteristic of man and believed it a desirable trait when in conformity with the general good. Inequalities in wealth were permissible to the point where the concentration of economic power in the few frustrated the ownership of property among the many. Taxation was a method of preventing an unwise concentration of wealth, but its administration was to extend rather than to destroy the benefits of the private property system.

Jefferson shared Hamilton's preference for the taxation of imports, holding that it bore chiefly on the rich and upon luxury goods. In later life Jefferson relaxed his opposition to an internal excise on whiskey, the precise item which had occasioned a bitter attack upon the internal revenue system of Hamilton. Although fiscal necessity called for additional revenue, Jefferson described his proposed excise as a "sanatory measure"

[36] Cf. Sidney Ratner, *American Taxation: Its History as a Social Force in Democracy* (New York: W. W. Norton & Co., 1942).

[37] To James Madison, October 28, 1795 [1785], *Works*, ed. Ford, VIII, 196.

[38] *Writings*, ed. Washington, VI, 574–75.

to discourage the consumption of the beverage which "claims to itself alone the exclusive office of sot-making."[39]

Opposition to the excise taxes had been a first principle with Jefferson's followers, and in April, 1802, the internal revenue system created by Hamilton was abolished by act of Congress. But the public finance of the Jefferson administration properly belongs in an account of the Treasury career of Albert Gallatin. Jefferson's interest in taxation was largely in its social rather than in its fiscal aspects. The intricacies of the budget and taxation tried Jefferson's patience, and he preferred to leave the details of finance to his trusted and able Treasury head, contenting himself with the formulation of the general fiscal policy of the government.

Jefferson struck the keynote of his attitude toward government regulation and encouragement of commerce in his "First Annual Message," declaring: "Agriculture, manufactures, commerce, and navigation, the four pillars of our prosperity, are the most thriving when left most free to individual enterprise. Protection from casual embarrassments, however, may sometimes be seasonably interposed."[40]

Jefferson preferred to leave undefined those casual embarrassments which might sometimes justify protective measures. A pragmatic definition might be obtained as circumstances calling for government interposition arose, but to develop a systematic theory of protection was contrary to the Jeffersonian theory of government. Between nations who favored our productions and navigation and those who did not favor them, he asserted that "one distinction alone will suffice. . . . . One act of moderate duties, ... for the first, and a fixed advance on these as to some articles; and prohibitions as to others for the last."[41]

In his "Second Annual Message" he declared the protection of manufactures "adapted to our circumstances" to be one of "the landmarks by which we are to guide ourselves."[42] This protection was not to be generally accorded, however. The protection of certain infant manufactures "until they are strong enough to stand against foreign rivals" might be in the general interest, he declared; but "when it is evident that they will never be so, it is against right to make the other branches of industry support them."[43] The use of direct subsidies to commerce in the form of bounties

[39] To Samuel Smith, May 3, 1823, *Works*, ed. Ford, XII, 285.

[40] December 8, 1801, *ibid.*, IX, 339.

[41] "Report on the Privileges and Restrictions of the Commerce of the United States in Foreign Countries," December 16, 1793, *Writings*, ed. Washington, VII, 650.

[42] December 15, 1802, *Works*, ed. Ford, IX, 415.

[43] To Samuel Smith, May 3, 1823, *ibid.*, XII, 285-86.

or drawbacks, Jefferson deprecated.[44] The granting of bounties or premiums he believed would require a constitutional amendment, but, if
thereby rendered lawful, their use might be condoned in certain well-
guarded instances.[45]

The encouragement of invention and discovery in science and technology
Jefferson would leave to private rewards through the system of patent
rights. Replying to a French inquirer concerning the policy of the American states toward inventions, he declared: "Though the interposition of
government, in matters of invention has its use, yet it is in practice so inseparable from abuse, that they think it better not to meddle with it."[46]
Jefferson was not convinced, however, that private patent monopolies
were for the good of society, and he observed that nations which refused
monopolies of invention were as fruitful in new and useful discoveries as
those which granted patents.[47]

Although Jefferson was willing to sanction some protection for commerce and manufacturing, he clearly did not favor such protections as a
matter of general policy. As he would not subject industry to governmental controls, so also he would deny to it governmental favors. It was a
major paradox that the Jeffersonian embargo was, in effect, the most
drastic piece of protectionist legislation in the nation's history. But special protection was not its purpose, and in the administration of its restrictive provisions Jefferson adhered as far as possible to the principles
which governed his general theory of government.[48] Gallatin, with a view
to the effective administration of the embargo, wished to centralize its
enforcement in the Treasury rather than to share responsibility with the
state governors. The regulation of permits required for coastwise shipping
of necessary foodstuffs was susceptible of great abuse, as Gallatin warned
the President. But Jefferson, favoring administrative decentralization,
preferred to rely on the co-operation of the governors, who, however, were
unavoidably subject to local pressures, rather than to rely on the revenue
collectors of the Treasury, who were clearly responsible to the federal

---

[44] To Benjamin Stoddert, February 18, 1809, *ibid.*, XI, 98–99; to William H. Crawford,
June 20, 1816, *ibid.*, pp. 537–40.

[45] To Dr. Maese, January 15, 1809, *Writings*, ed. Washington, V, 412–13.

[46] To M. L'Hommande, August 9, 1787, *Works* (Memorial ed.), VI, 255.

[47] To Isaac McPherson, August 15, 1813, *ibid.*, XIII, 334. This letter contains a comprehensive account of Jefferson's theory of patent rights.

[48] For a comprehensive account of Jefferson's administration of the embargo see Louis
Martin Sears, *Jefferson and the Embargo* (Durham, N.C.: Duke University Press, 1927), esp.
chap. iv.

executive. Where opposition to the embargo was not pronounced, the federal-state co-operative enforcement appears to have worked well, but in New York and Massachusetts, where local opposition was strong, the governors were unwilling to sacrifice their political futures to the enforcement of a federal measure. The administration of the embargo shows clearly that Jefferson was willing to apply his theoretic notions of government to the actual conduct of public affairs and to participate in that age of experiments in government of which he held high expectations.

Jefferson's opinions concerning the support of education reflected a somewhat more expansive view of governmental responsibility than did his attitude toward public works, commerce, and industry. His work in laying the foundations of public education in the state of Virginia and the Northwest Territory is well known and need not be described here. Significant, however, was his opinion that education was clearly a public governmental responsibility. In this distinction between education and governmental enterprise in general, Jefferson's view was characteristic of a growing American conviction to which his opinion surely added strength. In Great Britain the education of youth had never been deemed as public as the regulation of ferries, harbors, or lodging-houses, and on the European continent generally the church viewed education as a function peculiarly its own. Jefferson believed that democratic government made education a public interest of the first order, and in his Diffusion of Knowledge Bill (1779) he began a struggle for tax-supported, state-administered public education in which he persevered for the remainder of his life. In the "Report of the Revisors" submitted to the Virginia Assembly during the same year, Jefferson proposed to extend public support and control to the College of William and Mary and to establish a public library at state expense and under state direction. Thus the field of public education was recognized by Jefferson as appropriate to public regulation and support, and to him much credit must be given for the early development of this special field of public administration in America.

As a matter of national administrative policy, Jefferson would also have favored provision for educational enterprise, and his ideas forecast the rise of extensive scientific investigation and publication in the federal public service. Hamilton, though favoring a duty on imported books to encourage the development of a domestic printing industry, nevertheless urged that books imported by educational institutions should be exempt from taxation. Jefferson shared the opinion that the government should encourage education through its tax measures and held further that no tariff should be levied on imported books. He recommended the establishment of a national university, not to displace the existing private institutions, but to supplement them.

Education is here placed among the articles of public care, not that it would be proposed to take its ordinary branches out of the hands of private enterprise, which manages so much better all the concerns to which it is equal; but a public institution can alone supply those sciences which, though rarely called for, are yet necessary to complete the circle, all the parts of which contribute to the improvement of the country, and some of them to its preservation. The subject is now proposed for the consideration of Congress, because, if approved by the time the State legislatures shall have deliberated on this extension of the federal trusts, and the laws shall be passed, and other arrangements made for their execution, the necessary funds will be on hand and without employment. I suppose an amendment to the constitution, by consent of the States, necessary, because the objects now recommended are not among those enumerated in the constitution, and to which it permits the public moneys to be applied.

The present consideration of a national establishment for education, particularly, is rendered proper by this circumstance, also, that if Congress, approving the proposition, shall yet think it more eligible to found it on a donation of lands, they have it now in their power to endow it with those which will be among the earliest to produce the necessary income. This foundation would have the advantage of being independent on war, which may suspend other improvements by requiring for its own purposes the resources destined for them.[49]

Writing to Joel Barlow in 1807, Jefferson confessed his doubt that the project of a natural university could be soon realized. "There is a snail-paced gait for the advance of new ideas on the general mind, under which we must acquiesce," he explained, and, he added, "people generally have more feeling for canals and roads than education."[50] Thus, although Jefferson did not disfavor the national university idea, provided a constitutional amendment to permit its establishment could be obtained, he did not push the matter, and the project came to nothing. After his retirement from the presidency, Jefferson's great interest was in the University of Virginia, and he appears to have had no further concern about a national institution.

In considering the respective authority of the Union and the states over the disposal of the public lands of the United States, Jefferson favored a greater degree of centralization than in most other respects. Writing to James Monroe in 1785, he expressed the belief that the Union was safer than the states as a repository for the control and disposal of public lands.[51] With respect to the Indian lands, Jefferson stood for exclusive control by the general government. No state or individual could treat

---

[49] "Sixth Annual Message," December 2, 1806, *Works*, ed. Ford, X, 318–19.

[50] December 10, 1807, *ibid.*, p. 530.   [51] June 17, 1785, *ibid.*, IV, 418.

with the Indians without the consent of the general government and no act of a state could give a right to lands not ceded by the Indians.[52] Jefferson asserted that "if any settlements are made on lands not ceded by them, *without the previous consent* of the United States, the government will think itself bound, not only to declare to the Indians that such settlements are without the authority or protection of the United States, but to remove them also by the public force."[53]

The basis for Jefferson's desire to remove public land questions from state control appears to have been twofold. Most apparent was his desire to see the lands used to pay off the domestic debt of the Union.[54] Less emphasized in his writings but of great significance was Jefferson's desire to permit the new western states to develop free from subserviency to the interests of the Atlantic states. His "Report of Government for the Western Territory," March 22, 1784, provided the pattern upon which the better-known Ordinance of 1787 was to be shaped. Although he allowed the Congress considerable latitude in fixing the conditions of statehood, only in respect to the prohibition of slavery in *all* the western lands did his plan subject them to requirements not imposed upon the original states. The problem, as he phrased it, was: "How may the territories of the Union be disposed of so as to produce the greatest degree of happiness to their inhabitants?"[55]

Within his native state Jefferson sought to encourage a self-reliant property-owning democracy by the incorporation into his proposed Virginia constitution of 1776 of a homestead provision which provided that "every person of full age neither owning nor having owned [50] acres of land, shall be entitled to an appropriation of [50] acres or to so much as shall make up, what he owns or has owned [50] acres in full and absolute dominion."[56] He favored public encouragement of diversified agriculture and advocated the gradual abolition of slavery. The utilization of the land was basic to any society and particularly to the agrarian commonwealth which Jefferson envisaged, and it was therefore logical that he favored an extensive area of public authority in matters pertaining to the use of the soil.

[52] To the Secretary of War, August 10, 1791, *ibid.*, VI, 301.   [53] *Ibid.*, p. 302.

[54] E.g., to James Monroe, June 17, 1785, *ibid.*, IV, 418; to William Carmichael, December 15, 1787, *ibid.*, V, 367; to James Madison, January 30, 1787, *ibid.*, p. 256.

[55] To James Monroe, July 9, 1786, *ibid.*, V, 132.

[56] *Ibid.*, II, 178. In a letter written August 13, 1776, Jefferson expressed opposition to the sale of western lands by Congress. He favored their free appropriation in small quantities (*ibid.*, pp. 239–40).

The rationale which brings Jefferson's extensive use of public power into consistency with his pronouncements on the limitation of government is his objective of the public welfare. In his conception of the scope of public policy Jefferson was seldom doctrinaire, and neither the confirmed socialist nor the advocate of laissez faire can derive substantial support from his opinions. He was at the apex of his political power when he declared: "If we can prevent the government from wasting the labors of the people, under the pretence of taking care of them, they must become happy." Yet he was willing to see the government undertake positive measures on behalf of the people which they could not properly accomplish for themselves. There is no doubt that Jefferson rejected paternalism as a philosophy of government, but it is a common error to construe his political philosophy as essentially negative.

As Charles E. Merriam has observed, "Jefferson was for freedom, not only *from* something but *for* something."[57] He proposed to utilize the public power, not to take care of men, but to create a society wherein men could take care of themselves. He would use the public resources to enlarge the area of human freedom. In this desire he joined company with Alexander Hamilton, from whom he differed as to the way in which this end might best be realized. Whether Jefferson's domestic program expanded or contracted the area of public policy in America cannot, therefore, be categorically determined, for it did both.

FOREIGN POLICY AND NATIONAL DEFENSE

Foreign relations are our province: domestic regulations and institutions belong, in every state, to itself.—To CAESAR RODNEY.[58]

Although the fields of foreign relations, diplomacy, and military affairs lie for the most part outside the scope of this study, a brief description of Jefferson's theory of executive responsibility in these respects is necessary to a complete interpretation of his thought on administration.

As Henry Adams has observed, Jefferson's "ideas of presidential authority in foreign affairs were little short of royal. He loved the sense of power and the freedom from oversight which diplomacy gave, and thought with reason that as his knowledge of Europe was greater than that of other Americans, so he should be left to carry out his policy undisturbed."[59] Herein lies the explanation of what to some has seemed a major inconsistency in Jefferson's philosophy of limited government.

[57] Merriam and Bourgin, *op. cit.*, p. 284.   [58] December 21, 1800, *Works*, ed. Ford, IX, 161.

[59] *History of the United States during the Administration of Thomas Jefferson* (2 vols.; New York: Albert & Charles Boni, 1930), Book II, p. 245.

The explanation for this apparent dichotomy lies in Jefferson's contention that the federal government was the government for foreign affairs and possessed sole authority for negotiation with foreign states. In the conduct of foreign relations the Constitution plainly designated the President as the exclusive national agent. To be sure, the Senate participated in the making of treaties, but in this, as in the confirmation of nominations, Jefferson held the Constitution merely to modify executive power in the interest of caution and responsibility. These departures from the independence of the executive power he would construe strictly against expansive interpretations by friends of senatorial authority.

An aspect of his foreign policy significant to the development of the American administrative system was his political isolationism. As early as 1785, Jefferson declared that he wished to see America "stand with respect to Europe precisely on the footing of China. We should thus avoid wars, and all our citizens would be husbandmen."[60] In a letter to Thomas Paine on March 18, 1801, Jefferson translated this wish into the principles which were to govern his administration of foreign affairs:

Determined as we are to avoid, if possible, wasting the energies of our people in war and destruction, we shall avoid implicating ourselves with the powers of Europe, even in support of principles which we mean to pursue. They have so many other interests different from ours that we must avoid being entangled in them. . . . . We believe that we can enforce those principles as to ourselves by peaceful means, now that we are likely to have our public councils detached from foreign views.[61]

Several days later, writing to Dr. George Logan, he declared that "it ought to be the very first object of our pursuits to have nothing to do with the European interests and politics. Let them be free or slaves at will, navigators or agricultural, swallowed into one government or divided into a thousand, we have nothing to fear from them in any form."[62] And, again, to Philip Massei he wrote: "On the subject of treaties, our system is to have none with any nation, as far as can be avoided."[63]

Obviously, a foreign policy which aimed at the reduction of official foreign relations to a minimum, and which proposed to dispense with all treaties, afforded little opportunity for administrative authority in the diplomatic sphere. As there was little to occupy functionaries in the foreign service, Jefferson proposed to reduce their members to an absolute minimum. Writing to Elbridge Gerry in 1799, he declared himself in favor

[60] To Count Hogendorp, October 13, 1785, *Works*, ed. Ford, IV, 469.

[61] *Ibid.*, IX, 212-13.

[62] March 21, 1801, *ibid.*, pp. 219-20.

[63] July 18, 1804, *Writings*, ed. Washington, IV, 552.

of little or no diplomatic establishment.[64] Writing to William Short in 1801, Jefferson described his desire to relinquish all treaties, and added:

We call in our diplomatic missions, barely keeping up those to the most important nations. There is a strong disposition in our countrymen to discontinue even these; and very possibly it may be done. Consuls will be continued as usual. The interest which European nations feel, as well as ourselves, in the mutual patronage of commercial intercourse, is a sufficient stimulus on both sides to insure that patronage.[65]

Thus, although Jefferson may have added to the presidential prerogative in the field of foreign affairs, he actually diminished any role that public administration might otherwise have played in this field. In the struggle between Great Britain and Napoleonic France, Jefferson wished America to take no part. So far as America was to have foreign relations he would govern them by a policy of neutrality. To *enforce* American neutrality was quite another matter, but he believed that the European powers could be controlled through the interests of commerce. And, as Henry Adams has suggested, "Jefferson wanted no treaties which would prevent him from using commercial weapons against nations that violated American neutrality; and therefore he reserved to Congress the right to direct commerce in whatever paths the Government might prefer."[66]

Relying mainly on the geographic situation of the United States for protection from the contentions of the Old World, Jefferson was nevertheless willing to conclude international agreements where the national interests were clearly served. In October, 1801, he wrote to William Short: "We have a perfect horror at everything like connecting ourselves with the politics of Europe," and added that "it would be advantageous to us to have neutral rights established on a broad ground; but no dependence can be placed in any European coalition for that."[67] But when news of the French acquisition of Louisiana reached Jefferson, he declared that the day that France takes possession of New Orleans "seals the union of the two nations who in conjunction can maintain exclusive possession of the ocean. From that moment we must marry ourselves to the British fleet and nation."[68] The aggressions of Napoleonic France aroused Jefferson's fears, and he declared to Madison that "we should lose no time in securing something more than a mutual friendship with England."[69]

[64] January 26, 1799, *Works*, ed. Ford, IX, 18.

[65] October 3, 1801, *ibid.*, p. 309.

[66] *Op. cit.*, Book II, p. 355.   [67] *Works*, ed. Ford, IX, 308.

[68] To Robert R. Livingston, April 18, 1802, *ibid.*, p. 365.

[69] August 25, 1805, *ibid.*, X, 171. See also letter to Madison, August 27, 1805, *ibid.*, pp. 172–74.

Not only did Jefferson propose a treaty of alliance with Great Britain when the national interest appeared to require it but he further proposed a convention with the maritime powers of Europe to suppress the piracy of the Barbary States and the slave trade from Africa.[70] Although, in general, he opposed the maintenance of diplomatic missions abroad, he recognized the important role of Russia in the preservation of international peace, and, impressed by the humanitarian sensibility of the Emperor Alexander I, he proposed to establish a mission at the Russian court.[71] Aware of the opposition which this departure from earlier principles might arouse, Jefferson "thought it best to keep back the nomination to the close of the session, that the mission might remain secret as long as possible";[72] but the Senate had learned too well the lesson of unentanglement with Europe which Jefferson had preached, and with "unexampled precipitancy" and without explanation the senators rejected Jefferson's last official communication to them.

Although he favored peace as a national policy, Jefferson was prepared to marshal the nation's armed strength in the interest of security. He dispatched an American fleet to the Mediterranean to stop the depredations of the Tripoli pirates on American persons and property. As American minister at the court of France he observed the warlike disposition of the European powers and urged that the Confederation "may see the importance of putting themselves immediately into a respectable position" and declared that magazines and manufactures of arms should be established.[73] He was prepared to see the United States declare a state of war with Great Britain in 1812, for he held: "Two items alone in our catalog of wrongs will forever acquit us of being the aggressors: the impressment of our seamen, and the excluding us from the ocean. The first foundations of the social compact would be broken up were we definitively to refuse to its members the protection of their persons and property, while in their lawful pursuits."[74]

Standing armies he believed to be of greatest danger to the freedom of a people. Consequently, he would rely upon a citizens' militia for the national defense. This militia, however, he would classify and organize for effec-

---

[70] To John Adams, November 1, 1822, *ibid.*, XII, 270; *Autobiography, ibid.*, I, 100-103.

[71] To the Emperor Alexander of Russia, April 19, 1806, *ibid.*, X, 249-51; to William Short, March 8, 1809, XI, 102-4.

[72] To William Short, March 8, 1809, *ibid.*, XI, 103.

[73] To John Brown, May 26, 1788, *ibid.*, V, 399.

[74] To James Maury, April 25, 1812, *ibid.*, XI, 240.

tive military service. In his "Fifth Annual Message" to the Congress he declared:

> You will consider whether it would not be expedient, for a state of peace as well as of war, so to organize or class the militia, as would enable us, on any sudden emergency, to call for the services of the younger portions, unencumbered with the old and those having families. Upwards of three hundred thousand able bodied men, between the ages of eighteen and twenty-six years, which the last Census shows we may now count within our limits, will furnish a competent number for offense or defense in any point where they may be wanted, and will give time for raising regular forces after the necessity of them shall become certain, and the reducing to the early period of life all its active service, cannot be but desirable to our younger citizens of the present as well as future times, inasmuch as it engages to them in more advanced age a quiet and undisturbed repose in the bosom of their families. I cannot then but earnestly recommend to your early consideration the expediency of so modifying our militia system as, by a separation of the more active part from that which is less so, we may draw from it, when necessary, an efficient corps, fit for real and active service, and to be called to it in regular rotation.[75]

Jefferson proposed to divide the militia into land and naval units, and he drafted bills for the establishment of a naval militia, for classing the militia, and for assigning to each class its particular duties. To these recommendations, which would have brought uniformity and system into the national defense, Congress did not respond, and the War of 1812 found the nation poorly prepared for the military undertakings to which it aspired. Jefferson recognized the necessity for expert military leadership and declared to Monroe in 1813 that military instruction must be made a regular part of collegiate education. "We can never be safe till this is done."[76]

Unfortunately for Jefferson's expectations, an effective organization for national defense was not to be obtained by the procurement and organization of men alone. The disposition and numbers of the American forces on the Canadian frontier were such as could have achieved victory with competent leadership and effective administration. But Jefferson's reluctance to insist upon an energetic, well-organized federal administrative system had left a legacy of military incompetence in the Army and administrative ineptitude in the War Department which certainly contributed to the destruction of what he described as "the fairest expectations of the nation."[77]

Jefferson's views on the organization and maintenance of a navy were

[75] December 3, 1805, *ibid.*, X, 191–92.

[76] June 18, 1813, *Writings*, ed. Washington, VI, 131.

[77] To Dr. Benjamin Rush, March 6, 1813, *ibid.*, p. 106.

colored by the same passion for economy that conditioned his attitude toward the Army, but he deemed a navy less dangerous to civil liberties than the presence of a permanent military establishment. His attitude on the organization of national defense contrasted sharply with that of Hamilton, who advocated a substantial army, and of Adams, who favored an ample navy. Jefferson wanted neither, preferring to defend the shores of America from forts and gunboats and to man the nation's ramparts with a citizen army. The task of over-all administration in the armed forces, particularly in aspects of procurement and supply, he appears never to have fully appreciated. His own record as revolutionary governor of Virginia was attacked upon grounds of incompetence, and he sought refuge in resignation with the hope that someone versed in military affairs would be elected to succeed him.[78]

Although he employed great personal power in the conduct of foreign relations and national defense, it is doubtful if Jefferson extended the scope of public policy in either area beyond the limits established by the Federalists. Political success and the misfortunes of Europe provided him with occasions for the exercise of presidential prerogative which circumstances denied his predecessors. Yet the effect of his administration, although perhaps not his intention, was to diminish the independence and prestige which the executive departments had enjoyed under the Federalists. Jefferson took the conduct of foreign relations largely into his own hands. Madison, serving as his amanuensis, held a very different relationship than Jefferson had enjoyed as Secretary of State under Washington. The departments of War and Navy suffered from Jefferson's want of interest in their affairs and from his desire for economy and peace. The Treasury under Gallatin's able direction preserved something of its former strength, but its basic policies were determined by Jefferson and the congressional leaders, and Gallatin was never able to effect the administrative leadership which Hamilton had accomplished.

Although Jefferson as President played a major role in the formulation of public policy, he relied upon his political leadership in Congress rather than upon his independent executive powers to effect his purpose. John Marshall presaged this development in a letter to Hamilton, declaring: "Mr. Jefferson appears to me to be a man, who will embody himself with the House of Representatives. By weakening the office of President, he will increase his personal power. He will diminish his responsibility, sap

---

[78] *Works*, ed. Ford, I, xxiv (Introd.), and *Autobiography*, p. 79. See H. J. Eckenrode, *The Revolution in Virginia* (Boston: Houghton Mifflin Co., 1916). Eckenrode, however, appears to overemphasize Jefferson's administrative shortcomings.

the fundamental principles of the government, and become the leader of that party which is about to constitute the majority of the legislature."[79]

Likewise observing the trend but misreading the character of Jefferson's leadership was Oliver Ellsworth, who is reported to have remarked that, if Jefferson were President, "he would take little or no responsibility on himself. . . . . Everything would be referred to Congress. A lax, intriguing kind of policy would be adopted; and while arts were practiced to give direction to public sentiment, Mr. Jefferson would affect to be directed by the will of the nation. There would be no national energy."[80]

But Jefferson had always stood for the mutual independence of the executive and legislative branches, and "the influence he exerted could rarely be seen in his official and public language; it took shape in private, in the incessant talk that went on, without witnesses, at the White House."[81] It was a case of the Jeffersonian principle of harmony utilizing the new role of the President as party leader to smooth the path of administrative and congressional relations. The formulation of policy which Hamilton and the Federalists had believed largely an executive function henceforth became a matter of legislative-executive co-operation or contention and depended upon the partisan organization of Congress and presidential party leadership for its mechanism. Whether presidential leadership in policy-making was strengthened or weakened by Jefferson's career cannot perhaps be determined categorically. But certainly the theory of policy-making as a primary executive function independent of party leadership barely survived his administration. Marshall and Ellsworth were wrong in their belief that Jefferson would refuse responsibility. Rather Jefferson recognized a responsibility which differed from the Federalist conception. He recognized no plenary executive power to formulate policy after his own notion of the national interest, but rather he assumed leadership on behalf of the majority of the electorate to effect their interests within the limits of his constitutional authority. It was a move in the direction of democracy in public administration.

[79] *The Works of Alexander Hamilton Comprising His Correspondence and His Political and Official Writings* . . . . , ed. J. C. Hamilton (7 vols.; New York: Charles S. Francis & Co., 1850–51), VI, 501–3; Albert J. Beveridge, *The Life of John Marshall* (4 vols.; Boston: Houghton Mifflin Co., 1916–19), II, 537.

[80] William G. Brown, *The Life of Oliver Ellsworth* (New York: Macmillan Co., 1905), pp. 324-25.

[81] Adams, *op. cit.*, Book IV, p. 155.

CHAPTER XII

ADMINISTRATIVE POLICY AND THE PUBLIC SERVICE

ANY inquiry into Jefferson's thought on administrative policy and the public service must be concerned with his ideas on the holding of office. This chapter will therefore largely have to do with Jefferson's administration of the federal civil personnel and with his theories about the relation of the civil service to the rest of the government and to the public. In the following sections the distinction in Jefferson's mind between the higher offices (which he deemed honorable duties) and the lower offices (which he held necessary evils) will be emphasized. This distinction is important to an understanding of his attitude on many issues, for he did not necessarily apply his policies uniformly throughout the federal service—sometimes following contrary lines of action in the higher and lower levels.

The available material on Jefferson's theories of appointment, tenure, and removal is more than adequate to provide a comprehensive account of this aspect of his administrative thought. Several specialized studies have been made of Jefferson's use of patronage and the appointive power,[1] and these, together with his voluminous correspondence, afford a fairly complete picture of his attitude toward the holding of public office. Between Jefferson's theories and certain practical results of his administrative policies lies a confused area of contradiction into which the interpreter must attempt to bring some order. Jefferson's unsympathetic biographers have customarily dismissed his practical lapses from professed principles as evidence of "contemptible hypocrisy." Admirers of Jefferson's democratic faith and humane idealism resent the implications of his inconsistent conduct that he was either in fact hypocritical or that he lacked the force of character to insist upon the application of his principles in the face of determined opposition. But any penetrating reading of Jefferson's

[1] Gaillard Hunt, "Office Seeking during Jefferson's Administration," *American Historical Review*, III (January, 1898), 270–91; Worthington C. Ford, *Jefferson and the Newspaper* ("Records of the Columbia Historical Society," Vol. VIII [Washington, 1905]); Randolph C. Downes, "Thomas Jefferson and the Removal of Governor St. Clair in 1802," *Ohio Archeological and Historical Quarterly*, XXXVI (January, 1927), 62–77; Carl Russell Fish, *The Civil Service and the Patronage* (Cambridge: Harvard University Press, 1921); and Howard Lee McBain, "Jefferson and the New York Patronage," *DeWitt Clinton and the Origin of the Spoils System in New York* ("Columbia University Studies in History, Economics, and Public Law," Vol. XXVIII [New York: Columbia University Press, 1907]).

personality as revealed in his writings or in his political life will absolve him of failure on these grounds.

Jefferson's weakness, certainly not peculiar to himself but one that may account for the more pronounced contradictions in his political career, was an acute form of intellectual astigmatism which made certain acts when committed by others appear to him in a very different character than the same acts performed by himself or his friends. His observations on the conduct of political contemporaries were based upon a double standard of morality; one, censorious, applied to his rivals; another, colored by the conviction of good intentions, applied to himself and to his followers. Jefferson seemed never to have sensed his own defect and appears to have surely lacked a sense of the humorous position in which his contradictory behavior not infrequently placed him. His derogators have made much sport of his curious conduct, but these lapses from consistency are important indications of the care with which Jefferson must be read if an accurate evaluation of his opinions is to be attempted.

It is also true that Jefferson understood that practical political solutions may not conform to ideal standards. The responsibilities of public office require that the public business be done, not that the ideals of perfectionism be translated into reality. Jefferson was accordingly prepared to perform his public duties, although the conditions under which they must be performed sometimes required departure from his ideals. As T. V. Smith has observed, "means are as narrow as ideals are wide,"[2] and Jefferson as an administrator could not have effectively served the American people had he failed to recognize this axiom.

THE NATURE OF PUBLIC OFFICE

[Politics] is my duty.—To HARRY INNES.[3]

Throughout his long political career Jefferson professed a profound distaste for public office, which, regardless of the degree of sincerity which it may reflect, indicated an attitude that he wished his countrymen to associate with him. "No man had ever had less desire of entering into public office than myself," he declared.[4] "Public employment," he explained, "contributes neither to advantage nor happiness. It is but honorable exile from one's family and affairs."[5]

[2] "Thomas Jefferson and the Perfectibility of Mankind," *Ethics*, LIII (July, 1943), 297.

[3] March 7, 1791, *Works*, ed. Ford, VI, 209.

[4] *The Anas*, 1792, *ibid.*, I, 194.

[5] To Francis Willis, April 13, 1790, *ibid.*, VI, 46.

In justification of his retirement from public life after his unhappy experience as governor of Virginia, Jefferson rejected Monroe's contention that the people had an unqualified right to call forth his services, declaring that the doctrine that the state has a perpetual right to the services of its members would "annihilate the blessings of existence."[6] He held that uniform and multiplied precedents established the right of individuals to refuse as well as to accept public office. Yet although Jefferson was not prepared to admit that the state might demand, without cessation, the services of its citizens, he nevertheless agreed that an equal "tour of duty" might be asked of every individual. This duty to serve in public office was a favorite notion of Jefferson's, and he offered it as explanation of his many years of public service.

How long the tour of duty ought to be was a question which Jefferson found difficult to answer. At several points in his career, notably on retiring as governor of Virginia and as Secretary of State, he protested that his tour of duty was finished, only again to return to public life. Writing to Madison in 1793, he expressed the belief that four and twenty years in office had completed his *corvée*,[7] but he did not hesitate to serve four years more as Vice-President and eight more years as President of the United States.

Holding public office to be a duty rather than a privilege, Jefferson did not consider it a proper place for the acquisition of wealth or reputation. His notion of office-holding excluded the idea of a careerism and the existence of a distinct administrative class or profession. There was, indeed, a strong flavor of Virginia aristocracy in his conception of public office. In essence it postulated a body of gentlemen of independent means, talent, and high ideals of service to fill the upper posts of government. An agrarian economy based upon slave labor and large plantation units could and did supply such leadership. Four of the first five presidents, and a high proportion of cabinet and diplomatic officers, represented the southern planter class; and the rest of the higher administrative positions were to a considerable degree filled by northern men of moderate wealth, often inherited. Financial considerations, Jefferson believed, should be beneath men called to the higher public trusts. "I love to see honest and honorable men at the helm, men who will not bend their politics to their purses, nor pursue measures by which they may profit, and then profit by their measures."[8]

To Edward Rutledge, Jefferson declared that "there is a debt of service

---

[6] May 20, 1782, *ibid.*, III, 301.   [7] June 9, 1793, *ibid.*, VII, 373.

[8] To Edward Rutledge, December 27, 1796, *ibid.*, VIII, 258–59.

due from every man to his country, proportioned to the bounties which nature and fortune have measured to him."[9] He believed that there was a natural aristocracy of virtue and talents which he held the most precious gift of nature, "for the instruction, the trusts, and government of society." "May we not even say," he asked, "that that form of government is the best, which provides the most effectually for a pure selection of those natural *aristoi* into the offices of government?"[10] Mere wealth or birth did not constitute this aristocracy of talent, but in proportion to the talent and wealth which an individual enjoyed, so was his debt of service to the community to be measured. "Some men," he declared, "are born for the public. Nature by fitting them for the service of the human race on a broad scale, has stamped them with the evidences of her destination and their duty."[11]

To this picture of public office as a duty to be met by disinterested men of public spirit there was a reverse side. To desire public office either for power or for pelf was held by Jefferson a contemptible ambition; "and whenever a man has cast a longing eye on them, a rottenness begins in his conduct,"[12] wrote Jefferson (rather appropriately) to Tench Coxe. Writing to the governor of Pennsylvania, Jefferson explained why his administration had put down "the great mass of offices which gave such patronage to the president."

These had been so numerous, that presenting themselves to the public eye at all times and places, office began to be looked to as a resource for every man whose affairs were getting into derangement, or who was too indolent to pursue his profession, and for young men just entering life. In short, it was poisoning the very source of industry, by presenting an easier resource for a livelihood, and was corrupting the principles of the great mass of those who passed a wishful eye on office.[13]

Although Jefferson did not imply that the public service should not afford a livelihood to persons necessarily employed in its subordinate posts, he did not believe that it should afford opportunity for employment in excess of the actual needs of the service. Taken with other pronouncements upon the corrupting influence of office and the disparaging tenor of his reference to office-holders, one must conclude that he viewed public offices as necessary evils at best. The highest public offices he deemed arduous honors; the presidency he described as a "splendid misery" and

[9] *Ibid.*, p. 258.

[10] To John Adams, October 28, 1813, *ibid.*, XI, 343–44.

[11] To James Monroe, January 13, 1803, *Writings*, ed. Washington, IV, 455.

[12] May 21, 1799, *Works*, ed. Ford, IX, 70.

[13] To Thomas McKean, February 19, 1803, *ibid.*, pp. 450–51.

the lower positions were necessary but in the nature of unavoidable expenses which should be held to the minimum.

Fearing the concentration of power which long tenure of office might vest in public functionaries, Jefferson subscribed to the principle of rotation. With regard to the higher posts of government he favored "responsibilities at short periods,"[14] but with regard to the mass of offices he came to believe that some measure of stability must prevail. He declared to Gallatin that he never considered the length of time a person had continued in office, nor the money he had made in it, "as entering at all into the reasons for a removal."[15]

Jefferson at first opposed the re-eligibility of the President to election, insisting that "re-eligibility makes him an officer for life."[16] He described the chief executive office as "a bad edition of a Polish King";[17] and, although he acquiesced in the decision of the majority to retain the provision for perpetual re-eligibility, he deemed it a real defect which future generations might see fit to correct. He nevertheless justified his second term as President as a vindication of his first administration. "The abominable slanders of my political enemies have obliged me to call for that verdict from my country in the only way it can be obtained," he declared to Thomas McKean.[18]

A major source of Jefferson's anxiety over presidential re-election was that the President, with the patronage of the executive department at his disposal, could easily dictate his re-election for life! "And those who have once got an ascendency, and possessed themselves of all the resources of the nation, their revenues and offices, have immense means for retaining their advantage," he observed.[19] "The elective principle becomes nothing, if it may be smothered by the emormous patronage of the General government."[20] "I sincerely wish," he wrote to Moses Robinson, "we could see our government so secured as to depend less on the character of the person in whose hands it is trusted. Bad men will sometimes get in, and with such an immense patronage, may make great progress in corrupting the public mind and principles."[21]

[14] To James Martin, September 20, 1813, *Writings*, ed. Washington, VI, 213.

[15] To Albert Gallatin, December 12, 1806, *Works*, ed. Ford, X, 324–25.

[16] To Edward Carrington, May 27, 1788, *ibid.*, V, 401.

[17] To John Adams, November 13, 1787, *Writings*, ed. Washington, II, 316.

[18] January 17, 1804, *Works*, ed. Ford, X, 69.

[19] To John Taylor, June 1, 1798, *Writings*, ed. Washington, IV, 246.

[20] To Governor Thomas McKean, February 2, 1801, *Works*, ed. Ford, IX, 175.

[21] March 23, 1801, *Writings*, ed. Washington, IV, 380.

The net effect of Jefferson's expression on the subject of public office must surely have been to depress the lower civil service in public estimation. The frequency with which he articulated the popular dislike for public functionaries—a legacy of the Colonial past—must place him among those political figures responsible for the belated rise of careerism in American public life. Yet Jefferson does not seem to have entirely opposed professionalism in the public service, for his interest in public education as a preparation for self-government and his encouragement of the study of government at the University of Virginia suggest that he did not believe that the administration of public affairs could be altogether intrusted to amateurs.

THE APPOINTMENT OF OFFICE-HOLDERS

There is nothing I am so anxious about as making the best possible appointments.— TO NATHANIEL MACON.[22]

"Nothing presents such difficulties of administration as offices," exclaimed Thomas Jefferson at the close of his first month in the White House. He had once believed the difficulties about offices to lie chiefly in the removals he proposed to make; but he soon discovered that appointments of office-holders merely multiplied the clamors of disappointed office-seekers. For the lower civil posts a hundred office-hungry Republicans could be found for every office—whether vacant or filled. For the higher posts Jefferson sought in vain for suitable candidates. Offices indeed presented difficulties to the victorious leader of a popular party at a time when able men eschewed the unprofitable drudgery, and abuse, which the party battles of the preceding decade had associated with public administration. While Jefferson despaired of even filling his cabinet positions, the Republicans grew impatient for the spoils of victory. When removals were attempted to placate the party subordinates, the Federalists uttered cries of revolution and anarchy and rent the heavens with maledictions against Jefferson's perfidy. Unhappily, the man who elevated harmony to the level of a principle described his plight to John Dickinson: "My position is painful enough between federalists who cry out on the first touch of their monopoly, and republicans who clamor for universal removal. A subdivision of the latter will increase the perplexity."[23]

With the lower posts recruitment at least presented no problem. But in the higher orders the case was different. The difficulties of Washington and Adams in securing competent officers for the leading posts of the government had revealed a dearth of suitable administrative talent in Ameri-

---

[22] May 14, 1801, *Works*, ed. Ford, IX, 253.   [23] July 23, 1807, *ibid.*, p. 281.

ca. Unfortunately for Jefferson, most of the existing talent and experience belonged to the ranks of federalism, which represented not only the commercial and manufacturing element in the country but contained the larger share of men experienced in the business of the federal government. These men Jefferson could not appoint to his administration, nor would many of them have willingly served under him. "Men possessing minds of the first order, and who have had opportunities of being known and of acquiring the general confidence, do not abound in any country beyond the wants of the country," Jefferson observed.[24] When these few men of talent refused to assume their responsibility to lend their aid in the direction of public affairs, the prospect for republican government was indeed dismal. So thought Jefferson, and, when offering an executive post of Secretary of the Navy to Robert R. Livingston, he explained his reasons for desiring men of distinction to head his administration:

> It is essential to assemble in the outset persons to compose our administration, whose talents integrity and revolutionary name and principles may inspire the nation at once, with unbounded confidence and impose an awful silence on all the maligners of republicanism; as may suppress in embryo the purpose avowed by one of their most daring and effective chiefs, of beating down the administration. These names do not abound at this day. So few are they, that yours, my friend, cannot be spared among them without leaving a blank which cannot be filled. If I can obtain for the public the aid of those I have contemplated, I fear nothing. If this cannot be done, then are we unfortunate indeed![25]

Jefferson's arguments failed to convince, for Livingston politely refused the responsibility offered. Six months later (two months after his inauguration) Jefferson had still been unable to head the Navy Department. "It is the department I understand the least," he declared, "and therefore need a person whose complete competence will justify the most entire confidence and resignation."[26] Writing to Gouverneur Morris, Jefferson lamented, "I believe I shall have to advertise for a Secretary of the Navy."[27]

Faced with the contention of office-seekers in the lower orders and the refusals of desirable appointees to accept the burdens of the higher offices, Jefferson preserved a remarkable restraint of temper. But on rare occasions the perverseness of mankind proved more than his placid disposition could bear, and in a moment of exasperation he exclaimed to

[24] To Robert R. Livingston, February 16, 1801, *ibid.*, p. 180.

[25] December 14, 1800, *ibid.*, pp. 152–53.

[26] To Samuel Smith, April 17, 1801, Jefferson manuscripts, cited in Henry Adams, *History of the United States during the Administration of Thomas Jefferson* (2 vols.; New York: Albert & Charles Boni, 1930), I, 223.

[27] May 8, 1801, *Works*, ed. Ford, IX, 251.

Gallatin, "But for God's sake get us relieved from this dreadful drudgery of refusal."[28] So embarrassing was the frequency of these refusals in the initial tender of an office that Jefferson deemed it of advantage to the public to "ask of those to whom appointments are proposed, if they are not accepted, to say nothing of the offer, at least for a convenient time." The refusal, he explained, "cheapens the estimation of the public appointments and renders them less acceptable to those to whom they are secondarily proposed."[29]

In determining the fitness of a candidate for office, Jefferson distinguished between the higher offices of state and those of subordinate nature. Writing to his friend, John Page, he described a measure for political preferment which suggested a compound of veteran's preference and reward for party loyalty: "In appointments to public offices of mere profit, I have ever considered faithful service in either our first or second revolution as giving preference of claim, and that appointments on that principle would gratify the public, and strengthen that confidence so necessary to enable the executive to direct the whole public force to the best advantage of the nation."[30]

To a record of military service and party regularity, marriage on at least one occasion proved a desirable attribute in an applicant for appointment. During his administration of the State Department in 1792, the office of chief clerk became vacant, and the two subordinate candidates for the post were equally qualified save that one was married. Upon grounds of the greater pecuniary needs of family life Jefferson forthwith appointed the married man.[31]

Jefferson placed high value upon the political recognition accorded to candidates for federal offices by their native states. The state and local offices occupied by a candidate were considered "public evidences of the estimation in which he is held."[32] Writing to J. F. Mercer in 1804, Jefferson, explaining his reasons for a particular appointment, declared: "The grounds on which one of the competitors stood, set aside of necessity all hesitation. Mr. Hall's having been a member of the Legislature, a Speaker of the Representatives, and a member of the Executive Council were evidence of the respect of the State towards him, which our respect for the State could not neglect."[33]

[28] December 8, 1808, *Writings*, ed. Washington, V, 398.

[29] To General John Armstrong, May 26, 1804, *Works*, ed. Ford, X, 79–80.

[30] July 17, 1807, *ibid.*, p. 468.   [31] To Jacob Blackwell, April 1, 1792, *ibid.*, VI, 456–57.

[32] To Elias Shipman and others, July 12, 1801, *ibid.*, IX, 270.

[33] October 9, 1804, *Writings*, ed. Washington, IV, 562–63.

Although Jefferson prophesied an age of experiments in government, he did not propose to pioneer the unexplored paths in the administration of the appointive power. When his Secretary of the Treasury recommended the appointment of a woman to a federal office, Jefferson replied, "The appointment of a woman to office is an innovation for which the public is not prepared nor am I."[34]

Jefferson had once declared to Washington, and continued to maintain, that "talents and science are sufficient motives with me in appointments to which they are fitted."[35] The occasion was a justification of his appointment of Philip Freneau as translating clerk in the State Department. But Jefferson well understood the political value of appointments which involved talents in the appointee more significant than those called for by the office in question. Nevertheless, talents and knowledge were not in themselves conclusive evidence of the fitness of a man for public affairs. Although political expediency might sometimes dictate the appointment to office of a man of doubtful ability, Jefferson held that "an unprincipled man, let his other fitnesses be what they will, ought never to be employed."[36] How closely Jefferson read the character of his appointees was another question. His intentions were of the best. To his friend Archibald Stuart, he declared, "There is nothing I am so anxious about as good nominations, conscious that the merit as well as reputation of an administration depends as much on that as on its measures."[37]

The test of character was not applied so rigorously in cases of removal as in initial appointment to office. Remarking upon the untruthful allegations of a federal office-holder in New York, Jefferson observed that "such rejection of all regard for truth, would have been sufficient cause against receiving him into the corps of executive officers at first; but whether it is expedient after a person is appointed, to be as nice on a question of removal requires great consideration."[38]

Unfortunately for his reputation as a judge of men, the characters of some of his most prominent appointees evidenced a lack of principle which even the dearth of suitable candidates for administrative posts could hardly mitigate. Most unfortunate in this respect was Jefferson's appointment of General James Wilkinson as civil and military governor

[34] January 13, 1807, *Works*, ed. Ford, X, 339.

[35] September 9, 1792, *ibid.*, VII, 145.

[36] To Dr. Gilmer, June 28, 1793, *Writings*, ed. Washington, IV, 5.

[37] April 8, 1801, *Works*, ed. Ford, IX, 248.

[38] To DeWitt Clinton, October 6, 1804, *ibid.*, X, 105.

of Louisiana.[39] Over the appointment of a man who was perhaps already implicated in the notorious affair of Burr's conspiracy, and who was a sub rosa pensioner of the King of Spain, Jefferson expressed satisfaction. "Not a single fact has appeared," he observed to Samuel Smith, "which occasions me to doubt that I could have made a fitter appointment than General Wilkinson."[40]

The methods which Jefferson employed in the recruitment of suitable appointees for the subordinate civil posts differed from those of his predecessors chiefly in the reliance he placed upon the partisan leaders in the states for recommendations. In part, this reliance reflects a well-organized party machine unavailable to Washington and only imperfectly to Adams, and in part it also reflects Jefferson's desire to preserve party and private harmony and to shift the burden of making the decisions to other shoulders. Much of the burden fell upon Gallatin, who received as well the onus of unpopularity when decisions displeased Republican stalwarts. To Jefferson's lieutenants in the states was shifted more of the burden, but the Clintons and McKeans accepted it gladly, as recruitment was not merely a process of selection among a host of anxious office-seekers but an invaluable aid in the building of a party machine.

Jefferson invited suggestions concerning pending appointments but was unwilling to divulge the information which he received, either to the nominees concerned or to members of the Congress. Explaining his policy in this regard, in a letter prepared in answer to a request from a Senate committee for information concerning certain nominees, he declared:

> The Constitution has made it my duty to nominate; and has not made it my duty to lay before them the evidences or reasons whereon my nominations are founded. . . . . During nearly the whole of the time this Constitution has been in operation I have been in situations of intimacy with this part of it and may observe from my own knowledge that it has not been the usage for the President to lay before the Senate or a committee, the information on which he makes his nominations.[41]

To exhibit recommendations, Jefferson averred, would be to turn the Senate into a court of slander and to expose the character of every man

---

[39] Although the two senators and four representatives of Tennessee united in recommending Andrew Jackson for governor of Louisiana, Jefferson refused to consider him. He described Jackson as a man of "violent passions" and "despotic principles" (Edward Channing, *The Jeffersonian System, 1801–1811*, Vol. XII of *The American Nation: A History*, ed. A. B. Hart [New York: Harper & Bros., 1906], p. 20). Years later Jefferson declared Jackson unfit for the presidency (*Private Correspondence of Daniel Webster*, I, 364 ff., cited in *Works*, ed. Ford, XII, 392).

[40] May 4, 1806, *Works*, ed. Ford, X, 264.

[41] To Uriah Tracy, January, 1806, *ibid.*, p. 218 (not sent).

nominated to an ordeal, without his consent, subjecting the Senate to heats and waste of time.[42]

During his own presidential terms Jefferson was frequently embarrassed by the appeals for office and recommendations for appointment from his old friends and from prominent political leaders. Upon his retirement from office he foresaw that many persons would seek to take advantage of his friendship with the new President to press for recommendations. To forestall this annoyance, he issued, as he left the presidency, a public letter in which he announced his determination to refuse all efforts to elicit his assistance. Although the effect of this letter was not all that Jefferson desired, and although his resolution did not always equal the persistence of the office-seekers, a recent study of his influence on the appointments made by Madison supports his contention that he customarily refrained from the recommendation of candidates for public office.[43]

Considering nomination to be a strictly executive power, Jefferson throughout his political career had consistently opposed the interference of legislative bodies in the naming of executive officers. Writing to Samuel Kercheval, Jefferson criticized the influence of the Virginia legislature over appointments:

> Nomination to office is an executive function. To give it to the legislature, as we do, is a violation of the principle of the separation of powers. It swerves the members from correctness, by temptations to intrigue for office themselves, and to a corrupt barter of votes; and destroys responsibility by dividing it among a multitude. By leaving nomination in its proper place, among executive functions, the principle of the distribution of power is preserved, and responsibility weighs with its heaviest force on a single head.[44]

During Washington's administration Jefferson, as Secretary of State, had fought against the pretensions of the Senate to negative the grade of persons nominated to fill foreign missions.[45] Nor did Jefferson believe that the Senate could indirectly interfere with the grade of presidential nominees. He declared: "It may be objected that the Senate may by continual negatives on the *person*, do what amounts to a negative on the *grade*, and so, indirectly, defeat this right of the President. But this would be a breach

---

[42] To Albert Gallatin, February 10, 1803, *ibid.*, IX, 444.

[43] Roy J. Honeywell, "President Jefferson and His Successor," *American Historical Review*, XLVI (October, 1940), 64–75.

[44] July 12, 1816, *Works*, ed. Ford, XII, 8.

[45] *Opinion on the Powers of the Senate*, April 24, 1790, *ibid.*, VI, 51; *Works* (Memorial ed.), III, 15.

of trust; an abuse of the power confided to the Senate, of which that body cannot be supposed capable."[46]

In nominations to subordinate posts Jefferson believed that the Senate should accept the wishes of the President in all but exceptional cases. He declared to Gallatin that "the selection made by the President ought to inspire a general confidence that it has been made on due enquiry and investigation of character, and that the Senate should interpose their negative only in those particular cases where something happens to be within their knowledge against the character of the person, and unfitting him for the appointment."[47] That the Senate did not share Jefferson's view of its responsibilities was evident when it refused to confirm his appointment of Benjamin Harrison as commissioner of loans at Richmond.[48]

Writing to President Madison, Jefferson recommended the removal of Post Office appointments from control by the Senate, observing the habit of senators to use their power of confirmation actually to usurp the appointive functions,[49] and in defense of the independence of the executive and the stability of the public service Jefferson opposed the "Four-Year" or Tenure of Office Act passed during Monroe's administration at the behest of William H. Crawford, Secretary of the Treasury, which made virtually every executive appointment subject to Senate confirmation:

> The late mischievous law vacating every four years nearly all the executive offices of the government . . . . saps the constitutional and salutary functions of the President, and introduces a principle of intrigue and corruption, which will soon leaven the mass, not only of Senators, but of citizens. It is more baneful than the attempt which failed in the beginning of the government, to make all officers irremovable but with the consent of the Senate. This places, every four years, all appointments under their power, and even obliges them to act on every one nomination. It will keep in constant excitement all the hungry cormorants for office, render them, as well as those in place, sycophants to their senators, engage these in eternal intrigue to turn out one and put in another, in cabals to swap work; and make them what all executive directories become, mere sinks of corruption and faction. This must have been one of the midnight signatures of the President when he had not time to consider, or even to read the law; and the more fatal as being irrepealable but with the consent of the Senate, which will never be obtained.[50]

The senatorial power of confirmation had cost Jefferson one of his bitterest humiliations. At the very close of his second administration, in re-

---

[46] *Works* (Memorial ed.), III, 17.

[47] To Albert Gallatin, February 10, 1803, *Works*, ed. Ford, IX, 444.

[48] *Executive Journal of the Senate*, II, 88; Edward Channing, *A History of the United States* (6 vols.; New York: Macmillan Co., 1927), IV, 56.

[49] To James Madison, March 10, 1814, *Works*, ed. Ford, XI, 392.

[50] To James Madison, November 29, 1820, *ibid.*, XII, 174–75.

sponse to a wish expressed by Emperor Alexander I of Russia, Jefferson had arranged for an exchange of ministers and had dispatched his old personal friend, William Short, to the new post. Waiting until two weeks before the close of his term, Jefferson made the appointment of Short the subject of his last message to the Senate. No one had exceeded Jefferson in expressing distaste for diplomatic missions; he had berated the Federalists for their alleged extravagance and had suggested that no permanent missions were necessary, consuls and special envoys being sufficient for representation abroad. But the mortification of the retiring President was keen when the Senate "abruptly and unanimously" rejected his last request.[51]

PATRONAGE AND THE PUBLIC SERVICE

Every office becoming vacant, every appointment made me donne un ingrait, et cent ennemis.—TO JOHN DICKINSON.[52]

The major issue concerning appointments during Jefferson's presidency was the question of the extent to which political party affiliation should govern the holding of public office. In his answer to the New Haven committee which had protested the removal of a Federalist appointee from the collectorship in that city, and the appointment of a Republican to the office, Jefferson reviewed carefully his theory concerning the relation of politics to appointments. The real purpose of this letter Jefferson revealed to his Attorney-General, Levi Lincoln, observing that the moderate policy of the administration concerning appointments and removals had "produced impatience in the republicans, and a belief we meant to do nothing. Some occasion of public explanation was eagerly desired, when the New Haven Remonstrance offered us that occasion. The answer was meant as an explanation to our friends."[53] So clearly does this letter illustrate Jefferson's thinking upon this matter that it deserves citation at length:

Of the various executive duties, no one excites more anxious concern than that of placing the interests of our fellow citizens in the hands of honest men, with understandings sufficient for their stations. No duty, at the same time, is more difficult to fulfill. The knowledge of characters possessed by a single individual is, of necessity, limited. To seek out the best through the whole Union, we must resort to other in-

[51] Adams, *op. cit.*, Book IV, pp. 465–68; also letter to William Short, March 8, 1809, *Works*, ed. Ford, XI, 102–3.

[52] January 13, 1807, *Works*, ed. Ford, X, 342.

[53] August 26, 1801, *ibid.*, IX, 289. The objections of the New Haven merchants were not entirely unreasonable in terms of Jefferson's professed principles, for it was generally suspected that the appointment of the aged Samuel Bishop was in fact designed to reward his son Abraham Bishop for political services. Jefferson, as in the instance of the patronage of John Page, was encouraging nepotism.

formation, which, from the best of men, acting disinterestedly and with the purest motives, is sometimes incorrect. In the case of Samuel Bishop, however, the subject of your remonstrance, time was taken, information was sought, and such obtained as could leave no room for doubt of his fitness. From private sources it was learned that his understanding was sound, his integrity pure, his character unstained. And the offices confided to him within his own State, are public evidences of the estimation in which he is held by the State in general, and the city and township particularly in which he lives. He is said to be the town clerk, a justice of the peace, mayor of the city of New Haven, an office held at the will of the legislature, chief judge of the court of common pleas for New Haven County, a court of high criminal and civil jurisdiction wherein most causes are decided without the right of appeal or review, and sole judge of the court of probates, wherein he singly decides all questions of wills, settlements of estates, testate and intestate, appoints guardians, settles their accounts, and in fact has under his jurisdiction and care all the property real and personal, of persons dying. The two last offices, in the annual gift of the legislature, were given to him in May last. Is it possible that the man to whom the legislature of Connecticut has so recently committed trusts of such difficulty and magnitude, is "unfit to be the collector of the district of New Haven," . . . .

The removal, as it is called, of Mr. Goodrich, forms another subject of complaint. Declarations by myself in favor of *political tolerance*, exhortations to *harmony* and affection in social intercourse and to respect for the *equal rights* of the minority, have, on certain occasions, been quoted and misconstrued into assurances that the tenure of offices was to be undisturbed. But could candor apply such a construction? It is not indeed in the remonstrance that we find it; but it leads to the explanations which that calls for. When it is considered, that during the late administration, those who were not of a particular sect of politics were excluded from all office; when, by a steady pursuit of this measure, nearly the whole offices of the United States were monopolized by that sect; when the public sentiment at length declared itself, and burst open the doors of honor and confidence to those whose opinions they more approved, was it to be imagined that this monopoly of office was still to be continued in the hands of the minority? Does it violate their *equal rights*, to assert some rights in the majority also? Is it *political intolerance* to claim a proportionate share in the direction of the public affairs? . . . .

I lament sincerely that unessential differences of political opinion should ever have been deemed sufficient to interdict half the society from the rights and blessings of self-government, to proscribe them as characters unworthy of every trust. It would have been to me a circumstance of great relief, had I found a moderate participation of office in the hands of the majority. I would gladly have left to time and accident to raise them to their just share. But their total exclusion calls for prompter correctives. I shall correct the procedure; but that done, disdain to follow it, shall return with joy to that state of things, when the only question concerning a candidate shall be; is he honest? Is he capable? Is he faithful to the Constitution?[54]

This reply to the New Haven committee serves as a text upon which to develop Jefferson's theory of patronage. He would not agree that the alleged Federalist incumbent, Elizier Goodrich, had in fact been removed.

[54] To Elias Shipman and others, July 12, 1801, *ibid.*, pp. 270–74.

He had been appointed by President John Adams after the latter's defeat in the election of 1800 had become a certainty, thus being one of the "midnight appointees" whose claim to office Jefferson considered void. Of these appointees, Jefferson declared: "I shall not consider the persons named, even as candidates for the office, nor pay the respect of notifying them that I consider what was done as a nullity."[55] To this theory that an outgoing President was not entitled to make appointments after assurance that he would not succeed himself, Jefferson adhered consistently, for, upon the election of Madison to the presidential office in 1808, Jefferson determined to "make no new appointments which can be deferred until the 4th of March, thinking it fair," he said, "to leave to my successor to select the agents for his own administration."[56]

In the notion that appointees should in general represent the opinions of the dominant political element Jefferson struck no new note in political history. But the circumstances of his accession to the presidency brought his policies on removals and appointment into sharp focus. For three administrations the Federalists had controlled the distribution of federal offices. The Republicans having become the dominant party in 1800, Jefferson believed that they should have a share in offices proportionate to their numerical strength in the electorate. "Deaths, resignations, delinquencies, malignant and active opposition to the order of things established by the will of the nation," would, Jefferson believed, "within a moderate space of time, make room for a just participation in the management of the public affairs; and that being once effected, future changes at the helm [would] be viewed with tranquillity by those in subordinate station."[57]

Jefferson's wish to avoid an indiscriminate purge of all Federalists in civil office did not imply a lack of determination to discharge Federalists whom he deemed detrimental to the public good and to the harmony of the administration. He proposed to proceed carefully with all cases of dismissal, but he made clear to all that he would appoint no Federalists to office until the political balance in the public service was redressed in favor of the Republicans. "I have firmly refused to follow the counsels of those who have desired the giving offices to some of their [Federalist] leaders in order to reconcile," he declared to James Monroe; "I have given and will give only to republicans, under existing circumstances."[58] He deter-

[55] To Dr. Benjamin Rush, March 24, 1801, *ibid.*, p. 231.

[56] To Dr. George Logan, December 27, 1808, *Writings*, ed. Washington, V, 404–5.

[57] To William Judd, November 15, 1802, *ibid.*, VIII, 114.

[58] February [March] 7, 1801, *Works*, ed. Ford, IX, 204.

mined to reinstate officers whom he believed that the Federalists had removed for political reasons. Writing to Gallatin, he remarked concerning two of Adams' removals, "with respect to Gardner and Campbell . . . . I think we are bound to take care of them. Could we not procure them as good berths as their former at least, in some of the custom houses?"[59] To Elbridge Gerry he explained: "The safety of the government absolutely required that its direction in its higher departments should be taken into friendly hands. Its safety did not even admit that the whole of its immense patronage should be left at the command of its enemies to be exercised secretly or openly to reestablish the tyrannical and dilapidating system of the preceding administration, and their deleterious principles of government."[60]

The pressure upon Jefferson for wholesale removals of Federalists appears to have been very great. It is apparent from his correspondence that he received many protests from disappointed partisans, and his letter to William Duane of Pennsylvania, written in reply to an address by the Ward Committee of Philadelphia calling for more removals, illustrates the gradual weakening of his earlier resolution:

Many vacancies have been made by death and resignation, many by removal for malversation in office, and for open, active and virulent abuse of official influence in opposition to the order of things established by the will of the nation. Such removals continue to be made on sufficient proof. The places have been steadily filled with republican characters until of 316 offices in all the U.S. subject to appointment and removal by me, 130 only are held by federalists. I do not include in this estimate the judiciary and military because not removable but by established process, nor the officers of the Internal revenue because discontinued by law, nor postmasters or any others not named by me. And this has been effected in little more than two years by means so moderate and just as cannot fail to be approved in future.[61]

Jefferson's letter to Duane revealed the extent to which political pressure had forced the unhappy President to depart in practice from his professed desire for moderation in removals. Writing to Samuel Adams shortly after his inauguration, he declared that "a few examples of justice on officers who have perverted their functions to the oppression of their fellow citizens, must, in justice to those citizens be made."[62] To Benjamin Rush he suggested that those would probably not exceed twenty in num-

[59] September 18, 1801, *ibid.*, pp. 304–5. In *The Anas*, March 8, 1801, Jefferson gives a list of contemplated removals and appointments, and notes explanations for the action proposed (*ibid.*, I, 363).

[60] August 28, 1802, *ibid.*, IX, 392.

[61] July 24, 1803, *ibid.*, X, 23 (not sent).   [62] March 29, 1801, *ibid.*, IX, 240.

ber.[63] Yet, writing to Duane in 1803, he explained that, of 316 offices removable by the President, only 130 remained in Federalist hands.

To the efforts of Gallatin to resist the use of federal patronage in the interests of party intrigue, Jefferson would lend little aid. He did not encourage Gallatin's attempt to stop the removal of the subordinate officers and to prevent the abuse of patronage in Pennsylvania and New York, which was assuming the proportions of a scandal.[64] It is this failure of Jefferson to enforce the principles which he had preached that complicates the evaluation of his policy on removals. Although the greater portion of his correspondence and public papers could be read as pronouncements against the abuse of patronage, nevertheless one is inclined to concur with the conclusion of Carl Russell Fish that Jefferson's administration opened the gates to the floodtide of spoils politics which was to come later.[65]

In appointments to federal offices Jefferson, like Hamilton, did not wish to be bound by an equal or proportional distribution of patronage among the several states. As Secretary of State he had explained to Colonel Henry Lee that it was not expedient to apportion all appointments among the states. "I am sensible," he had declared, "of the necessity as well as justice of dispersing employments over the whole of the U.S. But this is difficult as to the smaller offices, which require to be filled immediately as they become vacant and are not worth coming for from the distant states."[66] However, writing to Horatio Gates to explain why a recommendation for appointment had not received favorable action, Jefferson explained that "talents alone are not to be the determining circumstance, but a geographical equilibrium is to a certain degree expected. The different parts in the union expect to share the public appointments."[67] Although unwilling to be bound rigidly by any apportionment scheme, Jefferson nevertheless inclined to accept apportionment as a general principle. "Where an office is local we never go out of the limits for the officer," he declared.[68] Writing to one of the Republican leaders in Pennsylvania in 1803, Jefferson reviewed his policy on patronage and explained that "whether a participation of office in proportion to numbers should be effected in each state separately, or in the whole states taken together is

[63] March 24, 1801, *ibid.*, p. 231.

[64] Adams, *op. cit.*, Book I, pp. 234–36; cf. McBain, *op. cit.*

[65] *Op. cit.*, p. 50.

[66] April 26, 1790, *Works*, ed. Ford, VI, 52–53.

[67] March 8, 1801, *ibid.*, IX, 205.

[68] To Caesar Rodney, December 5, 1805, *ibid.*, X, 323.

difficult to decide, and has not yet been settled in my own mind. It is a question of vast complications."[69]

An exception to the general rule that states were entitled to some form of proportional distribution of federal patronage was Connecticut. The state during Jefferson's administration occupied a position roughly analogous to that of Rhode Island during Washington's first term.[70] Both cases constitute a forecast of the influence of federal patronage on state-federal relationships. In both cases the dominant political elements in the states were entirely out of step with the dominant national party and the policy of the federal administration. In both cases the federal administration attempted to coerce the recalcitrant states by denying them full participation in federal offices, although some effort was made by both Washington and Jefferson to strengthen their friends in the opposition in those states by appointing them to such offices as were made available. Jefferson expressed his policy toward the Connecticut Federalists in a letter to his Attorney-General, Levi Lincoln: "When they will give a share in the State offices, they shall be replaced in a share of the General offices. Till then we must follow their example."[71] But the spirit of Connecticut which Madison described as "perverse"[72] continued to resist the cure which Jefferson wished his measures to effect, and Jefferson, in a letter to Wilson Cary Nicholas, announced his intention to sweep the opposition out of all federal offices in the state:

> In Connecticut alone, a general sweep seems to be called for on principles of justice and policy. Their legislature . . . . are removing every republican even from the commissions of the peace and the lowest offices. There then we will retaliate. Whilst the federalists are taking possession of all the states offices, exclusively, they ought not to expect we will leave them the exclusive possession of those at our disposal. The republicans have some rights: and must be protected.[73]

Jefferson made much of his disinterest in appointments. "I know none but public motives" in making appointments, he declared.[74] "I did not think the public offices confided to me to give away as charities," he wrote to Monroe.[75] He held that, where a choice of appointments prevailed,

[69] To William Duane, July 24, 1803, *ibid.*, pp. 23–24.

[70] Gaillard Hunt, "Office Seeking during Washington's Administration," *American Historical Review*, I (January, 1898), 270–91.

[71] July 11, 1801, *Works*, ed. Ford, IX, 269.

[72] Adams, *op. cit.*, Book I, 225.   [73] June 11, 1801, *Works*, ed. Ford, IX, 266.

[74] To the Speaker of the House of Representatives, December 26, 1807, *Writings*, ed. Washington, V, 223.

[75] July 15, 1802, *Works*, ed. Ford, IX, 389.

those appointments which would be most repected by the public should prevail. He professed to use the bestowal of office, not for self-elevation, but for the public good "without regard to ties of blood or friendship."[76]

The question of nepotism was raised immediately upon Jefferson's inauguration to the presidency, and, as far as he was personally concerned, he refused all favors to his relatives. Channing suggests that Jefferson might have been willing to provide some patronage to his relatives provided the matter could be effected without arousing criticism.[77] Jefferson's well-known sensitivity to criticism may have been the greatest deterrent to this practice, although, in fact, he had few relatives whom he was in position to help. His apparent indifference to nepotism practiced by members of his own party diminishes the strength of his criticism of John Adams on this score.

Although Jefferson was able to resist the claims of blood, the ties of friendship sometimes proved stronger than political principles. His letters to his friend John Page furnish, as Paul Leicester Ford has observed, perhaps the most curious instance of the use of public office for private benefit and are collected in the Federal edition of Jefferson's *Works*.[78] Several excerpts deserve citation here to illustrate the extent to which Jefferson in practice could depart from Jefferson in theory.

We have reason to consider as very near at hand a vacancy in an office, which indeed could offer you no amusement, little emolument, but also no labor. The death of the present worthy loan officer [Mr. Jones] is considered as inevitably close at hand. This opinion I have from the best medical judge, and the proposing it to you occurs from the information of Mr. Walker's letter. The salary is 1500 D a year, and 150 or 200 D more as commission on payment of pensions. Stationary is allowed, but neither office hire nor fuel. 1000 D additional are permitted to be divided between two clerks as the principal pleases. Mr. Gallatin says that a residence so near to Richmond as that you could ride there once or twice a week, would be sufficient, and that the office books being deposited with the Richmond bank a little before quarter day, they would make all the payments without charge, considering as a sufficient emolument the deposit of the public money with them, which would at the same time save you from trouble and risk. The business can be done by one clerk, but there must still be two. However, nearly all the salary is given to the efficient clerk, and a minimum to the one who is merely nominal, or at least, this may be the arrangement, if it is not so at present. There is probably a clerk in the office well skilled in the business, and whom it might be necessary to keep some time. In the meanwhile if one of your sons could come in as a secondary, in proportion as he advances in his knowledge of the business, he might divide in the salary more and more largely, and finally take the principal place and salary, to the Commissioner of loans himself. The office is a perfect sinecure.

[76] To Governor Sullivan, March 3, 1808, *Writings*, ed. Washington, V, 252.

[77] *History of the United States*, IV, 254.   [78] *Works*, ed. Ford, IX, 350–56.

The introduction of one of your sons into the office, besides adding the benefit of the additional thousand dollars to the family, would, by placing him as it were in possession of the office, secure his succeeding to it in that event which you and I ought now to consider as not very remote.[79]

I have, moreover, heard that you have been particularly afflicted by want of health latterly, insomuch as to make it probable the indispensable attentions to your office are burthensome to you. Would it be a relief to transfer the office to your son Francis for your use with an understanding that it should afterwards continue with him for the benefit of the family? Or would you rather retain it in your own name during your life, with the probability (for we cannot be certain of what is distant) that he will succeed you for the same family benefit? Decide on this my friend, according to your own wishes, and if the execution falls within the compass of my time and powers, count upon it with the sacred confidence which your merits, my affections, and the gratitude of our country will justify.[80]

In these two letters Jefferson obviously violated nearly every principle of appointment which he had repeatedly stated in public and in private. He had proposed the use of public office not only for purely private benefit but for the benefit of a personal friend. Furthermore, he had encouraged nepotism. The man who had so often inveighed against the hereditary transmission of public office now inquired: "Would it be a relief to transfer the office to your son Francis for your use with the understanding that it should afterwards continue with him for the benefit of the family?"

Viewed broadly, Jefferson's ideas on appointment to office were temperate and conservative. Circumstances compelled him to a strongly partisan policy in appointment. He recognized as clearly as any political leader the value of patronage, but neither by temperament nor conviction was he a spoilsman. One cannot agree with Henry Cabot Lodge that Jefferson "founded the spoils system."[81] As Channing correctly observed, "it was an inheritance from the Federalist Presidents and by them had been built upon colonial and English precedents."[82] But Jefferson's administration was the occasion of a rapid growth of spoils patronage from an inefficient and sometimes dishonest method for filling offices to a system of national politics in which office became the end of political action.[83] The distinction is a matter of degree, but it is nonetheless important. There may be little to choose between the morality of spoils politics for the few, administered with some regard for the reputation and efficiency of public office, and a system of wholesale distribution of office with personal and

[79] July 3, 1806, *ibid.*, p. 354.

[80] September 6, 1808, *ibid.*, p. 355.

[81] *Studies in History* (Boston: Houghton Mifflin & Co., 1892), p. 288.

[82] *A History of the United States*, IV, 56.   [83] Fish, *op. cit.*, p. 50.

party advantage as the only objective; but the effect of the latter upon the administration of the public service is certain to be more devastating Against the former—the system of the Federalists—Jefferson had de claimed, but as President he was forced into unwilling complicity in the extension of spoils patronage which was in later administrations to de- velop into a national system. It is also significant that, although Jefferson favored a large construction of the executive authority, he preferred to rely on his political leadership to translate his program into action. In consequence, considerations of party support weighed heavily in decisions concerning patronage and appointment.

Jefferson's use of the appointive power to favor his personal friends seems less justifiable. Certainly his letters to John Page contrast glaringly with his erstwhile protestations of disinterest. It is probably true that the majority of Jefferson's errors in appointment stemmed from an emotional bias on behalf of his friends and followers rather than from a conscious violation of his pronounced principles. But he cannot be entirely absolved from mistakes which were in his power to avoid could he have cleared his mind of the misconception that good intentions put all to rights.

CO-ORDINATION AND CONTROL

For measures of importance or difficulty, a consultation is held with the Heads of depart- ments, either assembled, or by taking their opinions separately in conversation or in writ- ing. The latter method is most strictly in the spirit of the constitution. . . . . It is better calculated too to prevent collision and irritation, and to cure it, or at least suppress its ef- fects when it has already taken place.—To Dr. WALTER JONES.[84]

In the management of the internal affairs of his presidential administra- tion, Jefferson was governed by those same principles of harmony and simplicity that he sought to apply in his relations with the Congress. Sev- eral months after his inauguration he prepared and sent to the heads of the executive departments a statement of the procedure by which the busi- ness of the administration might be conducted with uniformity and with satisfaction to its members and to the public. The procedure which he rec- ommended was that followed in the first administration of General Wash- ington, of which he had been a member.

Letters of business came addressed sometimes to the President, but most frequently to the heads of departments. If addressed to himself, he referred them to the proper department to be acted on: if to one of the secretaries, the letter, if it required no answer, was communicated to the President, simply for his information. If an answer was requisite, the secretary of the department communicated the letter and his pro- posed answer to the President. Generally they were simply sent back after perusal,

[84] March 5, 1810, *Works*, ed. Ford, XI, 137–38.

which signified his approbation. Sometimes he returned them with an informal note, suggesting an alteration or a query. If a doubt of any importance arose, he reserved it for a conference. By this means, he was always in accurate possession of all facts and proceedings in every part of the Union, and to whatsoever department they related; he formed a central point for the different branches; preserved an unity of object and action among them; exercised that participation in the suggestion of affairs which his office made incumbent on him; and met himself the due responsibility for whatever was done. During Mr. Adams' administration, his long and habitual absences from the seat of government, rendered this kind of communication impracticable, removed him from any share in the transaction of affairs, and parcelled out the government, in fact, among four independent heads, drawing sometimes in opposite directions. That the former is preferable to the latter course, cannot be doubted. It gave, indeed, to the heads of departments the trouble of making up, once a day, a packet of all their communications for the perusal of the President; it commonly also retarded one day their despatches by mail. But in pressing cases, this injury was prevented by presenting that case singly for immediate attention; and it produced us in return the benefit of his sanction for every act we did. Whether any change in circumstances may render a change in this procedure necessary, a little experience will show us. But I cannot withhold recommending to heads of departments, that we should adopt this course for the present, leaving any necessary modifications of it to time and trial.[85]

The objective of Jefferson's effort to bring the business of the departments under his immediate surveillance was to insure unity of policy and to avoid the schisms which had rent the preceding administration. In his relations with the departmental heads Jefferson proved to be a good manager, recognizing that in the pursuit of harmony he must himself lead:

For our government, although in theory subject to be directed by the unadvised will of the President, is, and from its origin has been, a very different thing in practice. The minor business in each department is done by the head of the department on consultation with the President alone; but all matters of importance or difficulty are submitted to all the heads of departments composing the Cabinet. Sometimes, by the President's consulting them separately and successively, as they happen to call on him, but in the gravest cases calling them together, discussing the subject maturely, and finally taking the vote, on which the President counts himself but as one. So that in all important cases the Executive is in fact a directory, which certainly the President might control; but of this there was never an example, either in the first or the present administration. I have heard, indeed, that my predecessor sometimes decided things against his counsel by dashing and trampling his wig on the floor. This only proves what you and I know, that he had a better heart than head.[86]

Jefferson justified his practice of assembling the department heads and taking their opinions verbally "because the harmony was so cordial among us all, that we never failed, by a contribution of mutual views on the sub-

[85] "Circular to the Heads of the Departments," November 6, 1801, *ibid.*, IX, 311–12.

[86] To William Short, June 12, 1807, *ibid.*, X, 414–15.

ject, to form an opinion acceptable to the whole."[87] However, because he believed that this practice transformed the executive into a directory, Jefferson held the submission to the President of opinions in writing to be the more constitutional procedure. Toward the middle of his second administration the increasing tension in foreign and domestic politics and the necessity for frequent consultations regarding administration policy induced Jefferson to counsel separately with his administrators rather than to summon them as a group. He invited them "to call on me at any moment of the day which suits their separate convenience, when, besides any other business they may have to do, I can learn their opinions separately on any matter which has occurred, and also communicate the information received daily."[88]

In the management of the subordinate executive offices Jefferson did not propose to meddle. Offices which he described as the second grade he preferred to leave to the administration of the department heads.[89] However, in matters of conduct involving the reputation of his administration, he laid down the principles by which federal employees should be governed. He declared that "no man who has conducted himself according to his duties would have anything to fear from me, as those who have done ill would have nothing to hope."[90] Although he wished to see Republicans appointed to office whenever possible, he did not propose to turn out faithful and disinterested public servants, nor was he willing to continue a dishonest or insubordinate functionary in office because he professed Republican principles.

Concerning the political activities of the federal office-holders, Jefferson drew a sharp distinction between mere political opinion and the support of opposition candidates by personal vote and active electioneering activity. Inquiring of Caesar Rodney the grounds for the requested dismissal of a federal officer in Delaware, Jefferson wrote: "If he has been active in electioneering in favor of those who wish to subvert the present order of things, it would be a serious circumstance. I do not mean as to giving his personal vote, in which he ought not to be controlled; but as to using his influence (which necessarily includes his official influence) to sway the votes of others."[91] Writing to Levi Lincoln, Jefferson declared: "Our principles render federalists in office safe, if they do not employ

[87] To Dr. Walter Jones, March 4, 1810, *ibid.*, XI, 138.

[88] To Albert Gallatin, July 10, 1807, *ibid.*, X, 452.

[89] To John D. Burke, June 21, 1801, *ibid.*, IX, 267–68.

[90] To Dr. Benjamin S. Barton, February 14, 1801, *ibid.*, p. 177.

[91] June 14, 1802, *ibid.*, p. 376.

their influence in opposing the government, but only give their own vote according to their conscience. And this principle we act on as well with those put in office by others, as by ourselves."[92]

To what extent political activity other than the casting of a ballot was permissible to federal office-holders, Jefferson did not say. Mere attendance at political gatherings was evidently not opposed, but active participation in party meetings apparently would have been deemed grounds for disciplinary action. Writing to Gallatin about a charge against a New England office-holder, Jefferson observed: "Although meddling in political caucusses is no part of that freedom of personal suffrage which ought to be allowed him, yet his mere presence at a caucus does not necessarily involve an active and official influence in opposition to the government which employs him."[93]

The form of political activity which Jefferson deemed most obnoxious in federal officials was interference with election activity. This form of misconduct he opposed in Republicans as strongly as in Federalists. Writing to Thomas McKean in 1801, Jefferson promised that "interferences with elections, whether of the State or General Government, by officers of the latter, should be deemed cause of removal."[94] Although Jefferson had proposed soon after coming into office to restrain executive officers from interfering with elections, the proposition was laid over for consideration; but by 1804 he was convinced that the growing abuse by federal employees called for admonition. "I think the officers of the federal government are meddling too much with the public elections. Will it be best to admonish them privately or by proclamation?" he inquired of Gallatin.[95] In reply Gallatin suggested that the proper occasion for such admonishment had passed and implied that more harm than good might react to the reputation of the administration if misconduct of federal officials were aired on the eve of a national election.[96]

Of the use of the removal power for disciplinary purposes, the greater number of instances in Jefferson's presidency involve questions of political misconduct. The removal of the brother of Elbridge Gerry from a federal office in Massachusetts because of continued irregularities in his

---

[92] March 23, 1806, *Writings*, ed. Washington, V, 264.

[93] December 12, 1806, *Works*, ed. Ford, X, 325.

[94] February 2, 1801, *ibid.*, IX, 175.

[95] September 8, 1804, *ibid.*, X, 101.

[96] Gallatin to Jefferson, September 18, 1804, *The Writings of Albert Gallatin*, ed. Henry Adams (3 vols.; Philadelphia: J. B. Lippincott & Co., 1879), I, 209.

accounts was primarily a disciplinary move but may have been influenced by political considerations.[97]

A notable instance of Jefferson's use of the removal power to punish insubordination occurred while he served during Washington's administration as the leading member of the commission charged with the planning of the city of Washington. The personality of Major Charles L'Enfant, the engineer employed to lay out and execute the plan for the federal capitol, was compounded of an explosive mixture of perfectionism, ability, and volatile temperament. After a series of disagreements between L'Enfant and the commissioners in which the Major followed his own inclination in disregard of the wishes of the commission, Jefferson appealed to Washington to clarify the authority of the commissioners over the engineer.[98] Washington supported the authority of the commission; and Jefferson, declaring that it had become impractical to employ L'Enfant "in that degree of subordination which was lawful and proper," secured his dismissal.[99]

The L'Enfant episode may have been influenced by personal disagreement between Jefferson and L'Enfant over the planning of the city, for Jefferson was an architect in his own right and had his own ideas as to the way in which the capitol should be laid out. Nevertheless, the incident demonstrates Jefferson's readiness to use the removal power to secure the degree of subordination which he felt due executive authority.

THE RESPONSIBILITY OF PUBLIC ADMINISTRATION

Responsibility is a tremendous engine in a free government.—To ARCHIBALD STUART.[100]

In chapter ix the contention was made that Jefferson understood "responsibility" in the particular sense of strictly defined duties for the execution of which the executive could be held accountable to the legislature or the people. Jefferson favored well-defined methods prescribed by law for the execution of administrative powers but held that, at least for the higher officers, a degree of flexibility in adapting means to ends was essential to the accomplishment of the public business. He recognized an ascending scale of responsibility and believed that the highest responsibilities of a chief executive officer take precedence over established methods of procedure when duties conflict. In the purchase of Louisiana he be-

[97] To Elbridge Gerry, August 28, 1802, *Works*, ed. Ford, IX, 390–91.

[98] November 6, 1791, *Works* (Memorial ed.), VIII, 251–58.

[99] To Johnson, Carroll and Stewart, March 6, 1792, *ibid.*, p. 307.

[100] December 23, 1791, *Works*, ed. Ford, VI, 351.

lieved that his responsibility for the national welfare in matters of foreign relations must take precedence over his duty to act only within his lawful powers. Writing to Governor Claiborne of Louisiana, Jefferson explained that the constitutional responsibility of an officer might require him to exceed his defined authorities: "On great occasions every good officer must be ready to risk himself in going beyond the strict line of law, when the public preservation requires it; his motives will be a justification as far as there is any discretion in his ultra legal proceedings, and no indulgence of private feelings."[101]

In the interpretation of organic and statutory law Jefferson postulated two theories of executive responsibility. In construing the Constitution of the Republic, Jefferson held that each of the three great departments intrusted by the people to uphold the fundamental law was entitled to judge of its meaning in cases properly within its jurisdiction. Accordingly, he held that each division of the government "has an equal right to decide for itself what is the meaning of the Constitution in the cases submitted to its action; and especially, where it is to act ultimately and without appeal."[102] Jefferson declared that he pardoned offenders of the Sedition Act of 1798 because, although passed by the Congress and therefore presumably deemed constitutional by it, he, as President, considered the measure unconstitutional and null and therefore refused to enforce it.[103]

"The true key for the construction of everything doubtful in a law, is the intention of the law-makers," he declared to Albert Gallatin.[104] To the criterion of legislative intention as a guide to executive interpretation of statutes Jefferson repeatedly referred. Writing to Gallatin on a point of law, he declared: "We are to look at the intention of the Legislature, and to carry it into execution while the lawyers are nibbling at the words of the law. It is well known that on every question the lawyers are about equally divided . . . . and were we to act but in cases where no contrary opinion of a lawyer can be had, we should never act."[105] In cases where the word of the law could bear two meanings, the true purpose of the legislature in enacting the measure was to determine its application. "In a statute, as in a will, the intention of the party is to be sought after," he said.[106]

---

[101] February 3, 1807, *Writings*, ed. Washington, V, 40.

[102] To Judge Spencer Roane, September 6, 1819, *Works*, ed. Ford, XII, 137.

[103] *Ibid.*, p. 138.

[104] May 20, 1808, *Writings*, ed. Washington, V, 291.

[105] September 20, 1808, *ibid.*, p. 369.

[106] July 29, 1808. *ibid.*, p. 328.

In a letter to W. H. Cabell, the governor of Virginia in 1807, Jefferson developed at some length his theory of the executive interpretation:

In the construction of a law, even in judiciary cases of *meum et tuum*, where the opposite parties have a right and counterright in the very words of the law, the Judge considers the intention of the law-giver as his true guide, and gives to all the parts and expressions of the law, that meaning which will effect, instead of defeating, its intention. But in laws merely executive, where no private right stands in the way, and the public object is the interest of all, a much freer scope of construction, in favor of the intention of the law, ought to be taken, and ingenuity ever should be exercised in devising constructions, which may save to the public the benefit of the law. Its intention is the important thing: the means of attaining it quite subordinate. It often happens that, the Legislature prescribing details of execution, some circumstance arises, unforeseen or unattended to by them, which would totally frustrate their intention, were their details scrupulously adhered to, and deemed exclusive of all others. But constructions must not be favored which go to defeat instead of furthering the principal object of their law, and to sacrifice the end to the means. It being as evidently their intention that the end shall be attained as that it should be effected by any given means, if both cannot be observed, we are equally free to deviate from the one as the other, and more rational in postponing the means to the end. . . . .

It is further to be considered that the Constitution gives the executive a general power to carry the laws into execution. If the present law had enacted that the service of thirty thousand volunteers should be accepted, without saying anything of the means, those means would, by the Constitution, have resulted to the discretion of the executive. So if means specified by an act are impracticable, the constitutional power remains, and supplies them. Often the means provided specially are affirmative merely, and, with the constitutional powers, stand well together; so that either may be used, or the one supplementary to the other. This aptitude of means to the end of a law is essentially necessary for those which are executive; otherwise the objection that our government is an impracticable one, would really be verified.[107]

To this notion of executive discretion in the method of effecting the purpose of the legislature, Jefferson did not read an independence of executive judgment as sweeping as one might infer from his language. In times of national danger this latitude of discretion was expanded, and as governor of revolutionary Virginia he had admonished the county magistrates that "he is a bad citizen who can entertain a doubt whether the Law will justify him in saving his Country or who will scruple to risk himself in support of the spirit of a Law where unavoidable accidents have prevented literal compliance with it."[108]

Jefferson's conception of executive responsibility was not entirely logical. His notion of the responsibility of high executive officers for acts done personally contrasts with his attitude toward executive responsibility

[107] August 11, 1807, *ibid.*, pp. 158–59; cf. Hamilton's implied-powers doctrine.

[108] Circular letter to the county magistrates, January 20, 1781, *Works*, ed. Ford, III, 147.

for acts done by subordinates. Writing in a petulant mood to General Steuben during his unhappy experience as Revolutionary governor of Virginia, Jefferson declared: "We can only be answerable for the orders we give and not for the execution. If they are disobeyed from obstinacy of spirit or want of coercion in the Laws it is not our fault."[109] The notion that the executive was not responsible for the conduct of his agents or for the proper enforcement of his orders was an anomaly of the first order. Equally paradoxical was Jefferson's theory that a retiring executive should be "an unmeddling listener to what others say,"[110] taking no active part in the direction of public policy beyond that absolutely required by circumstances. The notion that the executive could continue to hold an office the functions of which he deemed improper to execute was an absurdity which Jefferson's closest friends recognized and from which they tried without success to dissuade him. Unfriendly Josiah Quincy declared that Jefferson's inaction during the last months of his presidency resulted from "fear of responsibility and love of popularity"[111] and contemptuously referred to the inactive executive as "a dish of skim milk curdling at the head of our nation."[112]

Jefferson certainly had no fear of responsibility, but he does appear to have had a distaste for commanding the actions of others, which distorted his view of responsibility on several occasions. There is evidence to indicate that it was this dislike of command rather than any defect of personal bravery or of unwillingness to accept personal responsibility that occasioned his difficulties as governor of Virginia during the American Revolution.[113] Why Jefferson virtually abdicated the functions of his presidential office after the election of Madison is more difficult to explain. Jefferson's wish to leave to his successor the greatest possible freedom in the formulation of policy and the selection of personnel may have been the primary factor; but one cannot escape the feeling that, although Jefferson had no fear of the responsibility of executive office, he seized upon

[109] March 10, 1781, *ibid.*, p. 212.

[110] To Dr. George Logan, December 27, 1808, *Writings*, ed. Washington, V, 404.

[111] Edmund Quincy, *Life of Josiah Quincy of Massachusetts* (Boston: Fields, Osgood & Co., 1869), p. 146.

[112] Adams, *History of the United States during the Administration of Thomas Jefferson*, Book IV, p. 356.

[113] Cf. Allan Nevins' appraisal of Jefferson's gubernatorial career in *The American States during and after the Revolution, 1775–1789* (New York: Macmillan Co., 1924), pp. 331 ff. See also Margaret B. Macmillan, *The War Governors in the American Revolution* (New York: Columbia University Press, 1943).

the certainty of his retirement as an occasion for reducing to a minimum the exercise of duties which he deemed onerous.

In their recognition of the responsibility of chief executives to fulfil the highest duties of their offices even at the sacrifice of lesser obligations, Hamilton and Jefferson agreed. The contrast in their conceptions of responsibility lies in the methods by which they would enforce it. Hamilton would impose few restrictions on the exercise of executive power, holding that, as each officer should be personally responsible for his acts, public opinion and sanctions for the violation of his trust sufficed to insure reliable conduct. Jefferson preferred not to leave the conduct of the executive to chance but to "bind him down from mischief by the chains of the Constitution," yet to recognize his duty to exceed such restrictions as might frustrate the highest responsibilities of his office. To Hamilton this paradox seemed to encourage contempt for the laws, for the executive must do what his responsibility requires whether he oversteps the permissive authority of strictly construed statutes or whether he resorts to implied powers to sanction his acts. In the latter case the executive, according to Hamilton, remained accountable for his acts but presumably violated no measures in their execution, whereas Jefferson's theory might require the executive to break down the law in pursuit of his duty.

In retrospect Jefferson's theory of responsibility seems more appropriate to a government of divided powers than does Hamilton's notion of executive discretion. Under parliamentary government Hamilton's ideas would be consonant with executive accountability, but, applied by an executive virtually irremovable until the end of a fixed term, they would be hardly in keeping with the American tradition of limited government. Jefferson's solution to the problem of accountability seems the more practical as applied to the theory and actual structure of government in the United States. Because departures from legislative prescription might be necessary to preserve the general welfare, Jefferson did not, therefore, favor the virtual removal of legislative checks on the executive power. As in the purchase of Louisiana, he wished to see the extra-legal acts of the executive confined to clearly defined occasions of vital concern, and he believed that the jealousy of the legislature and the republicanism of the people would suffice to insure that the executive authority could not with impunity exceed what the exigencies of the occasion required.

PART III

HAMILTON AND JEFFERSON

CHAPTER XIII

ADMINISTRATIVE CONFLICT

The dissensions between two members of the Cabinet are to be lamented. . . . . They can-
not be greater than between Hamilton and myself, and yet we served together four years in
that way. We had indeed no personal dissensions. Each of us, perhaps, thought well of the
other as a man, but as politicians it was impossible for two men to be of more opposite
principles.—JEFFERSON TO JOEL BARLOW.[1]

THAT Jefferson and Hamilton represented sharply opposing principles of government has long been a widely accepted belief and
one to which the great opponents themselves subscribed. Yet in
retrospect the differences which separated them seem less fundamental
and more complex than either they or their more partisan interpreters
would perhaps admit. Chiefly confusion has been gained by the intermit-
tent cross-fire of Jeffersonian and Hamiltonian antagonists, and the substantial differences of opinion and temperament between the two politicians have been obscured by the proclivity of writers to translate their
dissensions into melodramatic terms. Both Hamilton and Jefferson had a
feeling for history and for the dramatic value of their careers, and each in
defense of his position emphasized the differences distinguishing him from
his opponent.

If the opposing assertions of Hamilton and Jefferson concerning their
differences are taken at face value, Hamilton was a monarchist committed
to the conversion of the Constitution of 1789 into a centralized government dominated by a plutocracy and administered by a hereditary no-
bility; Jefferson, a demagogue with an insatiable desire for popularity and
an unreasonable jealousy of power in the hands of others. Actually, both
characterizations are extreme—exaggerations of small truths into large
myths. The two leaders differed in temperament; Jefferson was in some
measure given to jealousy and love of popularity, and Hamilton was by
nature domineering and impressed by the power of wealth and the exercise of authority. It may be true that their contrasting dispositions ag-

[1] January 24, 1810, *Works*, ed. Ford, XI, 132.

gravated their dissensions in Washington's administration; however, men of equal contrast have worked well together, and, indeed, Hamilton and Jefferson did so until they found themselves first administrative and then political rivals.

Whether the administrative rivalry between them would have developed as acutely had not foreign affairs and Washington's method of cabinet consultation thrown them into opposing positions can hardly be determined. But it is apparent that the circumstances under which the executive powers of the government were divided among the several departments of the administration created areas of undefined and contested jurisdiction in which friction was almost certain to occur.

Although the President might have drawn up a plan for the organization of the executive departments, he did not do so, and the responsibility for their establishment was thrust upon a first Congress which was governed in its decisions by a jealous fear of the executive power and by a general indifference to considerations of administrative efficiency.

The debates on the executive departments began in the House of Representatives on May 19, 1789, when Elias Boudinot of New Jersey proposed the creation of a Department of Finance confined to fiscal affairs and restrained by statute from all concern over trade and commerce.[2] The management of the public debt being of greatest import to the new government, the prompt organization of its finances was held to take precedence over other matters of executive concern. However, several members of the House contended that some general disposition of executive powers should be made before specific departments were created. John Vining, of Delaware, proposed a Home Department for territorial and domestic concerns, and Madison presented a resolution calling for the establishment of departments of Foreign Affairs, Treasury, and War. To Vining's proposal and Madison's resolution Samuel Livermore of New Hampshire objected. He held the Department of Foreign Affairs of lesser importance than the Treasury, which, as the first department of the executive, deserved precedence in the resolution. A Domestic Department he thought unnecessary, contending that *its* duties could be spread among the three departments proposed by Madison, thus avoiding the expense of an additional department.

On the following day the debate was resumed, and the remarks of Gerry of Massachusetts presaged the jealous opposition which the Treasury Department was to encounter in the House. Gerry advocated a board rather

[2] *The Debates and Proceedings in the Congress of the United States* (Washington: Gales & Seaton, 1834), I, 368–84.

than a single administrator to head the Treasury, arguing vehemently against the abuses certain to follow from a single head, predicting that a single minister would exceed the influence of the President[3] and might supplant the Senate as his adviser.[4]

It is noteworthy in view of the later congressional opposition to Hamilton, and Hamilton's attempt to maintain influence in the House, that the debates in May and June, 1789, occurred without knowledge of the identity of the new Treasury head. Gerry's opposition to a unitary Treasury administration seems to have been in part inspired by jealousy of the former Superintendent of Finance, Robert Morris. Evidence that the House would not support Treasury initiative in matters of finance developed in the debates of June 25, when a majority refused to grant the Secretary power to *report* plans.[5] The House accepted a compromise permitting the Secretary to *prepare* plans, but the intention of a substantial body of the representatives to confine the Treasury to bookkeeping and tax collection is clear.

Vining's resolution to create a Home Department charged with the keeping of the great seal and authentic copies of public acts; to make out commissions; to report to the President plans for the protection and improvement of manufactures, agriculture, and commerce; and to administer the census, patents, post roads, and a geographical survey would have clarified the responsibilities of the remaining departments. But after brief debate the proposition was voted down on July 23 on grounds of economy, lack of necessity, and particularly because domestic concerns, except where specifically delegated to the federal government, were deemed beyond its jurisdiction.[6] The decision accordingly was to distribute the miscellaneous duties of the executive among the three great departments. In this distribution Congress in some cases took the initiative, as when it created a Department of Indian Affairs within the War Department and placed the Post Office under the Treasury; other decisions were left to the President. Washington appears to have concurred in this settlement, for Hamilton, requesting a transfer of the Mint to the Treasury Department, observed that "these observations proceed on the supposition that the President has adopted in principle and practice, the plan of distributing all the particular branches of the public service, except that of the law,

---

[3] Cf. Jefferson's remarks to Washington, February 28, 1792, that "even the future Presidents . . . . would not be able to make head against this department" (*Works*, ed. Ford, I, 192).

[4] *Debates and Proceedings in the Congress*, I, 384–96.

[5] *Ibid.*, pp. 592–607. [6] *Ibid.*, pp. 666–69.

among the three great departments; a plan which is believed to be founded on good reasons."[7]

Although the Treasury was last of the three departments created in 1789,[8] Hamilton was the first Secretary appointed by Washington, and he commenced his duties in September, 1789, some six months before the arrival of Jefferson at the seat of government. Although Washington had decided as early as September 25 to nominate Jefferson as Secretary of State, John Jay acted in that capacity until Jefferson's return from France, when his acceptance could be effected. Meanwhile Hamilton began his administration of the Treasury and soon indicated that he did not share the restrictive views of certain House members concerning the scope and nature of his responsibilities.

The first budget under the new government was reported by Gerry in the House of Representatives "from the committee appointed to prepare and report an estimate of the supplies requisite for the present year, and the nett proceeds of the impost."[9] However, the preparation of the budget for 1790 was undertaken by Hamilton at the request of the House and was submitted early in that year.[10] It was thereafter customary for Hamilton to submit the budget to the House over his own signature, save for the expenses of the Army, which were submitted as part of the general budget but over the signature of the Secretary of War, Knox. What influence the Secretary of the Treasury may have exercised over the expenses of the several departments does not appear in the record, although Hamilton sometimes prefaced his estimates with observations, usually concerning the debt and occasionally Treasury personnel. Jefferson's departmental expenditures were, however, open to scrutiny by Hamilton's department, whereas Treasury expenditures were placed beyond Jefferson's official cognizance.[11] The freedom with which Hamilton prepared the executive budget Jefferson attributed to Washington's being "unversed in financial projects and calculations and budgets, his approbation of them," Jefferson averred, being "bottomed on his confidence in the man."[12]

---

[7] January 31, 1795, *Works*, ed. Lodge, IV, 62.

[8] Department of Foreign Affairs, July 27, 1789; Department of War, August 7, 1789; Department of Treasury, September 2, 1789.

[9] *American State Papers, Finance*, I, 11–13.

[10] General Estimate for the Services of the Current Year," January 5, 1790, and "Additional Estimates for 1790," March 1, 1790 (*ibid.*, pp. 33–37, 38–43).

[11] Jefferson, however, seems to have obtained information concerning Treasury affairs from sources within the Treasury (Charles A. Beard, *The Economic Origins of Jeffersonian Democracy* [New York: Macmillan Co., 1915], p. 167).

[12] *The Anas*, 1791, *Works*, ed. Ford, I, 179.

Shortly after his first submission of the budget Hamilton drove another wedge into the House theory of Treasury subordination. The occasion was a message to the House recommending the remission of forfeitures exacted from certain merchants for violation of the new revenue measures. Phrasing his language in most solicitous terms, Hamilton asked the House to vest him with certain discretionary or rule-making powers to avoid continual resort to legislative action as similar cases arose from time to time:

The Secretary, however, begs leave to avail himself of the occasion, to represent to the House, that there are other instances which have come under his notice, in which considerable forfeitures have been incurred, manifestly through inadvertence and want of information—circumstances which cannot fail to attend the recent promulgation of laws of such a nature, and seem to indicate the necessity, in conformity to the usual policy of commercial nations, of vesting, somewhere, a discretionary power of granting relief.

. . . .

. . . . the Secretary begs leave to submit to the consideration of the House, whether a temporary arrangement might not be made, with expedition and safety, which would avoid the inconvenience of a legislative decision on particular applications.[13]

Emphasizing the necessity of "the constant existence of some power capable of affording relief,"[14] Hamilton was merely explaining that the continuing processes of regulation and supervision of public concerns are essentially administrative in nature and require a certain flexibility in administrative controls if the public welfare is to be served. Nevertheless, the practical effect of his contention would be to enlarge the sphere of executive discretion and reduce the frequency of executive recourse to Congress. In his recommendations for administering the excise on foreign and domestic liquor, Hamilton again urged executive independence, observing that "it may not be unadvisable to vest somewhere a discretionary power to regulate the forms of certificates which are to accompany, and the particular marks which are to be set upon casks and vessels containing spirits."[15]

A third device by which Hamilton was alleged to have broadened the scope of Treasury concern was the encouragement of references from Congress to the Treasury Department.[16] Thus Hamilton was requested by the House of Representatives to report on the establishment of a mint and upon the subject of manufactures, topics lying beyond the field of Treas-

[13] January 19, 1790, *American State Papers, Finance*, I, 37.

[14] *Ibid.*

[15] Spirits, Foreign and Domestic," March 5, 1792, *ibid.*, p. 155.

[16] E.g., Jefferson to Madison, April 3, 1794, *Works*, ed. Ford, VIII, 141.

ury jurisdiction as understood by Jefferson, who cited Washington to prove the Treasury was limited to "the single object of revenue."[17]

Jefferson contended that the references from Congress directly to the department heads were contrary to the constitution of the executive branch,[18] and he appears to have conferred early in January, 1792, with Gerry, Fitzsimmons, and perhaps others in Congress over methods of blocking references to the Treasury. On January 19 Fitzsimmons "moved that the *President of the United States* be requested to direct the Secretary of the Treasury to lay before the House information to enable the legislature to judge of the additional revenue necessary on the encrease of the military establishment."[19] The House, on debate, struck out the words "President of the United States." The fight against the direct reference to the Treasury was led by Madison and was narrowly frustrated by Hamilton, who, though apprised of the danger late, adopted measures of counteraction.

Unsuccessful in preventing references to department heads in Congress, Jefferson appears to have attempted to persuade the President to insist on "the constitutional course," and, although he declared that Washington in private conversation "expressed clearly . . . . his disapprobation of the legislature referring things to the heads of departments,"[20] he does not appear to have succeeded in committing the President and administration to his view in the cabinet meeting of April 2, wherein he averred that all but Hamilton were agreed that "neither the committee or House had a right to call on the head of a department, who and whose papers were under the President alone, but that the committee should instruct their chairman to move the house to address the President."[21] On this point Hamilton refused to concur, observing that the act constituting the Treasury made it subject to Congress in some points. Washington does not appear to have disapproved of Hamilton's position on this occasion or to have opposed references to the Treasury during the remaining years of Hamilton's service. Whether he actually agreed with Jefferson's view remains uncertain, particularly as he was reluctant to lose the assistance of Hamilton, who

[17] *The Anas*, February 29, 1792, *ibid.*, I, 195.

[18] March 12, 1792, *ibid.*, I, 213. Among Gallatin's notes on Jefferson's "First Annual Message" to Congress appears the observation that Hamilton claimed the "right of making reports and proposing reforms, etc., without being called for the same by Congress. This was a Presidential power, for by the Constitution the President is to call on the Departments for information, and has alone the power of recommending" (November, 1801, *ibid.*, IX, 330).

[19] *Ibid.*, I, 198.

[20] *Ibid.*, pp. 212–13.   [21] *Ibid.*, p. 214.

had declared that a certain consequence of the refusal of the House to make direct reference to the Treasury would have been his resignation.[22]

Although it is sometimes alleged that Hamilton considered himself the first minister of the administration, there is no evidence that Hamilton himself shared this view. He did, however, declare that he would not "make pecuniary sacrifices and endure a life of extreme drudgery without opportunity either to do material good or to acquire reputation."[23] His energy and foresight spurred him to undertakings which others hesitated to attempt, and he was not careful to refrain from interference in matters properly within the jurisdiction of his associates.

Hamilton's interest in military affairs, coupled with the acquiescent disposition of the Secretary of War, Knox, led to the increasing Treasury influence in the War Department of which Jefferson complained to Washington on February 29, 1792.[24] Suggestive of the way in which Hamilton's zeal for efficiency in the public service led him to extend Treasury influence into other departments is a letter to Washington suggesting a method of putting certain of Hamilton's ideas into effect in the War Department:

I have long had it at heart that some good system of regulations for the forwarding supplies to the army, issuing them there and accounting for them to the Department of War, should be established. On conversing with the Secretary at War, I do not find that any such now exists; nor had the intimations I have taken the liberty to give on the subject, though perfectly well received, hitherto produced the desired effect. The utility of the thing does not seem to be as strongly impressed on the mind of the Secretary at War as it is on mine.

It has occurred to me that if you should think fit to call by letter upon the Secretary of the Treasury and the Secretary at War to report to you the *system and regulations under which the procuring, issuing, and accounting for supplies to the army is conducted*, it would produce what appears to be now wanting. I submit the idea accordingly.[25]

Hamilton's tutelage of the War Department continued after his retirement from the government in his advice to Secretary McHenry, and, indeed, Hamilton was actually acting Secretary of War during the absence of Knox from the government in the late summer of 1794. No more striking evidence of Hamilton's urge to command military policy can be found than his insistence that he lead the troops dispatched to suppress the Whiskey Rebellion in western Pennsylvania. Logically, the responsibility

[22] To Colonel Edward Carrington, May 26, 1792, *Works*, ed. Lodge, IX, 521.

[23] *Ibid.*   [24] *The Anas, Works*, ed. Ford, I, 196.

[25] July 22, 1792, *Works*, ed. Lodge, IX, 542–43.

would have fallen upon the Secretary of War. But Knox was then absent from the seat of government, and Hamilton declared to Washington that he believed it "advisable for me, on public grounds, considering the connection between the immediate and ostensible cause of the insurrection in the western country and my department, to go out upon the expedition against the insurgents."[26]

When Jefferson commenced his duties as Secretary of State in March, 1790, Hamilton was thus already well on the road to establishing his conception of Treasury responsibility. Jefferson, however, came to New York with a very different understanding of the relative roles of the executive departments. Washington had first written to Jefferson to invite his acceptance of the State Department on October 13, 1789, declaring that this department, "under its present organization, involves many of the most interesting objects of Executive Authority."[27] Although Washington's letter indicated that the State Department included more than the administration of foreign affairs, it hardly justified the conclusion which Jefferson observed in his reply to Washington: when I contemplate that this office, "embracing as it does the principal mass of domestic administration, together with the foreign, I cannot be insensible of my inequality to it."[28] It is very likely that Jefferson derived his understanding of the responsibilities of the State Department from Madison, who had been active in the congressional debates which preceded the establishment of the executive departments and who had been criticized by Livermore of New Hampshire for placing the Department of Foreign Affairs above the Treasury in his list of executive agencies.[29] Yet writing to Washington, January 4, 1790, Madison reported the results of his efforts to persuade Jefferson to join the administration and declared that he was sorry to find him

so little biased in favor of the domestic service allotted to him, but was glad that his difficulties seemed to result chiefly from what I take to be an erroneous view of the kind and quantity of business annexed to that which constituted the foreign department. He apprehends that it will far exceed the latter which has of itself no terrors to

[26] To Washington, September 19, 1794, *ibid.*, VI, 441–42.

[27] *The Writings of George Washington, from the Original Manuscript Sources*, ed. John C. Fitzpatrick (37 vols.; Washington: Government Printing Office, 1931–40), XXX, 446.

[28] *Ibid.*, 447, n. 7. See also *Works*, ed. Ford, VI, 28.

[29] The debates in Congress over Vining's proposal, particularly Sedgwick's suggestion for incorporating the principal duty of a Home Department in a reorganized Department of Foreign Affairs, and the subsequent amendment of the Act of July 27, 1789 (1 *Statutes at Large*, 68, 97), creating the Department of State, give credence to Jefferson's interpretation of the powers of the executive departments (see Gaillard Hunt, *The Department of State of the United States: Its History and Functions* [New Haven: Yale University Press, 1914], pp. 54–78).

him. On the other hand it was supposed, and I believe truly, that the domestic part will be very trifling, and for that reason improper to be made a distinct department.[30]

Upon receipt of Madison's letter, Jefferson's acceptance still in doubt, Washington again wrote to Jefferson urging his prompt decision and explaining the function of the Secretary of State in terms which hardly seem to justify Jefferson's belief that his department was "residuary legatee" of all administrative activities not assigned elsewhere:

I consider the Office of Secretary for the Department of State as *very* important on many accts: and I know of no person, who, in my judgment, could better execute the Duties of it than yourself. Its duties will probably be not quite so arduous and complicated in their execution as you might have been led at the first moment to imagine. At least, it was the opinion of Congress, that, after the division of all the business of a domestic nature between the Departments of the Treasury, War and State that those wch. would be comprehended in the latter might be performed by the same Person, who should have the charge of conducting the Department of foreign Affairs. The experiment was to be made; and if it shall be found that the fact is different, I have little doubt that a farther arrangement or division of the business in the Office of the Department of State will be made, in such manner as to enable it to be performed, under the superintendence of one man, with facility to himself, as well as with advantage and satisfaction to the Public.[31]

Washington's opinion was not entirely clear, but a fair construction would seem to be that, whereas in the Indian Department the Secretary of War was assisted by two superintendents of Indian affairs, the variety of domestic duties comprehended by the State Department did not appear to warrant the addition of a special officer charged with their supervision. The Treasury Department had by congressional action already been charged with the care of lighthouses and services relating to the sale of public lands, and the basis for Jefferson's opinion of the scope of the State Department seems hardly in accord with actualities.

However, Jefferson appears to have retained his original view of the role of the State Department, and in justification of his opposition to the expansion of Treasury functions he declared that Washington had "considered the Treasury Department as a much more limited one going only to the single object of revenue, while that of the Secretary of State embracing nearly all the objects of administration, was much more important"[32] He further alleged that Washington had rejected the notion of appointing Governor Johnson of Maryland as temporary Secretary of State upon Jefferson's retirement and subsequently appointing him to the

[30] *Writings of Washington*, ed. Fitzpatrick, XXX, 448.
[31] *Ibid.*, p. 510.
[32] *The Anas*, February 29, 1792, *Works*, ed. Ford, I, 195–96.

Treasury when Hamilton withdrew, observing that "men never chose to descend: that being once in a higher department he would not like to go into a lower one."[33]

It is evident that Jefferson wished to establish the primacy of the State Department beyond question, and an important measure to this end was the Act of 1792, which Jefferson hoped would indicate the Secretary of State as the officer to administer the government in defect of the President and Vice-President. Here Hamilton confessed: "I ran counter to Mr. Jefferson's wishes; but if I had no other reason for it, I had already experienced opposition from him which rendered it a measure of self-defence."[34]

The origin of the administrative rivalry between Hamilton and Jefferson lies therefore in the indefinite manner in which the scope of the executive departments was defined by Congress and in the conflicting interpretations of Jefferson and Hamilton concerning their authority and responsibility in the administration, which Washington does not appear to have properly reconciled. One other factor of more personal nature seems pertinent. Jefferson, being Hamilton's senior and having outranked him in prior political responsibilities, appears to have considered himself properly Washington's equal and confidential adviser and to have increasingly resented the influence of the General's former secretary over presidential policy. The intimate association of Hamilton with Washington during the Revolution had created a bond of friendship and mutual understanding which Jefferson did not enjoy. In *The Anas* Jefferson suggests that Washington at first considered *him* as his closest adviser but, through the artifices of Hamilton, was gradually drawn into the counsels of the Federalists. He declared that "from the moment . . . . of my retiring from the administration, the federalists got unchecked hold of General Washington. His memory was already sensibly impaired by age, the firm tone of mind for which he had been remarkable, was beginning to relax, its energy was abated; a listlessness of labor, a desire for tranquillity had crept on him, and a willingness to let others act and even think for him."[35] Jefferson's resentment of Hamilton's position was seldom expressed in invidious terms, but, writing to Washington, September 9, 1792, the bitterness of a Virginian gentleman toward an immigrant upstart of uncertain parentage broke forth: "I will not suffer my retirement to be clouded by the slanders of a man whose history, from the moment at which history can stoop to notice him, is a tissue of machinations against the liberty of the country

---

[33] August 6, 1793, *ibid.*, p. 314.

[34] Hamilton to Colonel Edward Carrington, May 26, 1792, *Works*, ed. Lodge, IX, 530–31.

[35] *The Anas*, February 4, 1818, *Works*, ed. Ford, I, 183.

which has not only received and given him bread, but heaped its honors on his head."[36]

Specific instances of administrative conflict between Jefferson and Hamilton are numerous, and an exhaustive résumé of cases is hardly necsary to establish the fact of their friction over details concerning administrative policy and procedure. Notable evidence of disagreement appears over the regulation of manufactures, of foreign commerce, the administration of the mint, the post office, the sinking fund, public land policy, and board of patents. Most notorious were the differences between Jefferson and Hamilton concerning foreign policy; but, as this area of contention lies beyond the scope of administrative thought, it requires attention only in so far as it furnishes evidence of interdepartmental interference.

Although Elias Boudinot had proposed in the debates on the executive departments to restrain the Treasury from any concern over commerce and trade, his resolution failed to receive favorable action, and the important area of domestic and foreign commerce remained *territorium nullius* at the beginning of the new government. Meanwhile the tradesmen, manufacturers, shipwrights, and mechanics of the several cities and ports were already beseeching the new Congress for the encouragement and protection of American shipping and manufactures.[37] Thus on January 15, 1790, fully a month before Jefferson accepted the position of Secretary of State, the House of Representatives requested the Secretary of the Treasury to consider the subject of manufactures "and particularly to the means of promoting such as will tend to render the United States independent on foreign nations for military and other supplies."[38] The celebrated *Report on Manufactures* was therefore under way and the Treasury already deeply immersed in the subject of manufactures and commerce, both foreign and domestic, before Jefferson assumed office.

Following Jefferson's organization of his department, references on the subject of commerce and manufactures went out from both houses of Congress—sometimes to the Treasury, sometimes to the Department of State. On February 10, 1791, Hamilton reported to the House on trade with In-

---

[36] *Ibid.*, VII, 148. Jefferson's attempt to nullify the influence of Hamilton has been beveloped by Dr. Leonard D. White in the Bacon Lectures delivered at Boston University, spring, 1944, and published in the *Boston University Law Review*.

[37] E.g., "A Petition from the Citizens of Baltimore," April 11, 1789; ". . . . from the Mechanics and Manufacturers of the City of New York," April 18, 1789; ". . . . from the Master Shipwrights of Philadelphia," May 25, 1789; ". . . . from the Tradesmen and Manufacturers of the Town of Boston," June 5, 1789 (*American State Papers, Finance*, I, 5–11).

[38] *Report on Manufactures*, December 5, 1791, *Works*, ed. Lodge, IV, 70.

dia and China,[39] declaring this field of enterprise for mariners and merchants deserving of the patronage of the government. On December 9, only four days after Hamilton's *Report on Manufactures* had been submitted, Jefferson reported to the House on manufacturer's trade-marks[40] and, incidentally, formulated a theory of federal jurisdiction over commerce and industry which contrasted with the sweeping theories of Hamilton's report. "Manufactures made and consumed within a State," he described as "being subject to State legislation, while those which are exported to foreign nations, or to another State, or into the Indian territory are, alone, within the legislation of the General Government."[41]

Not only did the secretaries of the Treasury and of State present differing views of the competence of the federal government in matters of commerce, but the request of the French government for most-favored-nation treatment commenced a conflict in commercial policy complicated by differences in foreign policy and fiscal affairs.

The divergence between Hamilton and Jefferson began amicably enough when the French chargé d'affaires requested the exemption of French ships from certain tonnage duties. Jefferson, although not concurring with the reasoning of the French, inclined to accede to their request in some measure and, preparing a report for the President, sent a copy of it to Hamilton for his observations, with the salutation "affectionately and respectfully."[42] Hamilton politely disagreed [43] with Jefferson's view, but the report communicated to the Senate on January 19 leaned in the direction of Jefferson's position.[44]

A fragment of Hamilton's letter to Jefferson of January 13, 1791, is suggestive of the trouble which was to follow. Recalling that Jefferson believed commercial regulation more properly subject to State Department jurisdiction than to Treasury control, and holding Hamilton's interest to be chiefly confined to the revenue aspect of the matter, one can imagine his reaction to the phrases "my commercial system turns very much on giving a free course to trade. . . . . And I feel a particular reluctance to hazard anything in the present state of our affairs which may lead to a commercial warfare."[45]

---

[39] *American State Papers, Finance*, I, 107.

[40] *American State Papers, Commerce and Navigation*, I, 48.   [41] *Ibid.*

[42] Jefferson to Hamilton, January 1, 1791, *Works*, ed. Ford, VI, 175.

[43] *Ibid.;* cf. also *Works*, ed. Lodge, IV, 345–48.

[44] *Works*, ed. Ford, VI, 175–84; cf. *American State Papers, Foreign Affairs*, I, 109–11.

[45] *Works*, ed. Lodge, IV, 348.

In his letter to Washington of September 9, 1792, Jefferson described the interdepartmental controversy over foreign trade which had developed and accused Hamilton of deliberately frustrating State Department policy.

Has abstinence from the department committed to me been equally observed by him? To say nothing of other interferences equally known, in the case of the two nations with which we have the most intimate connections, France & England, my system was to give some satisfactory distinctions to the former, of little cost to us, in return for the solid advantages yielded us by them; & to have met the English with some restrictions which might induce them to abate their severities against our commerce. I have always supposed this coincided with your sentiments. Yet the Secretary of the treasury, by his cabals with members of the legislature, & by high-toned declamation on other occasions, has forced down his own system, which was exactly the reverse. He undertook, of his own authority, the conferences with the ministers of those two nations, & was, on every consultation, provided with some report of a conversation with the one or the other of them, adapted to his views. These views, thus made to prevail, their execution fell of course to me; & I can safely appeal to you, who have seen all my letters & proceedings, whether I have not carried them into execution as sincerely as if they had been my own, tho' I ever considered them as inconsistent with the honor & interest of our country.[46]

That Jefferson was not wrong about Hamilton's opposition was attested by Hamilton himself when he explained to Colonel Carrington that he had not favored the attempts of Jefferson and Madison "to produce a commercial warfare with Great Britain"[47] and was therefore comprehended in their displeasure. The Washington administration was thus in the unhappy situation of having two opposing policies regarding foreign commerce advocated by opposing cabinet officers each of whom believed the other to be transgressing the limits of his department. Hamilton's system was to favor nothing which would reduce trade with Britain, upon which the larger share of the customs revenues depended. He conceived good terms with the British government to be essential to national peace and prosperity. Jefferson, while certainly not favoring commercial warfare, yet believed that a policy of reciprocal trade advantages should be effected between America and France and extended to other nations which would trade on a basis of mutual advantage. His system was based on the cherished notion that American trade was so valuable to Britain that the threatened loss of it to other powers would soon bring from the British ministry the concessions which Americans desired. Jefferson's latter experiment with the embargo was to prove the error of his theory, but as Secretary of State he pursued his policy against Hamilton's determined opposition.

[46] *Works*, ed. Ford, VII, 139–40.   [47] May 26, 1792, *Works*, ed. Lodge, IX, 529.

Jefferson set forth his commercial program in his report of December 16, 1793, on *Commerical Privileges and Restrictions*.[48] He regretted that trade must be embarrassed "under piles of regulating laws, duties, and prohibitions"[49] but recognized that some degree of governmental control was required by circumstances. This regulation, he believed, should be as simple as practicable and instituted wherever possible on a basis of reciprocity between nations. He then countered the doctrines expressed in Hamilton's *Report on Manufactures* and described the states as the proper authorities for the regulation and promotion of domestic commerce, advocating the support of household manufactures which Hamilton had specifically exempted from the benefits which he would have the national government confer upon industry.[50]

Early in January, 1794, Jefferson's report was taken up in Congress, and Madison introduced a series of resolutions based on the report and proposing duties discriminating against Great Britain and favoring France. Unable personally to attack this policy in Congress, Hamilton prepared the draft of a speech which was delivered in the House on January 13 by William Smith of South Carolina.[51] Jefferson recognized the true author at once, declaring "every tittle of it is Hamilton's except the introduction." And he added: "We had understood that Hamilton had prepared a counter report, and that some of his humble servants in the Senate were to move a reference to him in order to produce it. But I suppose they thought it would have a better effect if fired off in the House of Representatives."[52]

Although Hamilton was able to prevent favorable action on Madison's resolutions, the controversy over the control of commercial policy, having assumed a partisan character, continued in Congress. On March 12, Samuel Smith, a supporter of Jefferson, reporting from a House committee appointed to consider the remission of duty on bar iron, proposed an arrangement apparently designed to humiliate the Secretary of the Treasury. The recommendation of Mr. Smith's committee would have made it the duty of the collector, naval officer, and supervisor of revenue at certain ports to inform the Secretary of State at regular intervals of the wholesale price of bar iron, and when the wholesale price reached a certain level the Secretary of State was to report to the President, who would direct by proclamation that the duty would cease to be collected for a two-year interval.[53]

[48] *American State Papers, Foreign Affairs*, I, 300–304.   [49] *Ibid.*, p. 303.

[50] *Ibid.*, pp. 303–4; cf. Hamilton's *Report on Manufactures, Works*, ed. Lodge, IV, 194.

[51] *Works*, ed. Lodge, IV, 205–21.

[52] Jefferson to Madison, April 3, 1794, *Works*, ed. Ford, VIII, 141.

[53] *American State Papers, Finance*, I, 275.

The controversy over the control of commercial policy was perhaps unavoidable, but it need never have resulted in bitter contention had Hamilton been more tactful in the promotion of his views. Foreign commercial policy obviously involved both State Department and Treasury Department responsibilities, and co-operation between the executive heads was indispensable to good administration. Unfortunately, Washington did not assume the lead in policy determination, and each secretary believed the initiative in commercial policy to belong to his department. The resulting dissension embittered the relations between the two men, but no fundamental principles were actually at stake, and the affair seems largely a case of administrative rivalry.

The administration of the Mint provided another area of contention between Hamilton and Jefferson. Although the coinage of money was closely related to Treasury concerns, it was a matter of peculiar personal interest to Jefferson. He had prepared a report on coinage and a mint for the Congress of the Confederation and considered himself something of an authority on media of exchange.[54] It was not unusual, therefore, that the House of Representatives requested a report from Jefferson on copper coinage, which he submitted on April 15, 1790;[55] and on July 13 of that year he reported a "Plan for Establishing Uniformity in the Coinage, Weights, and Measures of the United States,"[56] but said nothing about a mint. The report, however, recommended a standardization of the current English system of weights and measures and suggested the desirability of a decimal system for both coins and units of measurement. Hamilton appears to have dissented from this proposal, for he related to Colonel Carrington his frustration of an attempt by Madison to edit Washington's message to Congress of October 25, 1791, so as to join the subjects of coinage, measurements, and the Mint and to commit the President to Jefferson's point of view.[57]

In answer to the request of the House of Representatives, Hamilton submitted his *Report on the Establishment of a Mint*, January 28, 1791, and included therein his views on the coinage to be adopted.[58] The Mint as established by Congress April 2, 1792, corresponded closely to Hamilton's

---

[54] *Notes on the Establishment of a Money Unit and of a Coinage for the United States*, April, 1784, *Works*, ed. Ford, IV, 297–313; *American State Papers, Finance*, I, 105–07; Jesse P. Watson, *The Bureau of the Mint: Its History, Activities and Organization* ("Institute for Government Research Monographs," No. 37 [Baltimore: Johns Hopkins Press, 1926]).

[55] *American State Papers, Finance*, I, 44–45.

[56] *American State Papers, Miscellaneous*, I, 13–20.

[57] May 26, 1792, *Works*, ed. Lodge, IX, 523.   [58] *Ibid.*, IV, 3–58.

proposal, but the chagrin of the Secretary of the Treasury was acute when Washington placed the administration of the Mint under the direction of the Secretary of State. The Chief Justice, Secretary of State, Secretary and Comptroller of the Treasury, and the Attorney-General were designated by Congress to make an annual inspection of the coins. This arrangement does not seem to have proved satisfactory and was not continued after 1800. Departmental friction may have constituted an initial drawback, and it is evident that the relations between the Mint and the Treasury Department were never satisfactory during Hamilton's administration, for in 1795, as he concluded his official duties prior to his retirement from office, he urged Washington to transfer the Mint to the Treasury Department so as to co-ordinate the monetary operations of the government.[59]

Another bone of contention was the Post Office. Placed under the Treasury Department, it was at first conceived to be mainly an instrument for revenue, and on January 22, 1790, Hamilton submitted to the Representatives a "Plan for Improving the Post Office Department," which was signed by the Postmaster, Samuel Osgood, and which asserted that "unless a more energetic system is established than the present one, there will be no surplus revenue that will be worth calculating upon."[60] Jefferson was also interested in postal reform and devised a plan for doubling the velocity of post-riders, which he unfolded to Washington early in 1792.[61] Using this occasion for an opening, he proceeded to observe to Washington that the Post Office should be transferred to State Department jurisdiction:

I had hitherto never spoke to him on the subject of the post office, not knowing whether it was considered as a revenue law, or a law for the general accommodation of the citizens; that the law just passed seemed to have removed the doubt, by declaring that the whole profits of the office should be applied to extending the posts and that even the past profits should be refunded by the treasury for the same purpose: that I therefore conceived it was now in the department of the Secretary of State: that I thought it would be advantageous so to declare it for another reason, to wit, that the department of treasury possessed already such an influence as to swallow up the whole Executive powers. . . . .[62]

Washington appears to have been cool toward Jefferson's proposal and took no action in its favor. However, Hamilton would perhaps have been

---

[59] Ibid., pp. 59-63.   [60] American State Papers, Post Office Department, I, 5-7.

[61] Plan of Posts, February, 1792, Works, ed. Ford, VI, 382-83.

[62] The Anas, February 28, 1792, ibid., I, 192. Learning of Osgood's intention to retire, Jefferson had unsuccessfully promoted Tom Paine for Postmaster (to Madison, July 10, 1791, ibid., p. 279).

willing to have effected an exchange of duties with Jefferson, for, in writing to Washington concerning the Mint, he declared that the Post Office, if intended to be "an instrument of the improvement of the public roads instead of a means of revenue, may without inconvenience be placed under the Department of State, while the mint establishment is transferred to the Treasury."[63]

As might be expected, friction appears to have occurred between Hamilton and Jefferson in the administration of the sinking fund. The responsibility for the fund was largely Hamilton's, but Jefferson as a cotrustee was alleged to have opposed Hamilton "in almost every leading question."[64] Likewise in the administration of the public lands differences appear to have arisen between the two administrators. Their respective land policies and reports have been treated in earlier chapters, but the division of administrative duties in connection with land sales between the secretaries of State and Treasury and the Attorney-General did not promote harmony or uniformity in policy.[65] In general, Hamilton favored a slow development of the West, with provision for land sales in large as well as small amounts, whereas Jefferson leaned toward a more rapid development of the new areas and the discouragement of the sale of land in large units.

The issuing of patents represented another instance of divided authority in the Washington administration and of conflicting policies on the part of Hamilton and Jefferson. The Act of 1790 "to promote the progress of useful arts" constituted a board of three trustees—the secretaries of State and War and the Attorney-General—and authorized any two of them to grant patents. Although Jefferson delighted in scientific discovery and mechanical innovation, he did not favor direct government benefits to inventors. There was criticism of the membership of the board of patents for alleged hostility to industrial activity, and Hamilton's *Report on Manufactures* recommended a new system involving direct aids for promoting the arts, agriculture, manufactures, and commerce. Jefferson viewed direct bounty aids as beyond the constitutional competence of the government and, withal, unwise; furthermore, Hamilton's recommendations concerned a matter which Jefferson believed his particular responsibility.[66]

[63] January 31, 1795, *Works*, ed. Lodge, IV, 62. Jefferson had, of course, retired from the administration, which may explain Hamilton's willingness to relinquish the Post Office.

[64] Hamilton to Colonel Edward Carrington, May 26, 1792, *ibid.*, IX, 518.

[65] *American State Papers, Public Lands*, Vol. I.

[66] An interesting commentary on the present-day relevance of Hamilton's and Jefferson's theories of patent rights is found in Howland H. Sargent, "Scientists in Government," *Public Administration Review*, II (autumn, 1942), 342 ff.

Nearly a year before Hamilton's report appeared, Jefferson had drawn up a bill to revise the patent system and place its administration clearly under the jurisdiction of the Secretary of State.[67] The Act of February 21, 1794, which followed in general Jefferson's plan, precluded further Treasury initiative by making the issuance of patents clearly a State Department function.

The most obvious areas of administrative conflict between Hamilton and Jefferson were, of course, those of fiscal and foreign policy. Hamilton's financial system was already well developed and in process of ratification when Jefferson entered the administration, whereas foreign affairs became increasingly important after 1791. The matter of foreign loans had made necessary Hamilton's correspondence with American diplomatic representatives abroad. Hamilton commenced writing directly to the American ministers soon after taking office and continued the practice after Jefferson came into the government. Jefferson on at least one occasion attempted to discourage William Short, chargé d'affaires in France, from writing too freely to Hamilton.[68] As the foreign policy of the administration had not crystallized and as the international scene changed swiftly with the advent of the French Revolution, Washington established the habit of calling upon the heads of the departments and occasionally Jay and John Adams for advice. Foreign affairs, including Indian affairs, became the principle subject for consultation in the cabinet meetings in which Hamilton inevitably participated. Thus Jefferson and Hamilton were brought into direct opposition over matters involving Jefferson's department, whereas Treasury matters were seldom discussed, the main lines of policy having been decided, and Jefferson had no direct occasion to bring his influence to bear in Hamilton's department.

Jefferson's objections to Hamilton's fiscal policies appear to have crystallized early in 1791. Writing to Gouverneur Morris on November 26, 1790, he declared that he believed many of the foes of assumption actually used the measure to mask their disaffection for the government on other grounds, and suggested that Patrick Henry's interest in opposing the ex-

[67] "Draft of a Bill To Promote the Progress of the Useful Arts," February 7, 1791, *Works*, ed. Ford, VI, 189–93.

[68] *Ibid.*, VII, 269. Hamilton and Gouverneur Morris, minister to France, appear to have carried on a private correspondence on political affairs (*Works*, ed. Lodge, IX, 537–38). Hamilton appears also to have dealt directly with the foreign ministers to the United States (see *The Anas*, March 11, 12, 1792, *Works*, ed. Ford, I, 207–12). Hamilton's dealings with M. Ternant, the French minister, resulted in a frigid exchange of notes between the two cabinet officers (*Works*, ed. Lodge, X, 40–41).

tension of federal power was to protect his speculations in the Yazoo lands. Jefferson declared the financial outlook "really a bright one."[69]

On December 16, 1790, the General Assembly of Virginia protested against the assumption of state debts; Madison had already begun to oppose Hamilton's policies, and by February 4, 1791, Jefferson appears to have begun to doubt the wisdom of his earlier support of Hamilton's measures when he inquired of George Mason what was being said in Virginia of the federal fiscal arrangements.[70] Jefferson's "Opinion" on the bank, February 15, 1791, brought him closer to outright opposition to Hamilton. Jefferson's letter to Madison of May 9, 1791, suggests growing unfriendliness between Hamilton and Jefferson over matters of foreign policy; yet writing to Benjamin Vaughan on May 11, 1791, Jefferson still spoke favorably of the nation's fiscal affairs, but by midsummer of 1791 his hostility to Hamilton's financial measures was apparent.[71]

The contention between Hamilton and Jefferson seems, therefore, to have developed simultaneously in the areas of fiscal and foreign affairs as well as in the several areas of impinging administrative jurisdiction; and one can hardly avoid the conclusion that temperamental differences combined with rivalry for the direction of administration policy were the effective cause of their famous quarrel. Political rivals ever incline to attribute their differences to matters of principle, and if one accepts the testimony of Jefferson in particular, one would conclude that Hamilton's purpose to convert the federal Republic into a centralized monarchy was the basis of their dissension.[72] But the truth is often less dramatic and even more involved than is the rhetoric of statesmen. Had Congress or the President properly defined the respective spheres of the executive departments and had Washington exercised a more compelling personal leadership in his administration, the quarrel between Hamilton and Jefferson might have been less bitter.[73] Yet it seems hardly possible that opposition in some degree would not have arisen between them, for, as the following chapter will indicate, they were divided by certain basic convictions concerning the nature of public administration.

[69] *Works*, ed. Ford, VI, 153–54.   [70] *Ibid.*, p. 186.

[71] E.g., to James Monroe, July 10, 1791, *ibid.*, VI, 257 ff.; to Edward Rutledge, August 29, 1791, *ibid.*, pp. 307 ff.

[72] *The Anas, ibid.*, I, 167–80.

[73] Washington's admonitory letters to Jefferson and to Hamilton on August 23 and 26, 1792, failed to accomplish the unification of the administration. Measures more positive than Washington's personal wish and concern for the stability of the government were in order (*Writings of Washington*, ed. Fitzpatrick, XXXII, 128–32, 132–34).

CHAPTER XIV

COMPARATIVE CONTRIBUTIONS

ALTHOUGH in the opinion of the writer the political principles of Hamilton and Jefferson were not so far divided as most of their interpreters insist, it is their differences in administrative theory and practice which here require evaluation. Personal antipathies and political jealousies aside, the fundamental difference between the administrative ideas of Hamilton and Jefferson appears to be in their attitude toward the control of political power. But the factor of temperament surely marked the thinking of each, for Hamilton—sanguine, impulsive, dominating—had no fear of power when the responsibility for its exercise was clear; and Jefferson—cautious, deliberate, and restive of arbitrary control—held power innately dangerous, although he did not hesitate to employ it in the public interest. Thus Hamilton stood for responsible government and Jefferson for limited government. Hamilton admired the system of centralized ministerial responsibility which Walpole and Pitt had developed in Great Britain, but Jefferson preferred the accepted American notion of separation of powers and local home rule.

HAMILTON

. . . . I anticipate with you that this country will, erelong, assume an attitude correspondent with its great destinies—majestic, efficient, and operative of great things. A noble career lies before it.—HAMILTON TO RUFUS KING.[1]

The practical contributions of Alexander Hamilton to the administrative institutions and practices of the nation are very great and are largely obvious. One need only to cite his work in the establishment of the Treasury Department, the Mint, the first United States Bank, and the University of New York and to recall his proposals for the creation of a national military academy, a national university, and a board of industry and agriculture to confirm Hamilton's position as a builder of administrative institutions. His contributions to administrative practices in the funding of the national debt, in taxation, in the controlling of revenue, in purchasing, and in the organization of the Army of the United States were scarcely less valuable to the establishment of the national administrative system.

Had Hamilton's contributions to public administration been only to

[1] October 2, 1798, *Works*, ed. Lodge, X, 321.

form and vitalize the greater part of our first truly national government, he would rank as one of the greatest constructive statesmen in the history of the nation. But his genius for creative thought exceeded the limitations of his practical accomplishments. In the realm of ideas Hamilton's constructive imagination had free rein, unobstructed by the hazards of personal defect or political opposition; and his great contribution to thought on public administration might have been made entirely apart from his distinguished administrative career. He formulated his administrative philosophy long in advance of the practical application of his ideas to the establishment of the national government; and his practical contributions afford exemplification of the scope and quality of his thinking.

Hamilton's contribution to thought on administration, reduced to its essence, may be stated in three propositions. First, public administration is a unifying process which must operate unimpeded throughout the area of its constitution. Second, the function of public administration is leadership in the systematic and comprehensive development of the area which it is designed to serve. Third, constitutional government requires the fixing of responsibility upon those administrative leaders to whom the guidance of social development is intrusted.

The first proposition might be applicable to any administrative system, but to Hamilton the national Union was the object of its application. The area of national administration was the federal Union—states, counties, municipalities, the nation as an entirety. National administration must operate throughout the nation in the fullest sense, knowing neither sovereign states nor local preference where national issues were concerned. The systematic and comprehensive development of the nation being the responsibility of public administration, the necessity for national planning by administrative leadership was obvious. And the execution of systematic and comprehensive national plans required a unified administrative system of nation-wide scope, which, cutting through all layers of government, would bring into action throughout the Union the plans which responsible administrators deemed necessary to the national welfare.

Hamilton therefore favored the centralization of administrative initiative and responsibility, and this was the basis of Jefferson's charge that Hamilton wished to administer the Union from a federal into a "consolidated" government. In his definition of the administrative relationship between the national government and the states, Hamilton's purpose is evident and Jefferson's fear substantiated. Hamilton would push as far as possible federal administrative direction of the states. His proposals in the Constitutional Convention of 1787 to place the appointment of state governors in the hands of the national executive and to give the governors an absolute veto on all state legislation indicate his belief that, where national interests were concerned, the national administrative system must comprehend and control state administrative action. Thus the states would have certain legislative autonomy, but for all national purposes they would become administrative units of the national system. To insure state subordination, Hamilton wished to reduce the size of the larger units so that the strength of no state or of a likely combination of states would be adequate to challenge the authority of the Union. Hamilton not only intended the subordination of state to national administration in the interest of unity but proposed to allow national administration to operate wherever possible upon the people directly. In April, 1802, he wrote to Gouverneur Morris: "It has ever appeared to me as a sound principle to let the federal government rest, as much as possible, *on the shoulders of the people*, and as little as possible on those of the State Legislatures."[2]

Hamilton's conception of public administration as a unifying process reflected his dissatisfaction with the system of local home rule which then characterized American government. The dissensions of local governing bodies he saw only as obstructive of comprehensive national purposes. He did not share Jefferson's admiration for the New England town meeting. He believed that unified public policy required unitary government and that large measures required comprehensive organization. He did not object to local assemblies dealing with local measures, but with the greater issues of national policy and general welfare he believed they had no proper concern. Hamilton feared the jealous mischief of the states more than the provinciality of the counties and townships. His centralizing tendencies may have placed a higher value on efficiency and a lower value on local freedom than most Americans considered wise, but it was order and efficiency that America most needed in realizing the benefits of independence; local liberty she enjoyed in superabundance.

Thus Alexander Hamilton's conception of the unity of public administration represents a contribution to the theory of national-state relationship in the federal Union. He was the first and most persuasive advocate of national supremacy and a unified public administrative system; and it is fair to say that, without his contributions of thought and practical achievement, the unification of America would have been substantially more difficult to realize. In the realm of political thought his nationalist and centralizing tendencies were not unique, but in the building of the United States of America they were indispensable.

[2] *Ibid.*, pp. 431–32.

The second major proposition in Hamilton's administrative theory—that the systematic and comprehensive development of the area which it serves is the proper function of administration—implies a dynamic, a creative, role for administrators. Thus Hamilton's third proposition logically follows—that responsibility for guiding social development should be required of administrative leadership. Perhaps the best synthesis of these two propositions has been developed by F. S. Oliver in his *Alexander Hamilton: An Essay on the American Union:*

Hamilton's idea of statesmanship was the faithful stewardship of the estate. His duty was to guard the estate, and, at the same time to develop its resources. He viewed mankind and natural riches as material to be used, with the greatest possible energy and with the least possible waste, for the attainment of national independence, power and permanency. A means to this end was certainly the prosperity of the people, but the end itself was the existence of a nation.[3]

To guide the evolution of public policy was the supreme task of public administration. The representatives of the people would, indeed, participate in the formulation of policy through the Congress and the state legislatures, deliberating upon the objectives and methods to be adopted, rejecting that of which they disapproved. But Hamilton deemed leadership in the evolution of policy the particular responsibility of public administration.

To interpret the Hamiltonian conception of administrative responsibility as a forecast of the regimented economies and authoritarian philosophies of the twentieth century would be utterly to misunderstand Hamilton's point of view. If he rejected the laissez faire theories of late eighteenth-century liberalism, he likewise questioned the omniscience of public administrators. He favored a greater degree of governmental guidance and control than nineteenth-century America was willing to accept, but he ever insisted that the area of individual freedom and opportunity be enlarged. He would have government regulate in order to liberate, to conserve, and to develop the material resources of the nation, to increase the opportunities for individual development and prosperity. He encouraged the organization of private societies to co-operate with the government in this work. Government was not the master of individual enterprise but rather a senior partner. Thus in the cultivation of the national well-being, administration encountered the inevitable problem of reconciling freedom with order. To the solution of this problem Hamilton brought a breadth of mind and a depth of practical understanding adequate to the major contribution to administrative philosophy which the problem required.

[3] (London: Archibald Constable & Co., 1905), pp. 450-51.

Hamilton believed that people cannot attain their common needs without common effort and that there can be no common effort without common direction. The logical and accepted directive agency in society was the state and, in it, the administrative arm. Government was a public service and administrators "trustees for the happiness and interest of their nation."[4] But in fulfilment of its stewardship Hamilton held that government was entitled to use force when necessary to insure public order and the rights of the people collectively against individual or group abuse. He declared that "the public good must be paramount to every private consideration."[5] The evolution of his program of administration was governed by the belief which he expressed in the opening pages of *The Federalist* that "it seems to have been reserved to the people of this country, by their conduct and example, to decide the important question, whether societies of men are really capable or not of establishing good government from reflection and choice, or whether they are forever destined to depend for their political constitutions on accident and force."[6] The establishment of good government was only begun by the framing of the Constitution of 1787. To translate its rhetoric into effective reality was the objective of Hamilton's national administrative career. For he believed that Americans were "to decide forever the fate of republican government; and that if we did not give to that form due stability and wisdom, it would be disgraced and lost among ourselves, disgraced and lost to mankind forever."[7]

JEFFERSON

We think experience has proved it safer, for the mass of individuals composing the society, to reserve to themselves personally the exercise of all rightful powers to which they are competent.—JEFFERSON TO DUPONT DE NEMOURS.[8]

During the greater part of the two centuries elapsed since the birth of Thomas Jefferson, his thought has been an undeniable influence in the shaping of American political institutions. This influence has been of two sorts: the popular traditions of Jeffersonian government and the actual beliefs and practices of Jefferson, which often vary from generally accepted notions. Jefferson was a practical idealist, and it is misleading to accept

[4] "Pacificus," No. IV, July 10, 1793, *Works*, ed. Lodge, IV, 465.

[5] To Gouverneur Morris, December 26, 1800, *ibid.*, X, 401.

[6] *The Federalist*, No. 1, Edward Mead Earle (ed.), *The Federalist* (Washington: National Home Library Association, 1937), p. 3.

[7] James Madison, *Journal of the Constitutional Convention*, ed. E. H. Scott (Chicago: Scott, Foresman & Co., 1893), p. 244.

[8] April 24, 1816, *Works*, ed. Ford, XI, 520.

his speculations on what ought to be as invariably descriptive of his actual policy. Throughout his long political and administrative career Jefferson deprecated the enjoyment of authority and command. "I have no inclination to govern men," he declared; "I should have no views of my own in doing it."⁹ He avowed himself never so well pleased as when he could shift power from his own shoulders to those of others. Actually, Jefferson did not lack political ambition, but his desire was to lead a host of willing followers. His wish was to reflect the will of the majority, but he sometimes read his preferences into his interpretation of public opinion. He preferred to exercise power through political leadership rather than through executive authority.

Jefferson's letters and public addresses expounded doctrine as often as they described practice, and much of the Jeffersonian tradition derives from the doctrine, whereas many of Jefferson's actual administrative contributions obtain from the practice. His theoretical desire for isolation from European political intrigue was tempered by his realistic judgment of what the national safety required, and the ideal of no treaties and few envoys gave way to proposals for an alliance with Great Britain and a diplomatic mission to Russia. His oft-voiced opposition to military expenditures and standing armies seemed to some the counsels of pacificism, but he favored selective military service from all male citizens and would include military science in collegiate training. He opposed executive expenditures of money without specific legislative approval, but in the purchase of Louisiana he contracted on behalf of the nation for an expenditure exceeding anything approaching the amounts his predecessors had spent out of general appropriations. He insisted that the power to put the nation into a state of war belonged to the Congress, and yet he directed an undeclared war against the Tripoli pirates upon the basis of his presidential responsibility for the defense of the national interests.

Jefferson was fond of speaking in generalities, and hence he was often misunderstood by persons with a literal turn of mind. Hamilton declared him a "contemptible hypocrite," and his more charitable colleagues often believed him inconsistent. That there was a large element of paradox in his thinking cannot be denied, but where fundamental principles were concerned Jefferson's position was unmistakable. The key to his administrative theories was his concern over the control of power. He understood with Hamilton that power is indispensable to civil society, and he was prepared to exercise a degree of personal authority which he deemed dangerous in the hands of others less devoted to the freedom and welfare of men.

⁹ To Comte de Volney, January 8, 1797, *Writings*, ed. Washington, IV, 158.

But he believed also that power corrupts its possessor, and he therefore endeavored to find ways of controlling the power which any individual or group might possess. He observed the growth of federal powers under the administrations of Washington and Adams and feared that the centralization of political authority would destroy the equilibrium of the Union and lead to an ultimate monopoly of public policy for the exclusive benefit of "the one, the few, the well born or the many."[10]

Jefferson's attempt to restrict the sphere of federal activity did not, however, imply a negative approach to administrative problems. He would have favored the use of federal revenue for the "great purposes of the public education, roads, rivers, canals, and such other objects of public improvement as it may be thought proper to add to the constitutional enumeration of federal powers,"[11] but the actual administration of these public works (a national research university excepted), he preferred to see in the hands of the states[12] or at least to insure by law that the federal proportion of each state should be expended within that state.[13]

Jefferson's desire to decentralize the administration of public affairs reflected his belief that government was republican in direct proportion to the participation of each citizen in its administration. The purest republics were those in which each citizen personally participated, and of these Jefferson described the New England township as "the wisest invention ever devised by the wit of man for the perfect exercise of self-government, and for its preservation."[14] He believed decentralized democratic government to be the strongest in the world, for had he not seen the concentrated despotism of Louis XVI rendered impotent when the people would no longer obey; and had he not felt the foundations of the federal Union shaken under his feet by the New England townships resisting the enforcement of his embargo? He was convinced that the ultimate power of the New England town meeting exceeded whatever consolidated force generals and bureaucrats might muster, and he tried without success to promote the establishment of the township system in the southern states.

The principle of decentralization therefore emerges as one of Jefferson's major contributions to thought on public administration. Not only would he control the exercise of power in terms of space, but his theories of rotation in office reflect a desire to control the use of power in terms of time.

[10] To Joseph C. Cabell, February 2, 1816, *ibid.*, VI, 544.

[11] "Sixth Annual Message," December 2, 1806, *Works*, ed. Ford, X, 317–18.

[12] December 24, 1825, *ibid.*, XII, 418–21.

[13] To Edward Livingston, April 4, 1824, *ibid.*, p. 351.

[14] To Samuel Kercheval, July 12, 1816, *ibid.*, p. 9.

He was concerned with the tenure of office in the policy-determining posts of government because he believed that it is in the nature of man to look upon that which he has long held as a personal possession. "The functionaries of every government have propensities to command at will the liberty and property of their constituents,"[15] he declared. He recognized the value of continuity of policy in public administration, but he believed that republican government required a change of hands at the helm at regular intervals. How long the tenure of office might safely be intrusted to the same person was a question to which Jefferson gave no precise answer, although he declared to a correspondent in 1813 that he preferred a presidential term of four years to that of seven, which he had first suggested with the proviso that perpetual ineligibility should follow the second quadrennial election of any one man.[16]

The ultimate purpose of Jefferson's desire to decentralize government and limit the tenure of office was not the reduction of the public power but rather its control. Jefferson has often been described, and in a sense correctly, as an apostle of limited government, but his career and considered pronouncements show that he was prepared to carry the public authority to great lengths when necessary to effect the public welfare. He favored the limitation of power to the degree which he believed necessary to insure its control but never to an extent incommensurate with the public need.

From this practical view of the role of power the significance of Jefferson's theory of administrative responsibility becomes apparent. In the absence of constitutional or legislative guidance it was incumbent upon the executive to determine the nature and degree of power which the exigencies of society required. When constitutional and statutory measures directed executive conduct, the independent responsibility of the chief executive required that he interpret, in accordance with his understanding of the purpose of the measures, what they required of him. Thus the control of power required the accountability of an executive who must in large measure be the judge of his responsibility and authority. Jefferson was willing to use the checks and balances of eighteenth-century political theory to guard against executive usurpation, but he was too astute a student of history and politics to believe that power could be restrained by mere constitutional mechanics. At the bottom of Jefferson's philosophy of government lay his profound belief in the perfectibility of man and his conviction that in the end only an informed and responsible electorate

[15] To Colonel Yancey, January 6, 1816, *Writings*, ed. Washington, VI, 517.

[16] To James Martin, September 20, 1813, *Works*, ed. Ford, XI, 336.

could exact responsibility from government. "If a nation expects to be ignorant and free, in a state of civilization, it expects what never was and never will be."[17] Thus, although beyond the scope of this inquiry, Jefferson's plans for universal public education must be considered as one of his positive contributions to thought on public administration.

Jefferson's insistence upon limited government can be properly understood only when read in the context of his equal insistence that government promote the public welfare and happiness. Although he believed that a large area of individual freedom was required for the public good, and therefore opposed paternalism as a philosophy of state, he recognized that the nature and degree of governmental authority required to serve the needs of societies varied with the dispositions of peoples. Because he feared the abuse of political power, he hoped that America would remain a nation of farmers and villagers and would avoid occasion for the elaborate administrative controls which he had observed in France. He encouraged the development of local government and opposed administrative centralization. Yet he was not doctrinaire in his attitude, for he recognized that among the warring powers of Europe and in small nations a centralized constitution, an executive office more permanent, and a leader more stable than the American system afforded would perhaps be necessary.[18]

Certainly it is true that Jefferson's administrative thought revolved about a focus quite distinct from that which lay at the center of Hamilton's thinking. Here political theory inevitably intrudes, for the *nation* was the hub upon which Hamilton's thought turned, whereas with Jefferson the *individual* was centermost. Both sought the general welfare, each by his own means. Hamilton believed that, given sufficient power, the government could guarantee the prosperity and happiness of the nation. Jefferson dissented, holding that government as such was incapable of creating conditions which obtained only from the free labor and responsible conduct of the mass of people. Thus Jefferson's wish that the government promote the public welfare was expressed not so much by the direct governmental aids which Hamilton proposed in the *Report on Manufactures* as by encouraging conditions favorable to freedom of labor, thought, and enterprise. Public education and a homestead law represented Jefferson's choice of methods to promote public happiness and prosperity.

Both leaders recognized the need for governmental leadership in the formulation of public policy. They agreed that public policies ought to be formed to promote the general interest in foreign affairs and in matters of

[17] To Colonel Yancey, January 6, 1816, *Writings*, ed. Washington, VI, 517.

[18] To M. Coray, October 31, 1823, *ibid.*, VII, 320–21.

common concern as indisputable as defense, public lands, Indians, and interstate commerce. But they differed in the method by which public policy was to be determined and common concerns defined. Hamilton advocated executive responsibility for the formulation and execution of policy, with the legislature accepting or rejecting the proposals of the administration. Public policy was therefore defined by the executive, subject to legislative ratification. Jefferson, although stoutly defending executive independence in the execution of the law, and the necessity of discretion to responsible administration, yet insisted that public policy was properly to be determined by the legislative branch. The right of legislative veto upon executive proposals he viewed as nugatory if the executive, reinforced with patronage, the prestige of official opinion, and a relative security of tenure, should have the primary right of determining the measures to receive legislative deliberation. Although he did not question the power of the executive to propose and promote certain measures in the legislature, he believed that these should be confined to instances defined by constitutional law, and he rejected Hamilton's notion of a general power of policy-making on the part of the administration.

The difference between Hamilton and Jefferson over the nature and extent of public policy was manifest in contrasting opinions in the details of administration. Hamilton, declaring that the general government must "not only have a strong soul, but *strong organs* by which that soul is to operate,"[19] favored lengthy tenure and substantial compensation for public officers. Jefferson declared conversely for rotation in office and considered it "a wise and necessary precaution against the degeneracy of the public servants" to offer them "drudgery and subsistence only."[20] Hamilton favored a lofty and formal tone in the chief executive when dealing with administrative subordinates or with members of the House of Representatives, contrasting with Jefferson's informal methods of consultation and deference to the representatives.

Clearly, Hamilton and Jefferson favored contrasting theories of organization. The nationalistic centralizing objectives of Hamilton encouraged his view of organization from the top down, whereas the democratic decentralizing hopes of Jefferson led him customarily to view organization from the bottom up. It is probable that Hamilton's familiarity with military organization influenced his thinking on the organization and adminis-

[19] "Brief of Speech on Submitting His Plan of Constitution" (1787), *Works*, ed. lodge, I, 374.

[20] To M. DeMeusnier, April 29, 1795, *Works*, ed. Ford, VIII, 174. See, however, Jefferson's letter to Archibald Stuart, December 23, 1791, *ibid.*, VI, 349–52. Jefferson knew that short tenure and frugality could be pushed to an extent injurious to good government.

tration of civil affairs and explains his emphasis on adequate executive power, clear lines of authority, the absolute responsibility of public officers, and the separation of auxiliary and staff from line functions.[21] His papers on the organization of the civil administration of the War Department, particularly his interest in the organization of the auxiliary services of supply, illustrate the consolidating, integrating character of his thought. Jefferson's theory of organization was dominated by his desire to give to every citizen personally some part in the administration of public affairs, and his concern with the development of effective local government exceeded his interest in the organization of the central administration.

The era of Hamilton and Jefferson was one of those notable periods of recession in the scope of government which Luther Gulick declares worthy of examination.[22] The formation of a national government between the years 1781 and 1789 should not obscure the general trend in thought in the late eighteenth and early nineteenth centuries which, with specific exceptions, moved from seventeenth-century mercantilism toward laissez faire. Jefferson propounded one of the major arguments for the minimized state, and his political success may be in part attributed to his movement with the popular current of opinion. Hamilton worked against that current and thus encountered popular distrust and a reputation for undemocratic tendencies.

Although his was one of the longest political careers in the history of the Republic, Jefferson never acquired the pro-government attitude which sometimes characterizes the conduct of career officers and which certainly marked Hamilton's thought. That Jefferson enjoyed the prestige of high office can hardly be doubted, but he was scarcely awed by the power and pomp of statecraft. His attitude toward government was utilitarian; he respected the authority of government but did not revere it, and he was prepared to defy it should it become unjust to the extreme of illegality.

Hamilton was impressed by the power of government. He was somewhat of an idealist in his attitude toward the forms, functions, and dignities of the state. His true state was "majestic, efficient, and operative of great things," and he was inspired by his conception of what a government should be, even as he deplored the weakness of the national constitution. His thought was tinged by the romantic idealization of the nation that colored much of the political thinking in the nineteenth century.

[21] See his suggestions for a military government for Santo Domingo (Hamilton to Timothy Pickering, February 21, 1799, *Works*, ed. Lodge, X, 343–45).

[22] "Notes on the Theory of Organization," in *Papers on the Science of Administration*, ed. Luther Gulick and L. Urwick (New York: Institute of Public Administration, Columbia University, 1937), p. 42.

And so one returns again to the basic disagreement of Hamilton and Jefferson over the control of political power. Hamilton is our great teacher of the organization and administration of public power; Jefferson, our chief expositor of its control. Jefferson's fear of unlimited centralized administrative authority inspired a corrective for Hamilton's overly sanguine expectation that the public interest would be served by responsible but unlimited public administration. The philosophy of government acting positively to promote the public welfare—a conception in which Hamilton and Jefferson concurred—is accepted by virtually all segments of public opinion, and it is as the great tasks of modern administration are undertaken that concern for effective execution and regard for individual liberties reveal the continuing relevance of the thought of Alexander Hamilton and Thomas Jefferson.

INDEX